FOUNDATION
FUNDAMENTALS

FOUNDATION FUNDAMENTALS

A Guide for Grantseekers

Seventh Edition

Kief Schladweiler, Editor

Library of Congress Cataloging-in-Publication Data
Foundation fundamentals : a guide for grantseekers / Kief Schladweiler, editor.— 7th ed.
    p. cm.
  Rev. ed. of: Foundation fundamentals / edited by Pattie J. Johnson. 6th ed. c1999.
  ISBN 1-59542-006-1 (pbk. : alk. paper)
 1. Endowments—United States—Information services. 2. Research grants—United States—Information services. I. Schladweiler, Kief.
  HV41.9.U5F686 2004
  361.7'632—dc22

                                    2004016814

Contents

List of Figures

List of Figures

Foreword

The Foundation Center was established in 1956 quite simply to be a useful resource for anyone seeking information about grantmaking foundations. As we approach our 50th anniversary, that remains our primary purpose. The impetus for our founding was the McCarthy-era hearings on foundations. In the current period of renewed public scrutiny of foundations, the Center's long history of advancing transparency for foundations, individually and as a field, through accurate and objective information stands us in good stead as the nation's leading authority on U.S. grantmakers and their grants.

Our charter suggests that the Center's principal activities should be to "collect, organize and make available to the public reports and information about foundations. . . ." Thus, from the beginning, the Center maintained a library of information and research on individual foundations and the foundation field. Now, however, we provide free public access to our resources not only at the library at our New York headquarters, but also at four other Center libraries in Washington, D.C., Cleveland, San Francisco, and Atlanta, and at the more than 230 public and academic libraries, community foundations, and other nonprofit organizations that make up the Center's network of Cooperating Collections. We also provide a full curriculum of educational programs about foundations and fundraising.

Almost as an afterthought, the Center's charter stipulated that "to the extent deemed advisable by its board of trustees," the Center might "compile and publish periodically a general directory of foundations." Beginning in 1960 with the first edition of *The Foundation Directory*, the Center developed a line of directories and grant guides covering the full universe of grantmaking foundations. The 1990s brought the possibility of convenient electronic formats, and the Center developed both a CD-ROM version of its information database on foundations and a free Web site that has become the "Gateway to Philanthropy on the Web," used by more than 30,000 people a day as of this writing. Since the prior edition of *Foundation Fundamentals*, we have taken our searchable database online with *The Foundation Directory Online*, which gives subscribers access to foundation and grant information that is updated on a weekly basis. Thus, while our purpose remains unchanged, the manner in which we accomplish it has evolved significantly.

The foundation field itself has also changed significantly in recent years. There has been an explosion in the numbers and types of institutional grantmakers. And increased public interest in foundations has led many grantmakers to communicate more actively about their work. Since staying abreast of the changes—and the burgeoning information sources—can be overwhelming, the Center is using new technologies to help grantseekers navigate a course through the sea of information. *Foundation Fundamentals*, however, remains the primary resource for those who want an in-depth, systematic orientation to the field, the funding research process, and the many resources for grantseekers that the Foundation Center offers.

We hope you'll find this guide of value in your work. Please call on our other resources, too, as you make your way through the challenging and exciting process of seeking foundation support.

Sara L. Engelhardt, President
The Foundation Center
May 2004

Introduction

The nonprofit sector plays an increasingly prominent role in society today. The downsizing of government that took place in the 1990s placed enormous pressure on voluntary agencies to find new ways of financing services previously supported with federal, state, and local tax dollars. Many looked to private generosity to offset decreases in government spending. The boom in U.S. investment markets, a surge of confidence in the economy, modest inflation, and strong corporate profits during much of the 1990s added tremendous value to existing foundation endowments, and spurred the creation of new foundations and the increased assets from which corporations make contributions. The dip in the economy in the early twenty-first century curbed some of this unprecedented growth, and for a short time foundation giving became comparatively flat. It is difficult to predict what the next few years will bring.

One thing is relatively certain, however: As it has in the past, the demand for philanthropic dollars far exceeds the supply. With all indications pointing to a continuation of this trend, the message for grantseekers is clear. In an increasingly competitive environment, the bulk of foundation and corporate giving will go to nonprofits that combine creativity and resourcefulness with a thorough knowledge and understanding of prospective funding sources. This guide is intended to help the grantseeker do just that.

As first-time grantseekers quickly discover, there is no dearth of information on grantmaking, nor in the ways this information can be accessed. If anything, the situation is one of information overload. Fully revised and updated, the seventh edition of *Foundation Fundamentals* is designed to help grantseekers make sense of the wealth of information available to them. Building on previous editions developed by Pattie Johnson, Carol M. Kurzig, Judith B. Margolin, Mitchell F. Nauffts, and Patricia Read, the first three chapters provide a context for understanding foundation giving, and the remaining chapters and appendices introduce the grantseeker to the resources of the Foundation Center, the oldest and most authoritative source of information on grantmaking and grantseeking, and outline a number of research strategies designed to help grantseekers develop a list of potential funders.

The organization and arrangement of the book, with one or two exceptions, follows that of the earlier editions:

Chapter 1 describes the various types of foundations, the regulations that govern their activities, and a brief history of their development. Chapter 2 looks at support from private foundations in relation to other private philanthropy and to other sources of support for nonprofits, including government grants, earned income, and individual donors. Chapter 3 examines who gets foundation grants in the context of nonprofit tax exemption.

Chapter 4 discusses the importance of planning your funding research strategies and includes a number of worksheets designed to facilitate the process.

The resources the Foundation Center makes available to grantseekers are described in some detail in Chapter 5. As distinct from prior editions of this guide, here the emphasis is placed on electronic as opposed to print resources, although books are still covered for those who prefer the traditional format. In particular, reference is made to the popular Web-based *Foundation Directory Online* and to *FC Search: The Foundation Center's Database on CD-ROM*, both of which now provide comprehensive information on foundations and their grants in conveniently searchable formats, and to the Center's information-rich, constantly evolving Web site at http://www.fdncenter.org.

Chapters 6, 7, and 8 introduce the reader to three research strategies designed to help identify potential funders. The subject, geographic, and types of support approaches effectively utilize the Center's electronic and print directories discussed in Chapter 5 and may be employed sequentially or simultaneously.

Chapter 9 is devoted to corporate giving, whether by company-sponsored foundations or direct corporate giving programs. Chapter 10 describes the critical process of presenting your ideas to a funder.

The bibliography in Appendix A has not only been updated, but significantly expanded to include relevant Web sites with brief descriptions.

This seventh edition of *Foundation Fundamentals* refers to the latest information technology as it relates to the field of funding research. While *The Foundation Directory Online* and *FC Search* are covered extensively along with the Center's Web site, other electronic databases, whether available on the Web or through other electronic media, are referenced in the text as well as in the bibliography in Appendix A. The illustrations and worksheets have been completely updated to reflect the many changes in the form and content of the Center's information resources, in both print and electronic formats, and to reflect the best fundraising practices in use today. You may use the table of contents to zero in on areas of specific interest, focus on particular chapters, or read *Foundation Fundamentals* from cover to cover.

Introduction

This revision of *Foundation Fundamentals* was truly a collaborative effort. I would like to thank Judith B. Margolin, who, having edited a previous edition of the book, was able to offer advice, guidance, and editing skills throughout the process. I also want to thank Marion Fremont-Smith (Senior Research Fellow, Hauser Center for Nonprofit Organizations, Harvard University; Of Counsel, Choate, Hall & Stewart, Boston), who provided a substantial review and revision of Chapter 1 (the essential context for the rest of the book).

While it is nearly impossible to thank everyone involved in creating this edition, in particular I would like to acknowledge contributions from the following: Jimmy Tom, Sarah Collins, Candace Springer, Ruth Kovacs, Beverly McGrath, and Erika Wittlieb for their assistance in researching and pulling together materials for the appendices. Margie Feczko and Lorna Mehta were invaluable in answering numerous questions related to *The Foundation Directory Online* and *FC Search* and Steven Lawrence was extremely helpful in providing statistical information from the Foundation Center's research database. Also, thanks are due to Christine Innamorato, Thomas Lam, and Cheryl Loe for their creative production and design efforts. Countless others on the Foundation Center staff also provided just the information I needed at particular points in the editing process. I thank these people collectively for taking time out of their busy work schedules to help me out when I needed it.

Kief Schladweiler, Editor

Chapter 1

What Is a Foundation?

Carnegie Corporation of New York, the Chicago Community Trust, the Duke Endowment, Rockefeller Brothers Fund—what's in a name? The answer is: not much, if you're looking for a grantmaking foundation. These four institutions are among the nation's top grantmaking foundations, but none has the word "foundation" in its name. Conversely, many nonprofit organizations that make no grants do call themselves "foundations."

The difficulty of identifying grantmaking foundations by name alone creates confusion and produces misunderstanding about the scope and activities of the foundation field. That is where the Foundation Center comes in. The Center enables those looking for grants to identify grantmaking foundations that might be good prospects, and it analyzes trends in growth and grantmaking patterns for the field as a whole. In this chapter, we will describe the various types of grantmaking foundations, with particular reference to the federal laws and regulations governing them, and we will provide a brief history of the major types.

Defining a Foundation

The Foundation Center defines a foundation as an entity that is established as a non-profit corporation or a charitable trust under state law, with a principal purpose of making grants to unrelated organizations or institutions or to individuals for scientific, educational, cultural, religious, or other charitable purposes. This broad definition encompasses two foundation types: private foundations and public foundations, a type of public charity.

The charitable universe is made up of private foundations and public charities, and different regulations apply to each category. The most common distinguishing characteristic of a private foundation is that its funds come from one source, whether an individual, a family, or a corporation. The term "public foundation" has come into common usage only recently to describe public charities that have a primary purpose of making grants. Like all public charities, public foundations generally receive their assets from multiple sources, which may include private foundations, individuals, government agencies, and fees for service. Moreover, a public foundation must continue to seek money from diverse sources in order to retain its status as a public charity. Historically, most of the scrutiny of foundations has focused on the private foundation universe, which is much larger than that of public foundations.

The best way to identify private foundations is to refer to the formal determination made by the Internal Revenue Service. Under the rules first set forth in the Tax Reform Act of 1969, those nonprofits determined by the IRS to be "private foundations" are treated differently from other categories of nonprofits, including those that are primarily charitable in purpose and those, such as social clubs and labor unions, that are not. To understand the differences between private and public foundations, it is helpful to trace the path that leads to an IRS determination letter. A nonprofit that has been legally established in one of the 50 states must obtain recognition as a charitable organization from the IRS in order for contributions to it to be tax deductible. Section 501 of the Internal Revenue Code covers many types of organizations that are exempt from federal income tax. Section 501(c)(3) covers those tax-exempt organizations that are "organized and operated exclusively for religious, charitable, scientific, testing for public safety, literary, or educational purposes. . ." and are eligible to receive tax-deductible contributions.

An organization that meets the definition of Section 501(c)(3) is then measured against Section 509(a) of the Internal Revenue Code, which declares that a 501(c)(3) organization is presumed to be a private foundation *unless* it can demonstrate that it falls into one of four categories of organizations:

- Organizations described in Section 170(b)(1)(A), which covers churches; schools, colleges, etc.; hospitals, medical research institutes, etc.; support organizations to educational institutions; governmental units; and publicly supported organizations (including community foundations);

- Organizations that normally receive more than one-third of their support from gifts, grants, fees, and gross receipts from admissions, sales, etc., *and* normally receive *not more* than one-third of their support from investment income;

- Supporting organizations, which, although not publicly supported, are controlled by and operated in close association with a public charity; or,

- Organizations operated exclusively for testing for public safety.

It is a rare grantmaking foundation that does not apply for Section 501(c)(3) status. When organizations receive their determination, those that do not meet the requirements for classification as "not a private foundation" are, by default, private foundations. Thus, the IRS defines a private foundation by exclusion: a private foundation is a nonprofit organization that does *not* meet one of the four criteria for exclusion. The IRS defines community foundations as a separate class of public charity, with special rules to enable them to retain their public charity status even when they have significant investment income. Since the IRS does not have a separate classification for public foundations other than community foundations, grantmaking public charities can be difficult to identify using IRS definitions and resources.

The federal rules for private foundations include, among other things, an excise tax on investment income, prohibition of "self-dealing," a minimum annual distribution requirement, limits on the proportion of a for-profit enterprise they may own, a standard of "care and prudence" in managing investments, and restrictions on foundation grantmaking and other activities. Most private foundations must make "qualifying distributions" of at least 5 percent of the average market value of their investment assets in any given fiscal year by the end of the following year, a rule often referred to as "the payout requirement." The excise tax, normally 2 percent of net investment income or 1 percent in special circumstances, counts as a credit toward the 5 percent minimum payout.

Although they are complex, the definitions of foundations contained in the Internal Revenue Code are important to the Center and others because they determine not only the way a foundation must operate but also the information it must make publicly available. All private foundations must file the Form 990-PF, which is a valuable source of information about their finances, board members, and grants. Copies of Forms 990-PF are available at the Foundation Center's Web site and can also be requested from the foundations themselves, the IRS, or the state attorney general's office where the foundation is located.

With the exception of community foundations, which have special IRS reporting requirements, public foundations follow the same reporting rules as other public charities. Public charities with gross receipts over $25,000 in any year must file an information return for that year with the IRS using Form 990. Because public foundations file the same information return as nongrantmaking public charities, these returns are not a ready means of identifying public foundations. Once identified, however, public foundations can be researched using their Form 990 to learn more about them.

The IRS publishes the *Cumulative List of Organizations Described in Section 170(c) of the Internal Revenue Code of 1986* as a three-volume annual set with quarterly supplements and as a searchable database at its Web site (http://www.irs.gov). Publication 78, as it is also known, is useful in determining whether an organization is a private foundation and thus files Form 990-PF, but it does not distinguish public foundations from other public charities. Publication 78 is available at Foundation Center libraries and at some Cooperating Collections (see Appendix F). Foundation Finder at the Center's Web site is a database of more than 70,000 private and community foundations, searchable by foundation name, and each entry indicates the foundation's type and usually includes a link to its Form 990-PF.

PRIVATE FOUNDATIONS

It is useful to differentiate the three types of private foundation—independent, corporate, and operating—because of the distinctive ways they function.

Independent foundations are the most prevalent type of private foundation, comprising 89 percent of those in the Foundation Center's database. An individual or family usually provides these foundations' assets in the form of gifts or bequests that are held as an endowment. Because of the narrow base of their support, they are subject to the private foundation laws, intended to assure that they serve the public good.

A subset of independent foundations are so-called family foundations, a term that is not a legal designation. Typically, the characteristic that distinguishes a family foundation from other independent foundations is that legal responsibility for the direction of the foundation rests to a large degree with family members. The Foundation Center periodically issues reports on family foundation facts and trends.

Company-sponsored or corporate foundations are normally structured as private foundations and receive their assets from a company rather than an individual or family. Although often closely tied to the company, a company-sponsored foundation and the company that established it are separate legal entities. A company-sponsored foundation often maintains a small corpus relative to its grants program, with the supporting company funding the bulk of its giving through annual gifts to the foundation. The company may augment the foundation's assets in some years to enable it to make grants from its corpus during years in which profits may be down or the company is expanding or for other reasons cutting back on gifts to the foundation. This permits the foundation to maintain a reasonably steady grants program despite business fluctuations.

Many companies make monetary or in-kind gifts to charities without using the foundation mechanism. Some make contributions both directly and through a foundation. While company-sponsored foundations established as private foundations are subject to the same IRS rules and regulations that apply to independent foundations, corporate direct giving programs have no IRS classification and are not subject to public disclosure requirements. Nonetheless, the Foundation Center includes information about them and their contributions, when available, in its database because of their significance in the total picture of corporate giving in the United States.

Recently, a few companies have established foundations as grantmaking public charities. The Ronald McDonald House Charities of Oak Brook, Illinois, is perhaps the best-known example of such a structure, while the King Benevolent Fund of Bristol, Virginia, is one of the largest. Funding comes from vendors, franchisees, employees, or some other base of support.

Operating foundations are a third type of private foundation. Like independent foundations, the source of their assets is usually an individual or a small group of donors, and they are subject to most of the same IRS rules and regulations. However, they accomplish their charitable purposes largely by operating their own programs rather than by making grants. The Foundation Center collects basic financial information on all operating foundations. It compiles more extensive information on the roughly one-half of operating foundations that also make grants, which are usually for purposes related to the programs they operate.

PUBLIC FOUNDATIONS

A public foundation is a nongovernmental public charity that operates a grants program benefiting unrelated organizations or individuals as one of its primary purposes. As previously discussed, the IRS does not have a special designation for public foundations, but a growing number of grantmaking institutions are classified by the IRS as "not a private foundation."

Community foundations are the best-known category of public foundation, and special rules apply to them. More than 650 of them currently serve specific geographic areas across the United States. Increasingly, public foundations have also been established to receive funds and make grants for populations with special needs, for specific subject areas, or around other nongeographic communities of interest. Many of these public foundations got their start as a fund within a community foundation, and they often limit their grants to a particular geographic area, but they do not fit the legal definition of a community foundation.

Community foundations receive funds from a variety of sources, including, in some instances, private foundations. They make grants primarily in support of the broad public needs of the geographic community or region in which they are located. Their investments are normally managed by several banks or investment firms, and their endowments are often composed of a wide assortment of individual funds, which may bear the donors' names. Their grantmaking activities are overseen by the governing body or by a distribution committee representative of various community interests, and grants are normally limited to charitable organizations within a particular city, county, state, or other geographically defined area. However, community foundations may administer funds intended to benefit other geographic areas, including those outside of the United States.

Community foundations usually qualify as public charities under the Internal Revenue Code because of the diverse sources of their funds and, therefore, do not file the Form 990-PF with the IRS. Instead they file the Form 990. Nonetheless, information about their programs is relatively easy to locate because nearly 85 percent of them issue annual or other reports on their work, and about 65 percent maintain Web sites. Community foundations are the only public foundations included in the Center's statistical analyses, such as our annual *Foundations Today Series,* because they are at present the only type of public foundation for which enough reliable information has been consistently available over time to permit statistical conclusions to be reached and patterns of change documented.

Other public foundations encompass a range of grantmaking institutions that raise and dispense funds around a particular community of interest. Women's funds that have been established in communities across the country to raise money and make grants to benefit women and girls are an example of population-oriented public foundations. Other public foundations focus their giving on the arts, health, the environment, social change, or any number of issues at a local, regional, national, or international level. Some public foundations receive funding primarily from an ethnic or religious community, but their grantmaking programs may extend beyond this particular community of interest.

OTHER FORMS OF GIVING

A ***donor-advised fund*** is a fund held by a public charity where the donor or a committee appointed by the donor may recommend eligible charitable organizations to receive grants from the fund. The donor receives a tax reduction for contributions to their donor-advised fund. The legal documents governing the transfer of funds should indicate that the fund's assets belong to the public charity, which must have the right to accept or reject the donor's recommendations. The operation of donor-advised funds hinges on the issues concerning direct or indirect donor control. The IRS holds that in receiving tax deductions for contributions to a donor-advised fund the donor gives up formal control of investments or distributions related to that fund.

Donor-advised funds are administrated by community foundations, federated giving programs, or other public charities, sometimes referred to as charitable gift funds. Charitable gift funds have been established by universities, hospitals, financial institutions, and others for the purpose of managing donor gifts to a variety of charitable organizations.

Recent years have seen the creation of other types of organized philanthropy, whereby groups of philanthropists pool their resources, which are then used to support selected eligible organizations of common interest to the donors. These can go by different names, such as giving circles or collaborative funds. Vehicles that allow the donors to be highly engaged in the management of a relatively small number of grantees are said to follow a venture capital model of investment. This approach has come to be known as "venture philanthropy."

Historical Background

Philanthropy dates back to ancient times, but legal provision for the creation, control, and protection of charitable funds (forerunners of U.S. foundations) was first codified in 1601 by England's Statute of Charitable Uses, which granted certain privileges to private citizens or groups of citizens in exchange for support or performance of charitable acts intended to serve the public good. Since then, legal doctrines in the common law countries have generally preserved this status for most types of charitable entities, including foundations, churches, hospitals, and schools, and have afforded them tax exemption, so long as they serve a charitable purpose.

Most early foundations in the United States were established for the benefit of a particular institution, such as a hospital or school, or to meet a specific social need, such as relief for the poor. Early in the twentieth century, a new kind of foundation began to emerge in the United States. Exemplified by Carnegie Corporation of New York (established in 1911) and the Rockefeller Foundation (established in 1913), these "general-purpose" foundations have large endowments and broad public purposes, enabling them to address major social issues. General-purpose foundations usually focus their grantmaking on one or more areas for a period of time, but their governing boards have considerable latitude to change their focus as social conditions change. Modern-day foundations may be limited by their charters to specific issues or geographic areas, but within those limitations they may periodically review and adapt their grantmaking strategies or programs.

RECURRING CONGRESSIONAL ATTENTION

American foundations began to attract congressional scrutiny soon after the Carnegie and Rockefeller foundations were created. The U.S. Commission on Industrial Relations of the U.S. Congress (called the Walsh Commission for its chairman) launched the first investigation of private foundations in 1915, looking into charges that wealthy capitalists were using the foundation mechanism to protect their economic power, but no major legislation or restrictions resulted. Two subsequent world wars and the Great Depression produced a relatively quiet period for foundations, as Congress focused on other issues. The 1950s ushered in a period of growth in the field, spurred by the creation of new wealth and a tax structure favorable to foundation formation, and foundations again became the target of congressional criticism. First the Select Committee to Investigate Foundations and Other Organizations (the Cox Committee) in 1952 and then the Special Committee to Investigate Tax-Exempt Foundations and Comparable Organizations (the Reece Committee) in 1954 looked into allegations that the large foundations were promoting "un-American activities" and Communist subversion of the capitalist system. The Cox Committee's *Final Report* found that, ". . .on balance, the record of foundations is good," and the very negative majority report from the Reece Committee hearings was generally discredited. Again, no major restrictive legislation resulted.

An open-ended investigation of foundations initiated in 1961 by Congressman Wright Patman, chairman of the Select Committee on Small Business, and a 1964 study of foundations by the Treasury Department ultimately led to a whole new legal and regulatory framework for foundations in the Tax Reform Act of 1969. This Act created the private foundation designation and included company-sponsored foundations in the rules governing them. At the time, it was assumed that the Tax Reform Act of 1969 spelled the end of private foundation formation, and this prediction seemed to be borne out by the sharp decline in their birth rate in the 1970s. To the surprise of many, the 1980s brought renewed growth in private foundation establishment rates, a trend that gathered momentum throughout the 1990s and continued into the twenty-first century.

THE EVOLUTION OF CORPORATE GIVING

Corporate contributions to nonprofit organizations go back to the 1870s, when railroad companies began supporting the development of Young Men's Christian Associations (YMCAs) at their divisional and terminal points to provide accommodations for their workers, and until World War I, the YMCA was the only major recipient of corporate contributions. The war prompted a major national fundraising drive aimed at corporations by the American National Red Cross, as well as the YMCA. It also led to the creation of "war chests" in local communities, which evolved into Community Chests following the war, with corporations leading the way in their support. The Revenue Act of 1935 greatly increased the corporate income tax, but it also provided, for the first time, a charitable deduction for corporate contributions.

Although a few corporate foundations existed prior to World War II, the higher corporate tax rates of the 1950s led to a boom in the creation of new ones. Only 81 corporate foundations currently in the Foundation Center's database existed at the opening of that decade; 323 were created during the 1950s. Also in the 1950s, regulation was increased to prevent the use of the foundation mechanism for private inurement or business purposes.

Formation of corporate foundations slowed considerably in the 1970s due both to the Tax Reform Act of 1969 and to the state of the economy. But with federal cutbacks in funding for social services, education, and the arts in the early 1980s, the call went out for private sources, notably business, to pick up the slack. In an unsuccessful bid to increase company giving levels during this time, the tax deduction limit for corporate charitable contributions was increased from 5 to 10 percent of a company's pretax earnings. The number of large corporate foundations grew substantially from the late 1970s through the early 1990s. From 1993 through 2000, however, corporate mergers and acquisitions led to foundation mergers and terminations, which undercut the rate of growth and resulted in a net gain in corporate foundations of only 3.2 percent over that seven-year period. In 2001 and 2002 the growth rate picked up again, by 7.5 percent and 8.8 percent, respectively. With pressure on corporations to demonstrate their social value, they are again focusing their giving more sharply to achieve direct benefit to major corporate constituencies and communities. Many also promote employee giving and volunteering with employee matching gifts and volunteer services.

THE COMMUNITY FOUNDATION MOVEMENT

The community foundation movement dates back to the early part of the twentieth century, with the establishment of the Cleveland Foundation in 1914. The idea of centralizing the governance of numerous separate trusts that were dedicated to charitable purposes in the community was welcomed by local trust offices, and community trusts or foundations were set up across the country, mostly at the initiative of banks and trust companies and of chambers of commerce. The movement lost momentum during the Great Depression, but following World War II, it was revived by leaders in the community planning arena as a suitable means of strengthening their cities and regions.

The 1969 Tax Reform Act recognized a special status and provided a separate category for community foundations, and the rate of community foundation formation increased dramatically when the regulations were finally issued in 1976. These clarified the significant new advantages that community foundations had over private foundations, including fewer limitations on their grantmaking, exemption from the excise tax on net income of private foundations, and greater deductibility of gifts as a proportion of donors' pretax income. In 2002, the 661 community funds tracked by the Foundation Center (up from 72 in 1975) accounted for just 1 percent of the foundations in the United States but more than 8 percent of the grant dollars awarded.

RECENT HISTORY

Overall, the twentieth century was one of tremendous growth for the foundation field. More than that, it was a century of innovation, seeing the emergence of the general-purpose foundation, the corporate foundation, and the community foundation. A legal and regulatory framework for the field was created, and an infrastructure of organizations and associations to improve practice, advocate policy, promote public understanding, and study outcomes grew up around it. At the end of the century, still other forms of institutional grantmaking, such as giving circles and venture philanthropy, came on the scene. These became especially visible as the stock market rise of the late 1990s created a great deal of new wealth, most notably among entrepreneurs in information technology.

Yet as the new century began, the economic downturn of 2000 combined with the events of September 11, 2001, precipitated a drop in foundation assets along with a modest decline in their grantmaking. A renewed examination of the social compact regarding the role of foundations in a changing society followed. A resurgence of criticism of private foundations in the media and by some legislators has resulted in a variety of suggested changes in the ways foundations operate and their activities are monitored. Lax oversight of foundations by the IRS and state authorities, however, makes it difficult to identify the real problems and evaluate possible solutions.

As of the writing of this chapter, the public debate continues, but those who represent foundations—the regional and national associations to which they belong, their affinity groups, and key foundation leaders—have taken the criticisms seriously and are addressing the issues in a variety of ways. Meanwhile, our nation's foundations continue to make significant contributions to a vital society.

Chapter 2

Where Foundations Fit in the Total Funding Picture

Patterns of Growth in the Foundation Field

The Foundation Center's analysis of trends since 1975 has examined three principal types of grantmaking foundations: independent, corporate, and community. These types of foundations are the most prolific and consistent in terms of levels of giving. Operating foundations are also included in the Center's trends analysis. However, they provide only a tiny percentage of overall giving and, since their principal activity is not grantmaking, their patterns of growth are far less predictable. According to the Center's 2004 edition of *Foundation Yearbook*, in 2002 there were 64,843 independent, corporate, community, and grantmaking operating foundations with a total of $435.2 billion in assets.

Independent foundations, which comprise the largest segment of this foundation universe (57,834 or 89.2 percent), reduced their giving in 2002. Independent foundations made contributions of $23.3 billion, down nearly half a billion dollars or 1.9 percent from 2001. The assets of independent foundations decreased 7.6 percent to $364.1 billion in 2002. This was the second consecutive decline in independent foundation assets reported since the Foundation Center began separate tracking of those foundations in 1987.

Corporate (or company-sponsored) foundations represent only one of many channels (direct cash and in-kind gifts, donations of staff time and expertise, etc.) that corporations use to make charitable contributions. However, corporate foundation giving is significant, comprising 11.4 percent of total foundation grants awarded in 2002. That year, corporate foundations paid out $3.5 billion in grants and contributions, up $173 million or 5.3 percent from 2001. Assets are not usually indicative of corporate foundation annual giving because companies frequently make annual gifts—based on profits—to their foundations for grantmaking purposes. Still, assets of corporate foundations decreased 7.4 percent between 2001 and 2002, from $15.6 billion to $14.4 billion. This decline can be attributed to a lower level of new gifts paid into foundations relative to grants paid out.

Community foundations represent a relatively small, but extremely vital, component of the foundation universe (661 or 1 percent of foundations in 2002). The number of community foundations in the Center's foundations database has grown by more than four-fifths from 353 in 1992. However, asset values of community foundations in 2002 decreased 1.7 percent, from $30.3 billion in 2001 to $29.8 billion. In 2002, community foundations distributed $2.5 billion in grants, up by $123 million or 5.1 percent from 2001.

Figure 1 provides a breakout of foundations by type, their aggregate assets, and their combined grant totals in 2002.

Figure 1. Aggregate Fiscal Data by Foundation Type, 2002 (Dollars in Thousands)*

Foundation Type	Number of Foundations	%	Assets	%	Gifts Received	%	Qualifying Distributions[1]	%	Total Giving[2]	%	PRIs/Loans[3]	%
Independent	57,834	89.2	$364,143,118	83.7	$13,951,579	62.9	$25,232,159	74.7	$23,253,690	76.4	$180,104	72.2
Corporate	2,362	3.6	14,428,397	3.3	3,001,839	13.5	3,514,870	10.4	3,457,186	11.4	5,184	2.1
Community	661	1.0	29,771,669	6.8	3,175,076	14.3	2,497,985	7.4	2,526,226	8.3	6,527	2.6
Operating	3,986	6.1	26,847,286	6.2	2,034,890	9.2	2,523,362	7.5	1,194,696	3.9	57,587	23.1
Total	64,843	100.0	$435,190,471	100.0	$22,163,384	100.0	$33,768,375	100.0	$30,431,799	100.0	$249,402	100.0

Source: The Foundation Center, *Foundation Yearbook*, 2004.

*Due to rounding, figures may not add up.

[1]Qualifying distributions are the expenditures used in calculating the required 5 percent payout for private foundations; includes total giving, as well as reasonable administrative expenses, set-asides, PRIs, operating program expenses, and the amount paid to acquire assets used directly for charitable purposes.

[2]Includes grants, scholarships, and employee matching gifts; excludes set-asides, loans, PRIs, and program expenses.

[3]Program-Related Investments (PRIs) include low- or no-interest loans and charitable investments for projects clearly related to the foundations' grantmaking interests. These disbursements count toward qualifying distributions.

Where Foundations Are Located

Foundations, whether independent, corporate, or community, are located in every state, as well as in Puerto Rico, the Virgin Islands, and American Samoa. However, the major concentration is in the Northeast. In 2002, New York foundations alone accounted for 17 percent of all foundation assets, while foundations in New England and the Middle Atlantic states combined controlled 30.6 percent of assets (see Figure 2).

The unequal distribution of foundation assets across the country is rooted in economic and industrial development patterns as well as in the personal preferences of the donors. This is offset to some extent by the funding policies of large national foundations, which give substantial amounts outside the states in which they are located. Moreover, since 1975, changing demographic patterns and relatively rapid economic and industrial growth in the West and South have stimulated a higher rate of growth in the number of foundations and foundation assets in those areas (see Figure 3). Western foundations, for example, have more than tripled their share of assets since 1975, up from 8.6 percent to 25.9 percent in 2002, and increased their portion of grants from 8.8 percent to 21.5 percent over the same period. California now ranks second to New York in foundation assets; it controls 13.8 percent of assets (compared with New York's 17 percent) and provides 11.9 percent of grant dollars (compared with New York's 18.4 percent). At the same time, Washington state held 7.1 percent of foundation assets and provided 5 percent of giving in 2002, up from 0.8 percent of assets and giving in 1975. The establishment of a single exceptionally large foundation accounted for nearly all of this growth.

Foundation assets of Southern states grew from 17.6 percent in 1975 to 21.4 percent in 2002 and grants from 16.9 percent to 22.5 percent. Foundation growth in this area reflects the economic growth of the region. Several established foundations received important additions to their endowments; large new foundations were formed; a few leading foundations relocated to the South; and corporate foundation activity increased.

Key Sources of Revenue for Nonprofits

While the distinctions among different types of foundations, the legal framework within which they exist, the evolution of foundations as philanthropic vehicles, and the scope of the foundation universe in terms of assets and giving are necessary building blocks for the funding research process, it is crucial for grantseekers to be able to distinguish

Figure 2. Fiscal Data of Grantmaking Foundations by Region and State, 2002*

Region[1]	Number of Foundations	%	Assets	%	Gifts Received	%	Qualifying Distributions[2]	%	Total Giving[3]	%
NORTHEAST	**20,323**	**31.3**	**$133,195,316**	**30.6**	**$ 7,357,637**	**33.2**	**$11,302,793**	**33.5**	**$10,244,875**	**33.7**
New England	**5,884**	**9.1**	**21,018,380**	**4.8**	**1,623,014**	**7.3**	**1,672,552**	**5.0**	**1,531,082**	**5.1**
Connecticut	1,337	2.1	5,586,541	1.3	373,237	1.7	508,915	1.5	484,113	1.6
Maine	268	0.4	771,910	0.2	55,037	0.2	59,372	0.2	47,571	0.2
Massachusetts	2,695	4.2	11,123,527	2.6	1,043,940	4.7	842,107	2.5	775,198	2.5
New Hampshire	272	0.4	890,393	0.2	38,388	0.2	71,975	0.2	57,527	0.2
Rhode Island	1,091	1.7	2,254,897	0.5	76,154	0.3	158,328	0.5	146,924	0.5
Vermont	221	0.3	391,112	0.1	36,259	0.2	31,855	0.1	19,750	0.1
Middle Atlantic	**14,439**	**22.3**	**112,176,937**	**25.8**	**5,734,623**	**25.9**	**9,630,240**	**28.5**	**8,713,792**	**28.6**
New Jersey	2,345	3.6	15,777,978	3.6	1,469,515	6.6	1,768,350	5.2	1,612,543	5.3
New York	8,716	13.4	73,882,209	17.0	3,653,294	16.5	6,221,126	18.4	5,597,543	18.4
Pennsylvania	3,378	5.2	22,516,750	5.2	611,814	2.8	1,640,764	4.9	1,503,706	4.9
MIDWEST	**16,364**	**25.2**	**95,991,709**	**22.1**	**4,926,600**	**22.2**	**7,205,916**	**21.3**	**6,789,225**	**22.3**
East North Central	**11,744**	**18.1**	**73,888,366**	**17.0**	**3,680,736**	**16.6**	**5,310,346**	**15.7**	**5,023,283**	**16.5**
Illinois	3,753	5.8	21,405,401	4.9	1,109,811	5.0	1,547,098	4.6	1,419,193	4.7
Indiana	1,119	1.7	15,618,278	3.6	491,341	2.2	932,735	2.8	896,075	2.9
Michigan	1,908	2.9	19,244,620	4.4	693,405	3.1	1,311,471	3.9	1,233,046	4.1
Ohio	3,033	4.7	12,105,343	2.8	1,031,993	4.7	1,002,958	3.0	988,284	3.2
Wisconsin	1,931	3.0	5,514,723	1.3	354,186	1.6	516,084	1.5	486,684	1.6
West North Central	**4,620**	**7.1**	**22,103,343**	**5.1**	**1,245,864**	**5.6**	**1,895,570**	**5.6**	**1,765,942**	**5.8**
Iowa	820	1.3	2,117,609	0.5	96,659	0.4	196,485	0.6	189,479	0.6
Kansas	663	1.0	1,775,229	0.4	52,518	0.2	105,172	0.3	97,486	0.3
Minnesota	1,281	2.0	8,870,746	2.0	509,283	2.3	738,158	2.2	689,073	2.3
Missouri	1,174	1.8	7,110,047	1.6	447,120	2.0	615,148	1.8	558,468	1.8
Nebraska	486	0.7	1,780,767	0.4	98,355	0.4	208,517	0.6	202,633	0.7
North Dakota	80	0.1	145,290	0.0	9,292	0.0	9,770	0.0	8,053	0.0
South Dakota	116	0.2	303,655	0.1	32,638	0.1	22,319	0.1	20,750	0.1
SOUTH	**16,925**	**26.1**	**93,048,535**	**21.4**	**5,115,944**	**23.1**	**7,544,495**	**22.3**	**6,843,806**	**22.5**
South Atlantic	**10,172**	**15.7**	**54,014,468**	**12.4**	**2,771,467**	**12.5**	**4,570,446**	**13.5**	**4,135,149**	**13.6**
Delaware	303	0.5	2,425,189	0.6	134,496	0.6	218,176	0.6	215,188	0.7
District of Columbia	384	0.6	4,039,055	0.9	240,149	1.1	380,742	1.1	327,515	1.1
Florida	3,205	4.9	13,100,249	3.0	611,622	2.8	1,078,443	3.2	970,052	3.2
Georgia	1,263	1.9	8,398,059	1.9	271,708	1.2	784,008	2.3	675,886	2.2
Maryland	1,371	2.1	9,511,501	2.2	254,655	1.1	740,082	2.2	669,803	2.2
North Carolina	1,855	2.9	8,868,862	2.0	444,060	2.0	736,339	2.2	739,642	2.4
South Carolina	358	0.6	1,195,749	0.3	60,075	0.3	95,962	0.3	95,075	0.3
Virginia	1,206	1.9	5,802,777	1.3	734,183	3.3	500,176	1.5	408,308	1.3
West Virginia	227	0.4	673,027	0.2	20,519	0.1	36,518	0.1	33,680	0.1
East South Central	**1,996**	**3.1**	**7,327,195**	**1.7**	**524,507**	**2.4**	**696,002**	**2.1**	**655,262**	**2.2**
Alabama	657	1.0	1,681,390	0.4	88,774	0.4	139,125	0.4	127,015	0.4
Kentucky	411	0.6	1,302,351	0.3	67,617	0.3	102,197	0.3	96,025	0.3
Mississippi	225	0.3	757,926	0.2	58,429	0.3	125,931	0.4	122,563	0.4
Tennessee	703	1.1	3,585,527	0.8	309,688	1.4	328,748	1.0	309,659	1.0
West South Central	**4,757**	**7.3**	**31,706,872**	**7.3**	**1,819,970**	**8.2**	**2,278,047**	**6.7**	**2,053,396**	**6.7**
Arkansas	252	0.4	1,865,642	0.4	130,366	0.6	229,272	0.7	218,898	0.7
Louisiana	429	0.7	1,994,216	0.5	103,784	0.5	178,985	0.5	159,043	0.5
Oklahoma	571	0.9	5,123,222	1.2	393,494	1.8	256,979	0.8	217,701	0.7
Texas	3,505	5.4	22,723,793	5.2	1,192,325	5.4	1,612,810	0.5	1,457,754	4.8
WEST	**11,220**	**17.3**	**112,911,772**	**25.9**	**4,759,427**	**21.5**	**7,710,150**	**22.8**	**6,551,003**	**21.5**
Mountain	**3,115**	**4.8**	**16,788,051**	**3.9**	**944,387**	**4.3**	**1,174,990**	**3.5**	**1,094,218**	**3.6**
Arizona	514	0.8	2,401,559	0.6	109,702	0.5	165,620	0.5	148,220	0.5
Colorado	1,075	1.7	5,976,066	1.4	403,164	1.8	370,007	1.1	341,819	1.1
Idaho	182	0.3	948,436	0.2	36,131	0.2	66,368	0.2	63,588	0.2
Montana	176	0.3	336,227	0.1	21,899	0.1	22,311	0.1	19,975	0.1
Nevada	401	0.6	3,370,280	0.8	86,047	0.4	278,297	0.8	271,745	0.9
New Mexico	198	0.3	1,035,260	0.2	47,389	0.2	76,069	0.2	59,498	0.2
Utah	403	0.6	1,777,244	0.4	125,332	0.6	143,757	0.4	142,085	0.5
Wyoming	166	0.3	942,978	0.2	114,723	0.5	52,561	0.2	47,289	0.2
Pacific	**8,105**	**12.5**	**96,123,721**	**22.1**	**3,815,040**	**17.2**	**6,535,160**	**19.4**	**5,456,784**	**17.9**
Alaska	64	0.1	297,171	0.1	31,074	0.1	19,005	0.1	16,538	0.1
California	5,929	9.1	60,190,097	13.8	2,841,268	12.8	4,371,337	12.9	3,611,135	11.9
Hawaii	275	0.4	1,579,388	0.4	57,339	0.3	101,888	0.7	77,256	0.3
Oregon	668	1.0	3,067,685	0.7	259,064	1.2	233,318	0.7	216,768	0.7
Washington	1,169	1.8	30,989,380	7.1	626,295	2.8	1,809,611	5.4	1,535,086	5.0
CARIBBEAN[4]	**10**	**0.0**	**41,970**	**0.0**	**3,776**	**0.0**	**4,980**	**0.0**	**2,849**	**0.0**
Puerto Rico	5	0.0	29,785	0.0	1,885	0.0	1,857	0.0	1,758	0.0
Virgin Islands	5	0.0	12,185	0.0	1,892	0.0	3124	0.0	1,091	0.0
SOUTH PACIFIC	**1**	**0.0**	**1,168**	**0.0**	**0**	**0.0**	**42**	**0.0**	**42**	**0.0**
American Samoa	1	0.0	1,168	0.0	0	0.0	42	0.0	42	0.0
Total	**64,843**	**100.0**	**$435,190,471**	**100.0**	**$22,163,384**	**100.0**	**$33,768,375**	**100.0**	**$30,431,799**	**100.0**

Source: The Foundation Center, *Foundation Yearbook*, 2004.
*Dollars in thousands. Due to rounding, figures may not add up.
[1]Geographic regions as defined by the U.S. Census Bureau.
[2]Qualifying distributions are the expenditures used in calculating the required payout; includes total giving, as well as reasonable administrative expenses, set-asides, PRIs, operating program expenses, and amount paid to acquire assets used directly for charitable purposes.
[3]Includes grants, scholarships, and employee matching gifts; excludes set-asides, loans, PRIs, and program expenses. For some operating foundations, program expenses are included.
[4]Private foundations in Puerto Rico, the Virgin Islands and American Samoa are not required to file Form 990-PF. Only a few voluntary reporters are represented.

between grants from foundations and other types of revenue nonprofit organizations may receive. According to INDEPENDENT SECTOR's[1] *New Nonprofit Almanac and Desk Reference* (San Francisco, CA: Jossey-Bass Publishers, 2002), earned income, such as fees for services, account for most revenue for nonprofits.

EARNED INCOME

Private payments for dues and services accounted for 38 percent of the total annual revenue for the organizations in the independent sector in 1997 according to the *New Nonprofit Almanac and Desk Reference* (see Figure 4). While some large nonprofits, like universities, hospitals, and social service agencies, have always relied heavily on fees for services, more and more smaller nonprofits have turned to income-producing ventures

Figure 3. Foundation Assets by Region, 1975 and 2002*

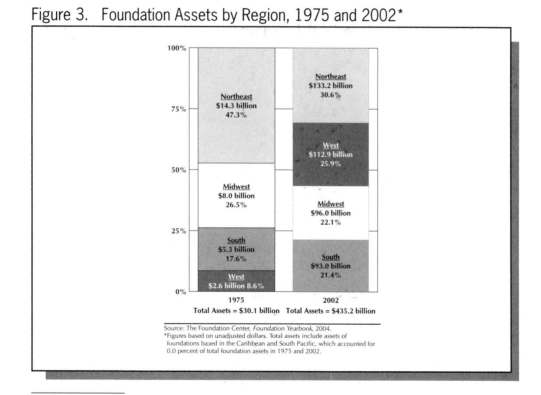

Source: The Foundation Center, *Foundation Yearbook*, 2004.
*Figures based on unadjusted dollars. Total assets include assets of foundations based in the Caribbean and South Pacific, which accounted for 0.0 percent of total foundation assets in 1975 and 2002.

---

1. INDEPENDENT SECTOR is a national forum promoting philanthropy, voluntarism, not-for-profit initiative, and citizen action.

and new dues and fee structures to help cover their operating costs. For some nonprofit organizations, this has meant simply establishing a fee structure for goods and services that they had previously supplied free of charge. Others have looked to capitalize on their existing resources by renting out unused office or meeting space; leasing computer time, services, or equipment; or offering consulting or information services to businesses and clients who can afford to pay. Still others have adopted a more ambitious approach to raising funds through profitable ventures such as gift shops, publications, travel services, and the like. Several books and articles on "nonprofit entrepreneurship" can be found in Appendix A.

GOVERNMENT FUNDING

Government funding is the second most important source of income for America's nonprofits. Government contracts, reimbursements, and grants accounted for 31 percent of the total annual revenue for the independent sector in 1997 according to the *New Nonprofit Almanac and Desk Reference*, reflecting a widespread pattern of partnership between government and the nonprofit sector in carrying out public purposes.

Figure 4. Nonprofit Sector: Sources of Revenue, 1987 and 1997

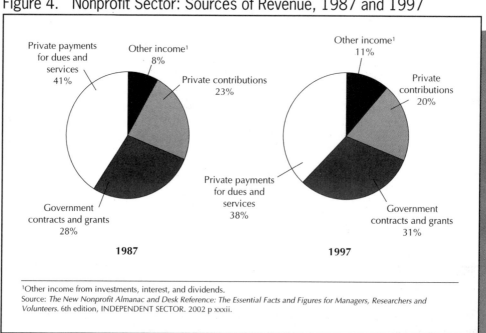

Private payments for dues and services 41%

Other income[1] 8%

Private contributions 23%

Government contracts and grants 28%

Private payments for dues and services 38%

1987

Other income[1] 11%

Private contributions 20%

Government contracts and grants 31%

1997

[1]Other income from investments, interest, and dividends.
Source: *The New Nonprofit Almanac and Desk Reference: The Essential Facts and Figures for Managers, Researchers and Volunteers.* 6th edition, INDEPENDENT SECTOR. 2002 p xxxii.

Loans/Program-Related Investments

In addition to grants, some foundations make loans to nonprofits, usually in the form of program-related investments (PRIs). A PRI, broadly defined, is an investment by a foundation to support a charitable project or activity involving the potential return of capital within an established time frame. Unlike grants, PRIs must be repaid—generally with interest—and are governed by strict regulations that mandate greater administrative attention than conventional grants. In addition, foundations must prove to the IRS that PRI funds are spent only for the designated charitable purpose and that the loan recipient could not have secured funding through traditional financial channels. Despite these restrictions, a number of foundations report an interest in, or have a history of, making program-related investments.

According to a study conducted by the Foundation Center in 2003, there were approximately 255 active PRI funders in the United States. From 2000 through 2001, a sample of 135 leading PRI funders made 667 charitable loans and investments exceeding $421 million. More than 85 percent of these funders were independent foundations, and they accounted for 79 percent of all PRI dollars and 83 percent of PRIs. The same number of community foundations made PRIs as did corporate foundations, but the corporate foundations gave more dollars in the form of PRIs.

Most grantseeking nonprofits will want to become familiar with the activities and funding programs of the federal, state, and local government agencies with responsibility for their service areas. In 1997, according to data provided by INDEPENDENT SECTOR, federal, state, and local governments were the source of more than half of the annual income of nonprofit organizations in the social and legal services field; 42 percent of the income in the health services sector; 19 percent in education and research; and only 10 percent in arts and culture.

If your organization is seeking funding from federal government sources, Grants.gov is a Web site you might want to visit. Grants.gov (http://www.grants.gov) allows organizations to find and apply for competitive grant opportunities from all

Although PRI funders represented all asset sizes, they tended to be among larger U.S. foundations. Fifty-seven percent of PRI funders held assets of $50 million or more, and they accounted for 80.3 percent of new charitable loans and investments.

Still, among the very largest U.S. foundations, many do not have PRI programs. For example, only seven of the 43 U.S. foundations with assets of $1 billion or more reported PRI transactions of $10,000 or more in 2000–2001. This finding suggests that asset size is not the principal determinant for making PRIs. Even foundations with significant resources, and therefore greater capacity to manage loans and charitable investments, have not opted to do so.

Although PRI financing remains closely associated with community development and housing, the practice of making, and using, no- or low-interest charitable loans and investments has spread to nearly all fields. In 2000–2001, more than three fifths of PRIs and of PRI dollars financed projects and organizations in fields other than development and housing, especially education, the environment, arts and culture, human services, health, and church support.

For more information about PRIs, see the Center's publication *The PRI Directory: Charitable Loans and Other Program-related Investments by Foundations* (2003).

federal grantmaking agencies. Grants.gov, a partnership of 11 agencies, led by the U.S. Department of Health and Human Services, provides a single location for information on, and the ability to apply for, more than $360 billion in annual grants from 26 federal grantmaking agencies and more than 900 individual programs.

You can search grant opportunities by keyword, funding opportunity number, Catalog of Federal Domestic Assistance number, funding activity category (such as agriculture, education, health, housing, and more), and by governmental agency. You can also register to receive automatic e-mail notifications of new grant opportunities as they are posted to the site.

Grants.gov features the ability to download a grant application package, and then view and complete it offline—giving you the flexibility to complete grant applications quickly and save them easily for future reference.

Information on other government publications, guides, and handbooks about government funding, is included in Appendix A.

In contrast to the wealth of information on federal government programs, information about funding by state and local governments is not always readily available. Most state and large municipal governments issue some type of guidebook or manual listing the addresses of departments and agencies along with brief descriptions of their program responsibilities. Sometimes the offices of state senators and congressional representatives may guide you to appropriate sources of local funding information. You'll want to check with your local public library for the specific resources available in your area.

PRIVATE GIVING

The *New Nonprofit Almanac and Desk Reference* reports that private contributions accounted for 20 percent of the total annual revenue for the independent sector in 1997. This compares with the previously cited 38 percent of revenues from private payments for dues and services and 31 percent from government contracts and grants (see Figure 4). However, the average proportion of revenue received from private contributions varied widely among areas of nonprofit endeavor.

According to estimates in *Giving USA* 2004, published by the AAFRC Trust for Philanthropy, philanthropic contributions in 2003 totaled $240.72 billion (see Figure 5). The largest portion of these contributions—$200.96 billion or 83.5 percent—came from individual donors through gifts or bequests. Independent and community foundations accounted for $26.3 billion or 10.9 percent of this total, while corporations, through their foundations or direct giving activities, were responsible for $13.46 billion or 5.6 percent of total estimated private giving.

Individual Donors and Bequests

Giving by individuals, historically the largest source of private giving, has grown steadily over the past three decades, reaching $179.36 billion in 2003, according to *Giving USA* 2004. As can be seen in Figure 5, these gifts by individuals accounted for 74.5 percent of all private giving in 2003. Giving by individuals in 2003 represents an increase of 2.5 percent over *Giving USA's* revised 2002 estimate of $175.04 billion. Over the previous four decades, individual giving ranged from a high of 2.26 percent of personal income to a low of 1.54 percent. The 2003 estimate of $179.36 billion is 2.1 percent of personal income.

Bequests accounted for 9.0 percent, or $21.6 billion, of all private giving in 2003. Because a few large bequests can skew the figures, bequest giving appears erratic when viewed from year to year. From the longer perspective, *Giving USA* reports that bequest giving has increased more than 1,000 percent since 1967, indicating that this type of giving is growing.

Individual contributions range from a few pennies to millions of dollars and from used appliances and clothing to priceless art collections. Many individuals also contribute another priceless resource—their time—although volunteer time is not consistently reported by all nonprofits in terms of its monetary value.

The list of techniques used by nonprofit organizations to raise money from individual donors is long and varied. It includes increasingly popular online and direct-mail appeals, door-to-door solicitation, membership programs, special fundraising events, and deferred giving programs. A good many guides and handbooks detailing these approaches have been published, and a number of them are listed in the bibliography in Appendix A.

Figure 5. Giving 2003: $240.72 Billion—Sources of Contributions

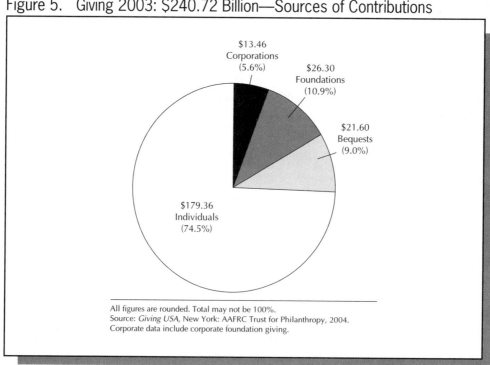

All figures are rounded. Total may not be 100%.
Source: *Giving USA*, New York: AAFRC Trust for Philanthropy, 2004.
Corporate data include corporate foundation giving.

Independent and Community Foundations

Independent and community foundation giving as a proportion of total private philanthropic giving grew during the 1960s from 6.4 percent in 1960 to 9 percent in 1970. During the 1970s the proportion of giving coming from independent and community foundations declined to a low of 5.2 percent in 1979. With a soaring stock market causing increases in foundation assets in the 1980s, independent and community foundation giving as a share of private contributions moved back up to 6.7 percent in 1989 and continued to rise in the 1990s as new foundations were created and existing ones received new assets. The 10.9 percent share captured in 2003 fell below the 12 percent share reported in 2000, which was the highest percentage level for independent and community foundations reported in *Giving USA* since 1970.

Corporate Giving

The *Giving USA* 2004 estimates for corporate foundation grants and their direct giving activities puts these contributions to the nonprofit sector at $13.46 billion in 2003. Of that amount, $3.4 billion is estimated to have been distributed by corporate foundations, which are believed to be responsible for roughly one quarter of total corporate giving. While corporate foundation giving can be documented through the Forms 990-PF that all private foundations must file with the IRS, corporate direct giving numbers, even historically, are based on estimates because no formal reporting is required and because corporate direct giving takes so many different forms. Studies of company donations show that as much as one third of the value claimed by companies as tax-deductible contributions are in the form of in-kind or noncash gifts.

According to *Giving USA* 2004, corporate giving represented between 5 and 6 percent of philanthropic giving throughout the 1990s, after a five-year period from 1984 through 1988 with between a 6 and 7 percent share. Corporate giving first outstripped independent and community foundation giving, according to *Giving USA* estimates, in 1983. The mid-1980s were initially hailed as a turning point in corporate philanthropy, with predictions that it would continue to gain in relation to independent and community foundation giving. However, this new equilibrium did not last long. In fact, in the late 1980s, the Foundation Center noted a growing gap between grants paid out by corporate foundations and new gifts into these foundations, indicating that companies were eroding their foundation asset base to maintain giving levels. This pattern reversed for several years in the prosperous mid- and late1990s, when corporations put more into their foundations than they paid out. However, while corporate gifts into their foundations have remained high in the first years of the new century, they have not kept pace with increases in giving.

Information on resources for corporate grantseeking will be found in Chapter 9 and in Appendix A.

Religious Funders

Churches, temples, and other religious organizations are usually thought of as recipients of charitable contributions, but many are also funding sources. Because religious organizations do not have to report to the government, there is little information about their finances on a national scale. While many religious institutions operate their own service programs, many also give to organizations *outside* their own denomination for activities they wish to promote. These activities include a range of direct social service programs, grassroots and advocacy activities, and education and research. According to the *Religious Funding Resource Guide* (Washington, D.C.: ResourceWomen, 2000), grants from religious sources average between $1,000 and $10,000, with a few religious funders making larger grants of $35,000 and up.

While relatively little has been written about how best to approach religious institutions for funding support, a few directories and guides have appeared in recent years. The *Religious Funding Resource Guide* states that seeking funding from religious bodies requires a different approach than seeking grants from foundations. The *Guide* offers guidelines for identifying, approaching, and building relationships with religious groups. Information on religious funding sources is included in Appendix A.

Summary

As detailed in this chapter, foundations may be important sources of support for organizations, but their grants represent a relatively small proportion of the total philanthropic dollars received by nonprofit organizations. And government funding and earned income sources vastly overshadow the entire field of philanthropy in accounting for nonprofit revenue. While the most successful nonprofit organizations develop strategic fundraising plans that encompass a range of income sources, this guide focuses on strategies for securing information on funding from foundations and corporations. In future chapters, we provide step-by-step assistance in identifying those foundations and corporate giving programs that will be most likely to fund your project, program, or organization. Next, we will examine who gets foundation grants.

Chapter 3

Who Gets Foundation Grants?

The overwhelming majority of foundation grants are awarded to nonprofit organizations that qualify for "public charity" status under Section 501(c)(3) of the Internal Revenue Code. An organization may qualify for this tax-exempt status if it is organized and operated exclusively for charitable, religious, educational, scientific, or literary purposes; monitors public safety; fosters national or international amateur sports competition (but only if its activities do not involve the provision of athletic facilities or equipment); or is active in the prevention of cruelty to children or animals. These tax-exempt organizations must also certify to the IRS that no part of their income will benefit private shareholders or individuals and that they will not, as a substantial part of their activities, attempt to influence legislation or participate in political campaigns for or against any candidate for public office.

Under federal law, foundations are permitted to make grants to individuals and organizations that do *not* qualify for public charity status, *if* they follow a set of very specific rules covering "expenditure responsibility." Essentially, the rules for expenditure responsibility involve submitting a number of financial and fiduciary reports certifying that the funds were spent solely for the charitable purposes spelled out in the grant agreement, and that no part of the funds was spent to influence legislation. As opposed to provisions regulating support for nonprofit organizations, those governing grants to individuals require advance approval of the program by the IRS and prohibit giving to "disqualified persons"—a broad category covering contributors to the foundation and their relatives, foundation managers, and certain public officials. Although some 6,000 foundations have, nonetheless, instituted giving programs that support individuals directly, they represent a small segment of the foundation universe.

Nonprofit Organizations

Foundations award grants to a wide variety of nonprofit organizations. The majority confine their giving to nonprofits that provide services in the foundation's home community. Others restrict their grants to specific types of institutions or organizations active in a particular subject area, such as medical research, higher education, or youth services. Still others limit their giving to specific purposes, such as capital campaigns, providing seed money, or bolstering endowments. The research strategies outlined in the chapters that follow are designed to help nonprofit grantseekers identify funders that are likely to fund organizations like theirs.

HOW TO FORM A NONPROFIT CORPORATION

Virtually every grantmaker you identify through your research will want to know that your organization is recognized as a 501(c)(3) organization by the IRS, and most will ask to see a copy of your IRS exemption letter. Depending on the particular state in which your organization is located, the foundation may also wish to see that you've received the appropriate state certification for tax-exempt charitable organizations. If your organization has not yet received tax-exempt status, you'll want to read the IRS booklet *Tax-Exempt Status for Your Organization* (IRS Publication 557), which includes the actual application forms for Section 501(c)(3) organizations as well as for most other tax-exempt organizations. The publication can be viewed and downloaded in PDF format from the IRS Web site (http://www.irs.gov/pub/irs-pdf/p557.pdf). Copies of the booklet can also be obtained by calling the tax information number (1-800-TAXFORM).

A corporation is a legal entity that allows a group of people to combine their money, expertise, time, and effort for certain activities, which can be for-profit (e.g., has the ability to issue stock and pay dividends) or nonprofit (cannot issue stock or pay dividends). Although most for-profit corporations can be formed for "any lawful purpose," state statutes usually require nonprofit corporations to be established to accomplish some specific purpose to benefit the public or a community. As previously stated, only those nonprofit corporations formed for religious, charitable, scientific, educational, or literary purposes of benefit to the public are eligible for tax-exempt status under Section 501(c)(3) of the Internal Revenue Code.

Once a nonprofit organization has been incorporated in one of the 50 states and has obtained a federal Employer Identification Number (EIN), it can then apply for tax exemption from the IRS. The nonprofit organization may also have to file for separate exemption under the state's revenue regulations. Thereafter, the nonprofit must report income receipts and disbursements annually to the IRS and to the state revenue department. Also, it will usually have to renew its registration with the appropriate state agency on an annual basis.

Figure 6 outlines the basic steps involved in forming a nonprofit corporation. Since the process of incorporating as a tax-exempt nonprofit organization is regulated under federal, state, and sometimes local law, it is advisable to consult an attorney, preferably one with nonprofit experience, to guide you through the process. There are also a number of handbooks that explain the application procedures and examine the legal ramifications and issues involved in structuring your organization. Many of these are listed in the bibliography in Appendix A and can be examined free of charge at Foundation Center libraries. Other resources for establishing a nonprofit organization can be found through the Foundation Center's Web site in the Learning Lab directory.

BENEFICIARIES OF FOUNDATION SUPPORT

The nonprofits that benefit from foundation grants are many and varied. As can be seen in Figure 7, education was the most popular subject category for grant dollars in 2002 (26.4 percent), followed by health (18.3 percent), human services (14.8 percent), arts and culture (12.2 percent), and public affairs/society benefit (11.4 percent). These five areas also received the most grants, but in slightly different percentages, with human services receiving the largest number of grants (26.0 percent), followed by education (20.7 percent), arts and culture (14.6 percent), public affairs/society benefit (12.1 percent), and health (11.9 percent).

Figure 6. How to Form and Operate a 501(c)(3) Nonprofit Corporation

	Steps	Applicable Form	Results
Articles of Incorporation	Reserve the name of your organization (optional).	File application for reservation of name with appropriate agency in your state. Obtain necessary consents for the name, where required.	Reserves your name so that no other organization can, for a limited period of time, incorporate under that same name in your state.
	Prepare Articles of Incorporation. Includes: purposes and incorporators of the corporation and any other clauses that are required by your state for-not-for-profit law.	File Articles of Incorporation with your Secretary of State.	The State recognizes your organization as an incorporated nonprofit organization (i.e., one conducting nonprofit activities for charitable, educational, religious, scientific, literary, cultural, or other purposes).
Federal Employer Identification Number	File with the Internal Revenue Service (IRS) as a nonprofit, even if you do not have employees.	IRS Form SS-4	Your organization has an identification number so the IRS can track your reports and IRS Form 1023 tax exempt application (see below).
Federal Tax Exemption	Determine the applicable section of the Internal Revenue Code.	IRS Publication 557 and IRS Forms 1023 or 1024.	Your organization is recognized by the IRS as exempt from paying income tax on most revenues related to your charitable functions.
	File with the IRS as a tax-exempt organization, preferably within 27 months of the date of incorporation.	IRS filing fee is maximum of $500. See IRS Form 8718.	In general, donations made to your organization are tax deductible only if you are a 501(c)(3) organization.
State Registration and Reporting	Contact the Secretary of State (Corporate Division) and Attorney General (Charities Division).	Registration forms and fiscal annual reports; fee will vary with size of your organization's operating budget.	Your organization is officially registered as a charity to solicit funds, do business or own property in your state.
			You may have to apply for a separate exemption under your state's regulations.
Reporting to the IRS	Report annually to the IRS. Certain types of organizations with gross annual receipts of less than $25,000 are not required to file.	IRS Form 990	Provides the IRS with a report of your organization's income and disbursements.

Adopted from a chart by the Nonprofit Connection, Inc., One Hanson Place, Suite 2504, Brooklyn, NY 11243

Figure 7.   Grants by Major Subject Categories, 2002

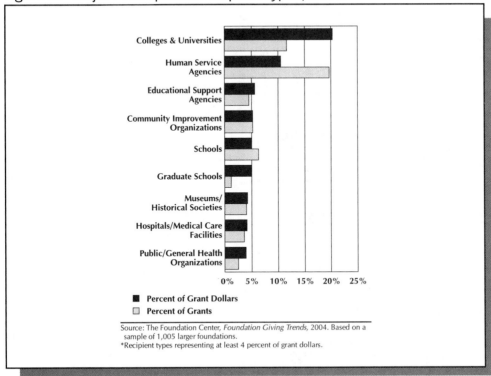

Source: The Foundation Center, *Foundation Giving Trends,* 2004. Based on a sample of 1,005 larger foundations.
[1] Includes Civil Rights and Social Action, Community Improvement and Development, Philanthropy and Voluntarism, and Public Affairs.

Figure 8.   Major Field-Specific Recipient Types, 2002*

Source: The Foundation Center, *Foundation Giving Trends,* 2004. Based on a
sample of 1,005 larger foundations.
*Recipient types representing at least 4 percent of grant dollars.

A look at beneficiaries by major field types of recipients (see Figure 8) shows that educational institutions, with 37.1 percent of the grant dollars distributed in 2002, were far and away the most likely nonprofits to receive foundation funding. Colleges and universities received most of these grants with 20.3 percent. Human service agencies with 10.5 percent of the 2002 grant amounts and community improvement organizations with 5.2 percent came in second and third, respectively. The distribution of grants by field-specific recipient type has remained fairly consistent since 1992.

The major types of support provided to nonprofit organizations in 2002 were program support, capital support, general/operating expenses, research grants, and student aid. While there were differences between the percentage of grant dollars received and the number of grants received by category, the distributions were generally consistent (see Figure 9).

FISCAL RESPONSIBILITY

Organizations that do not have tax-exempt status can still participate in the grantseeking process. However, doing so may be challenging. You may receive funds,

Figure 9. Major Types of Support, 2002

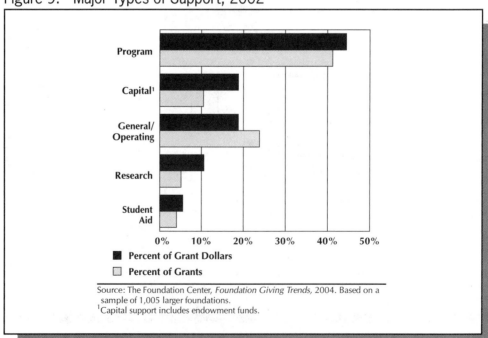

Source: The Foundation Center, *Foundation Giving Trends*, 2004. Based on a sample of 1,005 larger foundations.
[1]Capital support includes endowment funds.

for example, by affiliating with an existing organization that already is eligible to receive foundation grants and is willing to assume fiscal responsibility for your project, usually on a contract basis. Since grants would then be made directly to the sponsoring organization, your organization and the sponsor should have in advance a clear written agreement about the management of funds received and what fees (if any) may be subtracted by the fiscal sponsor. Since there is no master list of organizations willing to act as sponsors, you will need to investigate those with purposes similar to your own. Many of the general fundraising and nonprofit management guides listed in Appendix A outline this and other options in detail.

Profit-Making Organizations

While foundations generally cannot award grants to profit-making groups, they are permitted under the Tax Reform Act of 1969 to make grants to organizations that are not tax-exempt, or have not yet received their exemption, for projects that are clearly charitable in nature, so long as the funders exercise "expenditure responsibility." Most foundations do not have the staff to provide the necessary oversight for expenditure responsibility and, therefore, are unlikely to fund profit-making ventures or other organizations that do not have tax-exempt status.

Those seeking funding to start their own for-profit businesses will find information at their local office of the Small Business Administration (http://www.sba.gov), their local Chamber of Commerce, business libraries at colleges or universities, and/or the business sections of large public libraries. Foundations do not provide funding for starting private for-profit businesses.

Individuals

As noted previously, under the provisions of the Tax Reform Act of 1969, private foundations may make grants to individuals for "travel, study or similar purposes" if the foundations obtain, in advance, approval from the IRS of their selection criteria and procedures. These procedures must ensure an objective selection process and usually involve extensive follow-up reports that demonstrate adequate performance and appropriate expenditures of the grant funds by the individual receiving the grant. Although foundations may make grants to individuals, only a small percentage do.

Individuals seeking foundation grants should first look at the programs described in *Foundation Grants to Individuals* (issued as both an online database and print directory by the Foundation Center). Both resources contain descriptions of more than 6,000 foundations of all sizes that currently operate grant programs for individuals. Most of these programs have significant geographic and other limitations.

There are, as well, a wide variety of funding sources other than foundations that make grants to individuals. Individual grantseekers should also consult general reference books, such as *The Annual Register of Grant Support* (Medford, NJ: Information Today, Inc.), *The Grants Register* (New York, NY: Palgrave Publishers, Ltd.), *Awards, Honors and Prizes* (Farmington Hills, MI: Gale Group), and others that describe grant programs run by government agencies, corporations, associations, and nonprofit groups in such diverse fields as sports, religion, medicine, and the performing arts. The Foundation Center also maintains a For Individual Grantseekers area on its Web site (http://www.fdncenter.org/for_individuals) with a wide selection of references to specialized funding guides and links to Web sites for individuals seeking grants in specific subject areas or for specific population groups.

STUDENTS AND ARTISTS

Many individual grantseekers are either prospective students or practicing artists. Students seeking financial aid for their education should be sure to consult with the financial aid office at the school they plan to attend. Approximately 80 percent of the more than 6,000 foundations in the Center's *Foundation Grants to Individuals Online* and *Foundation Grants to Individuals* print directory fund programs for educational assistance, including scholarships, fellowships, and loans. There are a number of guides and directories that describe grant programs operated by local and state governments, corporations, labor unions, educational institutions, and a variety of trade associations and nonprofit agencies. Many high school and public libraries maintain, and make available free of charge, collections of funding information resources for students. Several Web sites may prove helpful as well in the quest for funding:

- Michigan State University Grants and Related Resources (http://www.lib.msu.edu/harris23/grants/3subject.htm) has a section on educational funding for individuals.

- FinAid's FastWeb (http://www.fastweb.com) has a free scholarship search engine for students (free registration required).

- College Board's Scholarship Search (http://apps.collegeboard.com/ cbsearch_ss/welcome.jsp) allows users to create a personal profile of educational level, talents, and background to search among 2,300 undergraduate scholarships, loans, internships, and other financial aid programs from noncollege sources.

Individual artists should conduct subject searches using *Foundation Grants to Individuals Online* or look in the "Arts and Culture" section of the print publication *Foundation Grants to Individuals* for potential funders. Fiscal agency is another possibility for artists (see below). Several Web sites may prove helpful as well:

- Art Deadlines List (http://www.xensei.com/users/adl) lists funding, residency, and internship opportunities; updated monthly.

- Arts Over America (http://www.nasaa-arts.org/aoa/aoa_contents.shtml) links to state arts agencies, many of which offer funding.

- New York Foundation for the Arts (NYFA)—For Artists (http://www.nyfa.org/level1.asp?id=1) includes NYFA Source, a national database of awards, services, and publications for artists of all disciplines.

A comprehensive bibliography of print and electronic sources on individual scholarships and grants for artists can be found in *Foundation Grants to Individuals* and on the Foundation Center's Web site in the Topical Resource Lists of the Learning Lab directory. Many of these materials are available for free use in Foundation Center libraries and Cooperating Collections (see Appendix F).

FISCAL AGENTS

Individuals seeking funds for research or special projects not related to their education may wish to do what organizations without tax-exempt status often do: affiliate with a nonprofit organization that can act as a sponsor, sometimes called a "fiscal agent," for a foundation grant. The typical fee a fiscal agent imposes is approximately 5 percent. Universities, hospitals, churches, schools, arts organizations, and theaters are just a few of the many types of nonprofits that receive and administer foundation grants for work done by individuals. The challenge to individual grantseekers is to identify those organizations with which they or their project have something in common. For more information about fiscal agents, see the Foundation Center's FAQs on fiscal sponsorship (http://www.fdncenter.org/learn/faqs/section_5c.html) that refer to several useful resources on this topic, including the Guide to Fiscal Sponsorship and Affiliation (http://www.fdncenter.org/for_individuals/fiscal_sponsorship/index.html) and *Fiscal Sponsorship: Six Ways to Do It Right* by Gregory L. Colvin (San Francisco, CA: Study Center Press, 1993).

Summary

Nonprofit organizations with tax-exempt status as public charities under section 501(c)(3) of the Internal Revenue Code are the most common recipients of foundation grants. The types of nonprofit organizations, the types of support they receive, and the subjects these grants cover vary widely. Individuals and nonexempt organizations can receive grants from foundations and other nonprofits; however, these individuals and groups must perform more research and be more creative in their approach to fundraising. Seeking fiscal sponsorship from a qualifying nonprofit is one such approach.

Nonprofits, as well as other organizations and individuals seeking grants, must plan their research strategies and learn about the resources available to help identify potential funders. In the next two chapters we outline a research strategy and then introduce you to the vast array of resources available today in the field of fundraising research.

Chapter 4

Planning Your Funding Research Strategy

Grantmakers receive thousands of requests for funding every year, as the competition for foundation resources grows ever more intense. Many requests go unfunded because there are simply not enough resources to go around; others are denied because the proposal clearly falls outside the funder's interest. Proposals may also fail because they are poorly prepared or do not reflect an attentive analysis of the applicant organization's needs, its credibility, or its capacity to carry out the project as proposed.

The key to any successful fundraising effort is homework, beginning with a careful inspection of your organization, the formulation of a clear idea of where it's going, and the development of a concrete plan for getting there. Once you have completed this assessment, you're ready to begin tracking those foundations whose stated objectives and grantmaking priorities are directly related to your organization's goals and needs. All of this takes time.

Faced with this reality, some grantseekers look for ways around the funding research process. They mail copies of their proposal to such easily targeted groups as the largest foundations in the United States, to all foundations in their own geographic region, or to foundations whose names are well known. Rarely does this approach work. Funders are only too familiar with the mass-mailing technique, and groups that employ it may do their causes harm. Grantseekers are well advised, instead, to do their home-work carefully and to be sure to let that preparation show. Explore all the resources described in this guide, including primary source material. And let the funders you approach know exactly why you believe your program matches their interests. It is help-ful to use the grantmakers' own words from Web sites, annual reports, IRS returns, and other sources in describing how your program and their interests coincide.

The process is lengthy. Therefore, six months or a year prior to actually needing the grant money is not too early to begin your research. Since many foundation boards meet only once or twice a year, and you would not want to miss a prospect's deadline, it is best to begin your search in a timely manner. As part of your plan, allow adequate time not only for your research at the beginning but also for the funder's review of your proposal at the end.

KNOW YOUR OWN PROGRAM

The importance of program planning cannot be overstated. Far too many grantseekers representing nonprofit organizations get so caught up in their day-to-day tasks and immediate concerns that they give the planning process short shrift. Simply stated, there is nothing more important than the precise examination and mapping out of your organization's programs and financial needs. Without such analysis, no amount of funding research will save the day. Scores of useful Web sites, guides, and hand-books on program planning and nonprofit management are available. Many of these publications are listed in Appendix A. Whatever procedures you adopt, however, there are several items you need to address before you can plot your research strategy. Ask yourself the following questions:

1. Is your organization structured so that it is eligible to receive foundation and corporate grants? As noted in Chapter 3, most foundations limit their giving to organizations that have received 501(c)(3) tax-exempt status from the IRS. Many foundations require that grantees also be classified as "not a private foundation" as described in Sections 509(a)(1) and 170(b)(1)(A)(vi) of the Internal Revenue Code. Individuals seeking grant support should refer to the resources mentioned in the previous chapter.

2. Can you transmit verbally and in writing a clear picture of the purpose of the program or project for which you are seeking support?

3. Can you delineate the type of support required, such as general operating support, capital support, or seed money? (See Appendix D for definitions of the different types of support.)

4. Do you have a formal budget indicating the projected costs of the project, the amount of money you hope to raise, and how you plan to cover other costs?

5. What are the distinctive features of your project/organization? Are you collaborating with, or do you have an affiliation with another organization? Does your service generate income? Are you creating a model program that other organizations can replicate? Does your organization provide direct services, or are you an advocacy or research group?

6. Have you carefully defined your project's goals, timeline, and budget to help you report back successfully to funders?

In preparation for planning your funding research strategies, complete the "Know Your Program" worksheet (see Figure 10). This comprehensive outline will help you make a realistic appraisal of your project.

RESEARCH STRATEGIES

Once you have analyzed and pinpointed your organization's funding needs, you can begin to develop a strategy for identifying potential funders. Although there are a variety of approaches to uncovering appropriate funding sources, they all boil down to three basic steps:

1. Develop a broad list of prospects—that is, cast a wide net to identify foundations and/or corporate grantmakers that have shown an interest in funding projects or some aspect of programs similar to your own based on subject, geography, or type of support.

2. Refine your list of prospects to eliminate those grantmakers that have giving restrictions making them seem unable or unlikely to fund projects in your subject field or geographic area, that do not provide the type or amount of support you need, or for some other reason.

3. Use primary and other sources to investigate thoroughly the funders remaining on your list and determine which ones are most likely to consider your proposal favorably.

Figure 10. Know Your Program

A successful funding research strategy must be based on a realistic appraisal of the types of funders that are most likely to be interested in your project. Your first step, then, is to get all relevant aspects of your own program clearly in focus.

1. Is your organization structured to receive foundation and/or corporate support? Does it have 501(c)(3) status?

_____

_____

2. What is the central purpose of the activity for which you are seeking funding? Does it address a significant issue? _____

_____

_____

    (a) What is the _subject_ focus of the activity? _____

_____

_____

    (b) What _population groups_ will benefit from the activity? _____

_____

_____

    (c) What _geographic_ area will be served by the activity? Will this project have an impact beyond that geographic area? _____

_____

_____

_____

Figure 10. Know Your Program (continued)

3. How does this activity fit into the central purpose of your organization?

_____

_____

_____

4. What unique qualifications of your organization and/or staff enable you to accomplish the proposed activity? What is your degree of credibility in relation to other nonprofits? _____

_____

_____

5. What are the distinctive features of your project/organization?

_____

_____

_____

6. What *type of support* (e.g., building funds, equipment, operating support) are you seeking? _____

_____

7. What is the total budget for the project? _____

(a) *How much* grant support are you seeking? _____

_____

(b) What *other sources* of income will be used to meet the project costs?

_____

_____

Figure 10. Know Your Program (continued)

(c) How will the project be funded for the *long term*? _____

_____

8. Who has supported or expressed an interest in your organization's programs? (Note past and current funders, members of the board of directors, volunteeers, community leaders, media coverage, etc.)

_____

_____

The Foundation Center

The key to success is doing your homework. Identifying potential funders requires serious, time-consuming research, but grantseekers often determine that it is well worth the effort.

STEP ONE: DEVELOP A BROAD PROSPECT LIST

The first step in funding research is to conduct a broad search to identify foundations and corporate grantmakers that have indicated in their statements of purpose or by their recent grantmaking activities an interest in funding programs or organizations similar to your own. In analyzing your organization and its funding needs, consider the subject fields in which your group is active, the geographic area it serves, and the type and amount of grant support it needs. Our experience at the Foundation Center has led us to recommend three basic strategies when developing a broad list of funding prospects:

1. The **subject approach** identifies funders that have expressed an interest in your specific subject field or population group focus.

2. The **geographic approach** identifies grantmakers that fund programs in a specific city, state, or region.

3. The **types of support approach** identifies foundations that provide specific types of support to nonprofit organizations (e.g., construction or

renovation funds, research funds, endowment money, program-related investments, and so on; see Appendix D for a complete list).

We'll examine each of these strategies in greater detail in Chapters 6, 7, and 8. If you use *The Foundation Directory Online* or *FC Search: The Foundation Center's Database on CD-ROM*, you will be able to combine the above approaches in various ways. If you rely on print resources, you will likely need to work on each strategy independently or sequentially.

The Prospect Worksheet (see Figure 11) we've provided is the format the Foundation Center recommends to grantseekers to focus on funders whose priorities match their projects. During the initial phase of your research you should concentrate on certain basic facts about the funders you uncover. While you may want to develop your own prospect worksheet, at a minimum it should include the following elements: the funder's name and location; the subject and geographic focus of its grantmaking activities; any stated restrictions or limitations it places on its grants; the size and type of grant it typically awards; and its application procedures, if any.

STEP TWO: REFINE YOUR LIST

Once you have developed a broad list of funding prospects, you will want to narrow it down to those grantmakers whose interests are similar to your own and therefore warrant further research. The Center recommends that you eliminate funders on your list that preclude your organization or project based on certain limitations, such as those that:

1. do not fund projects in your geographic area, even though they may have an interest in your subject field;
2. do not fund projects in your subject field, even though they are located in your community or provide the type(s) of support you are seeking;
3. do not provide the type(s) of support you need (e.g., they do not fund general operating expenses or endowment campaigns).

If you follow the research strategies presented in this guide, you should be able to compile a manageable list of funders that merit in-depth investigation.

STEP THREE: USE PRIMARY RESOURCES TO FIND YOUR MOST LIKELY PROSPECTS

The final phase of your research will focus on identifying those prospects that seem most likely to consider your proposal favorably. During this phase you will be gathering

Figure 11. Prospect Worksheet

PROSPECT WORKSHEET

Date:		
Basic Information		
Name of Funder		
Address		
Contact Person		
Financial Data		
Total Assets		
Total Grants Paid		
Grant Ranges		
Period of Funding		

Is Funder a Good Match?	Funder	Your Organization
Subject Focus (list in order of importance)	1.	1.
	2.	2.
	3.	3.
Geographic Focus		
Type(s) of Support		
Population(s) Served		
Type(s) of Recipients		
Typical Grant Size		
People (Officers, Donors, Trustees, Staff)		

Application Information	
Does the funder have printed guidelines/application forms?	
Initial Approach (letter of inquiry, formal proposal)	
Deadline(s)	
Board Meeting Date(s)	

Sources of Above Information

☐ 990-PF -- Year:	☐ Requested ☐ Received
☐ Annual Report -- Year:	☐ Requested ☐ Received
☐ Databases/Directories	
☐ Grantmaker Web site	

Notes:

Follow-up:

information on the funder's current financial status, its application procedures, and its most recent grantmaking activities. Primary resources, including a foundation's Form 990-PF, Web site, and/or printed materials, such as annual reports and guideline brochures, can be particularly helpful at this stage. Background information on the donors to the foundation or its sponsoring company, financial and institutional history, current program interests, and future plans will not only help you to eliminate prospects that are unlikely to provide funding for your proposal but will also assist you with coming up with a more compelling case directed to appropriate funders.

Learn More about Your Funding Prospects

In going through the process of identifying potential funding sources, you will gather names of grantmakers that, on the basis of initial evidence, appear to have an interest in some aspect of your project and do not preclude support to your organization based on stated limitations. Next, you will eliminate those that, on closer examination, seem unlikely to consider your proposal favorably. You will also be gathering important information on those funders whose priorities closely match those of your organization.

As you go through these steps and assemble the facts, you'll also be looking for answers to the following questions:

Does the funder accept applications? You may find it surprising that some do not. You'll want to find this out early in the research process so you don't waste your time. However, even when a funder says it does not accept applications and/or gives only to preselected organizations, grantseekers should not completely disregard it as a prospect. For such grantmakers a different approach is necessary. The grantseeker must cultivate a relationship with the grantmaker who funds only preselected organizations, and this takes time. Consult your board of trustees and list of volunteers for someone who may know someone on the foundation's board or begin the cultivation process by sending informational materials about your organization to the foundation (as a way of introduction, not as part of a request for funding).

Has the funder demonstrated a real commitment to funding in your subject field? You may have noted one or more grants by a particular foundation in your subject field. Upon examining the full grants list, however, you may find that these were the exceptions to their normal giving patterns. They may have been made for reasons other than a true commitment to the field, perhaps because of a special relationship between the recipient organization and a foundation board member, for example. Some foundations have historic and continuing relationships with particular institutions (due to a specified interest of the donor) that may cause them to fund activities that do not fall within their usual giving guidelines. In other cases, grants may have been awarded because the funder is committed to the recipient organization's location rather than to its primary field of endeavor.

Does it seem likely that the funder will make grants to organizations in your geographic location? Although it isn't necessary for a foundation to actually have made grants in your state or city to remain on your list, you should examine funding guidelines and grant records carefully for either explicit or implicit geographic restrictions. Be on the lookout for local or regional giving patterns or concentrations in rural or urban areas that might exclude your project. Corporate grantmakers, of course, generally restrict their funding to locales where they do business or have plants, subsidiaries, or corporate headquarters.

Does the amount of money you are requesting fit within the funder's typical grant range? Of course you should not request $25,000 from a foundation that has never made a grant larger than $10,000. At the same time, look for more subtle distinctions. If a foundation's arts grants range from $10,000 to $20,000 and its social welfare grants are in the $3,000 to $5,000 range, consider what that says about its emphasis. About 50 percent of this weeding out process is common sense; the rest is intuition and luck.

Does the funder have a policy prohibiting grants for the type(s) of support you are requesting? Some foundations will not make grants for operating budgets. Others will not provide funds for endowments, physical plant improvements, or equipment. Be sure the funder is willing to consider the type(s) of support you need.

Does the funder usually make grants to cover the full cost of a project or does it favor projects where other funders have an opportunity to participate? Since it is unlikely that a first-time donor will fund an entire project, it is entirely appropriate to approach multiple funders for the same project, asking each to contribute to the whole.

Does the funder put limits on the length of time it is willing to support a project? Some foundations favor one-time grants, while others will continue their support over a number of years. It is rare to find grantmakers that will commit funding to an organization for an indefinite period of time, however. Be sure you can point to possible avenues of income or support for the future before approaching funders. Many funders will expect you to have thought through and be able to present a long-term funding plan for any project in which they might be asked to participate.

What types of organizations does the funder tend to support? Does it favor large, well-established groups such as symphonies, universities, and museums, or does it lean toward grassroots community groups? A list of a funder's past recipients will give you an excellent feel for its focus. Look carefully at the mix of its recipients for clues that may not be stated explicitly in its printed guidelines.

Does the funder have application deadlines, or does it review proposals continuously? Note carefully any information you uncover about deadlines and board meeting dates so you can submit your proposal at the appropriate time. Since calendars fill up, and staff and/or board members have a limited amount of time to review and consider proposals, proposals should be sent well ahead of the stated deadline. Be aware, as well, that the time elapsed between the submission of your proposal and notification of actual receipt of a grant may be considerable—rarely less than three months and often up to six months or more. In planning ahead, be sure to allow enough time to obtain the necessary funding.

Do you or does anyone on your board know someone connected with the funder? You'll want to gather background information on the foundation or corporate funder's sponsoring company as well as its current trustees and staff. In doing so, you may find some unexpected connections between your organization and a potential funder that will make it easier to approach the funder. Make a list of individuals who have supported or expressed an interest in your organization and its programs. Include past and current donors, board members, volunteers, and "friends." See if there are any obvious links between these individuals and the funder's board and/or staff. The savvy fundraiser is constantly working to establish these kinds of connections. While knowing somebody who is affiliated with a prospective funder usually is not enough to win you a grant, it does tend to facilitate the process.

What are the financial conditions that may affect the foundation's ability to give? Carefully examine the available financial data. Although it's often mystifying to first-time grantseekers, data from foundation Forms 990-PF, annual reports, and published directories generally include information on assets, grants awarded, and gifts received. Learning to interpret these figures can provide important clues about the funding patterns of a particular grantmaker. Has the foundation or corporation received any large contributions in recent years that might increase its grantmaking potential? Has there been an increase or decrease in the funder's assets in recent years? Might it be "going out of business?" These are the factors that can affect the amount of money available for grants, as well as the size and type of grants awarded. Of course, general economic conditions also affect a foundation's assets and gifts received (especially for corporate grantmakers), which in turn impacts the amount of money it has to give away.

Do you have the most current and accurate details on the funder? You will need to be sure you have the most up-to-date information on those grantmakers you consider to be your best bets. Take time at the end of the research process to confirm not only the funder's current address and officer and trustee names, but also funding guidelines, assets, gifts received, application procedures, and actual grants awarded in a recent time period. Taking this extra step can help to ensure that you compensate for any information that may have changed since you began the research process.

Record What You Do

You must keep careful records of your findings during the research process and especially once you have made contact with a potential funder. It helps to think of the first activity as "data gathering" and the second activity as "record keeping."

DATA GATHERING

Throughout the research process you should gather as many pertinent facts about your funding prospects as possible. Develop careful files, either in hard copy or electronically. Each record of a potential funder should include the information in the Prospect Worksheet shown in Figure 11.

These records should be updated on a regular basis to provide a dynamic, consolidated base of funding information for your organization. Developing such a system helps to compensate for one of the biggest problems nonprofits face—the lack of continuity in fundraising efforts resulting from staff turnover.

It is important to document your research at every step along the way. As you gather facts about a funder, note the source and date of the information so that later on, if you come across conflicting information, you can quickly determine which is more current. While such attention to detail at the outset may seem needlessly time consuming, careful data gathering is guaranteed to save you and your organization time and money in the long run.

RECORD KEEPING

You need to keep track of each and every contact between representatives of your organization and a staff or board member at a funding institution. Your files should include copies of your letters of inquiry, formal proposals, and supporting documents, as well as reports, press releases, and invitations to events. Print out copies of any e-mail correspondence between you and a funding representative. In addition, you should keep careful notes regarding informational and follow-up phone calls, and your written summaries of interviews and site visits. Each record should include the date and the initials of the individual who made the contact. Figure 12 is a sample all-purpose form for keeping track of contacts with potential funders. It can also serve as a "tickler" or reminder sheet to let you know when the next steps need to be taken. While the Foundation Center does not track or evaluate software packages for nonprofits, there are a number of resources on commercially available record-keeping software programs in our FAQ "Where can I find information on fundraising and accounting software packages for my nonprofit organization?" (http://www.fdncenter.org/learn/faqs/html/software.html). You can also develop your own system using any versatile data management software package, such as Microsoft Access. The Notepad feature of *FC Search* enables fundraisers to create a basic prospect tracking and tickler system as well.

Summary

Doing your homework is your key to unlocking grant opportunities. Know your own program and develop a clear idea of what you are trying to accomplish. Formulate a plan and a timetable and calculate what it will cost to carry out your grant project. Then you are ready to compile a broad list of prospects that are interested in your subject field, give in your geographic area, and/or offer the types and amounts of support your organization needs. The list of prospects you compile will need to be refined, and the grantmakers clearly not interested in your program or geographic location eliminated. Then you can begin in-depth research on the remaining funders, using primary resources to answer several key questions. While this is all going on, you will need to keep accurate records of your efforts and continue to do so even after you have submitted a proposal. Chapter 10 offers further suggestions about record keeping and the proposal writing process.

The next chapter describes key resources for performing funding research. After that, subsequent chapters go into detail about the various research strategies.

Figure 12. Record of Funding Contact

Funder (name and address): _____

_____

Principal Contact (name and title): _____

_____

Telephone Calls

Date(s): _____

Time(s): _____

Call made by: _____

Spoke to: _____

Comments: _____

_____

MEETINGS	Date: Time: Outcome:	
PROPOSALS	Date submitted: Format: Signed by:	For project: Amount requested: Board meeting date(s):
TICKLER	Deadline: To do: Follow up:	By whom: By whom:
DECISION Yes/No: Notification date: Reason for rejection:		NEXT STEP Resubmit: Cultivation: Special activities: Send report:
The Foundation Center		

Chapter 5

Resources for Foundation Funding Research

A wide range of resources is available to help you identify sources of support for your organization or project. The types and number of tools you use will depend upon the grant project you have in mind and the search strategy you adopt to identify appropriate funding sources. Before you can plan an effective search strategy, however, you need to become familiar with the basic resources available to you.

Materials that describe the grantmaking universe can be accessed electronically or in traditional print format. Regardless of format, the information usually falls into one of five categories: (1) general grantmaker directories; (2) directories of grants awarded in the recent past; (3) specialized funding directories; (4) original or primary materials generated or published by grantmakers, including annual reports, brochures, information at their Web sites, and tax returns filed annually by foundations with the IRS; and (5) secondary resources such as newspaper or journal articles.

General grantmaker directories may be national or local in focus and can vary widely in the amount of information they provide. Many general grantmaker directories are now in electronic format, with search capabilities that allow them to serve also as specialized funding directories. In this chapter we focus on the national directories published by the Foundation Center, but refer to other directories and databases in Appendix A. When possible, your research should encompass all pertinent resources.

Directories of foundation grants, in whatever format, provide listings of actual grants awarded, enabling you to determine the specific subject interests of a foundation, the types and locations of the organizations it funds, the size of the grants it makes, and the types of support it awards. Such directories usually do not, however, list grants *available*. For information on grants available, you should refer to requests for proposal (RFPs), an increasingly popular vehicle for foundations to notify the public of grant programs. Links to recently posted foundation RFPs are a feature of *Philanthropy News Digest* at the Center's Web site (http://www.fdncenter.org/pnd/rfp). You can also subscribe to the Center's *RFP Bulletin*, an electronic newsletter providing a weekly roundup of recently announced RFPs from private, corporate, and government funding sources.

Specialized funding directories enable you to concentrate on a particular aspect of your fundraising needs, be it a specific field (e.g., the arts, health), population group (e.g., women, minorities), type of support (e.g., equipment, research), or type of grantmaker (e.g., corporations, community foundations). Some of the more specialized directories are listed in Appendix A, but you should check with your colleagues or local library to learn about others related to your field. A number of Web sites, journals, periodicals, and newsletters, particularly those issued by professional, educational, and alumni associations, include features or columns on funding opportunities in specific fields. So be sure to look for such listings as well.

Primary materials issued directly by funders, such as annual reports or application guidelines, whether in written format or at a Web site, can be used to secure detailed information about those grantmakers you have identified as potential funding sources for your organization or project. However, only a small percentage of funders provide written or electronic information about themselves. (Only about 5 percent of grantmakers tracked by the Foundation Center have Web sites.) The annual information returns filed by private foundations (Forms 990-PF) are often the only source of information on the grantmaking activities and interests of smaller foundations.

Secondary narrative sources, available both online and in print, such as newspapers and magazines, can provide up-to-date information about grants awarded, changes in leadership, and/or priorities within a foundation or corporation. Indexes to newspapers and other periodicals are your key to unlocking this resource. There are several resources on the Web that are particularly helpful in locating articles about specific donors and about philanthropy in general. The *Literature of the Nonprofit Sector Online* (http://lnps.fdncenter.org) and the Philanthropic Studies Index (http://cheever.ulib.iupui.edu/psipublicsearch) are two Web-based searchable bibliographic tools that cover periodicals from the philanthropic sector. *Philanthropy News Digest* (http://www.fdncenter.org/pnd) is a compendium in digest form of philanthropy-related news articles and features culled from print and electronic media outlets nationwide. A listing of other nonprofit news and publication resources will be found in the Nonprofit Links section of the Researching Philanthropy directory on the Foundation Center's Web site. Major newspapers in the United States also often have searchable indexes at their Web sites.

People are important sources of information as well. Often just chatting with a colleague or veteran fundraiser can yield useful information. Beware of unsubstantiated information, however. On the other hand, a telephone chat with a foundation's grants officer or a face-to-face interview with a representative of a foundation can produce just the information you are seeking. Public forums where grantmakers speak openly about their interests and procedures can also prove quite helpful to the nonprofit grantseeker. All Foundation Center libraries host such forums, called either "Meet the Grantmakers" or "Dialogue with Donors." Some Cooperating Collections also sponsor similar forums for the public to hear grantmakers talk about their funding interests and share issues and ideas. Online communities, such as listservs and message boards, help people from anywhere in the world establish and strengthen ties, facilitate collaboration, disseminate knowledge, build new audiences, and inform others of the important work they are doing.

SOME IMPORTANT CONSIDERATIONS

Once you have a general overview of the available resources, we'll explore the ways you can put those resources to work for you. Most, if not all, of the materials described here can be consulted at the five Center-operated libraries or the more than 230 Cooperating Collections listed in Appendix F. Although some of the databases and publications described may be useful additions to your organization's library, we recommend that, initially, grantseekers invest their time rather than their money. Visit one of our libraries or Cooperating Collections and examine the materials relating to your area of interest before making a decision as to which publications or databases will prove most useful.

For those lacking the time or expertise, an alternative way to get the fundraising information you need is the Foundation Center's Associates Program. The Associates Program provides its members with exclusive access to information specialists who will comb through electronic databases, research publications, Forms 990-PF, and grantmaker files to answer questions and reply by e-mail or telephone. More details on the Associates Program are provided in Appendix E.

When conducting research on your own, pay attention to the quality of the information in the publication or electronic resource, as well as its relevance to your funding search. It is especially important to:

- determine the reputation of the publisher or database compiler since different resources have varying degrees of reliability;

- note the date the book was published or when the database was last updated and whether or not it contains the most current information available;

- read the introduction and any instructions on how to use the material, paying particular attention to how the information was obtained, how current it is, and what verification procedures, if any, were used in obtaining it;

- familiarize yourself with the format, indexes, and the kinds of information about potential funding sources contained in the book or database.

Taking the time to evaluate resources for their accuracy and thoroughness prior to using them can save you countless hours that might otherwise be wasted.

The Foundation Center's Databases

The Foundation Center first implemented its computerized database in 1972. Since that time the database has grown in size, scope, and quality. Its millions of records provide detailed information on more than 2.3 million grants and more than 75,000 currently active grantmakers, including: background data on the grantmaker; its purpose and programs; application procedures; the names of its trustees, officers, and donors; its current financial data; and more.

Information stored in the Center's database is drawn primarily from one of three sources: (1) information voluntarily provided by grantmakers, including responses to questionnaire mailings, online update forms, electronically transmitted grants lists, and grantmaker-issued reports, including application guidelines, financial statements, and informational brochures; (2) annual IRS information returns—Forms 990-PF, filed by private foundations, and Forms 990, filed by public foundations, both of which the Center receives from the IRS; and (3) grantmaker Web sites and other Internet-based resources. Center staff verify and update the majority of the entries from the latter two sources. The Center then makes the verified information available through several media: online databases (including *The Foundation Directory Online*, *Foundation Grants to Individuals Online*, and Foundation Finder), CD-ROMs such as *FC Search: The Foundation Center's Database on CD-ROM*, printed directories, and other publications.

The Foundation Center began to record and categorize grants in 1961 and established a computerized grants classification system in 1972. In 1989, following explosive growth in the number of grants indexed annually, the Center introduced a new classification system based on the National Taxonomy of Exempt Entities (NTEE). The NTEE is a comprehensive coding scheme developed by the National Center for Charitable Statistics that established a unified standard for classifying nonprofit organizations while permitting a multidimensional structure for analyzing grants. The Center's classification system provides a concise and consistent hierarchical method with which to classify and index grants and the nonprofit organizations receiving foundation funding. With this system, hundreds of specific terms can be researched with consistent results, and grant dollars can be tallied to determine distribution patterns. (For more information about NTEE and the Center's Grants Classification System, see Appendix C.)

The Center makes the grantmaker and grants information in its databases available to the public electronically and in printed format. The electronic formats are comprehensive and flexible. You can combine several elements—for example, subject or intended population group, type of support, and geographic limitations—in one search. In a short amount of time, thousands of foundation profiles and grant records can be accessed with a few simple key strokes. In printed format, grantmaker information is either general, such as in the comprehensive *Guide to U. S. Foundations, Their Trustees, Officers, and Donors*; targeted by subject, such as in the *National Guide to Funding in Arts and Culture* or by population served, such as *Grants for Women and Girls*; or based on some other criteria, such as assets, annual giving, or geographic location.

THE FOUNDATION DIRECTORY ONLINE

Since its introduction in 1999, *The Foundation Directory Online* (http://fconline.fdncenter.org), the Center's Web-based database, has become the most popular way to search the grantmaking universe for potential funders. *The Foundation Directory*

Online, a subscription-based service updated weekly, allows searches across 18 fields, including full-text searching, to return targeted lists of funding prospects. With a few short steps, you can use *The Foundation Directory Online* from your desktop at home or at work to give you instant access to information on thousands of grantmakers and their giving interests. It is the most comprehensive online foundation funding research tool available anywhere. New data (updated information on existing foundations as well as new foundations) and features are being added on an ongoing basis to further enhance your funding research.

Levels of Subscription Service

The Foundation Directory Online offers four levels of access to information from the Foundation Center's database.

- The first level of service, *The Foundation Directory Online Basic*, contains current descriptions of 10,000 of the largest foundations in the United States based on annual giving. At the *Basic* level, the Trustees, Officers, and Donors search field and its corresponding index allow users to search more than 64,000 trustee, officer, and donor names.

- The second level of service, *The Foundation Directory Online Plus*, includes access to the database of the 10,000 largest foundations, plus access to a grants file of information on nearly 400,000 grants made by the nation's largest foundations.

- The third level of service, *The Foundation Directory Online Premium*, provides access to the grants file plus a database of the 20,000 largest foundations in the nation. At the *Premium* level, the Trustees, Officers, and Donors search field and its corresponding index allow users to search more than 110,000 trustee, officer, and donor names.

- The most comprehensive level of service, *The Foundation Directory Online Platinum*, provides access to the grants file, plus the Center's entire database of more than 75,000 grantmakers, including foundations, grantmaking public charities, and corporate givers (the latter two are available only at the *Platinum* level). At the *Platinum* level, the Trustees, Officers, and Donors search field and its corresponding index allow users to search more than 340,000 trustee, officer, and donor names. Only *The Foundation Directory Online*

Platinum offers extensive program details for more than 1,500 foundations; expanded application guidelines for more than 7,200 foundations; and sponsoring company information for corporate givers.[1]

There are varying subscription fees for the different levels. Subscriptions to *The Foundation Directory Online* are offered at monthly and yearly rates, and there are discounts available for multiple-user plans. For a comparison of the four subscription levels of *The Foundation Directory Online*, see Figure 13.

Foundation Search

The foundations database of *The Foundation Directory Online* has eight indexed searchable fields and four non-indexed fields, including a "catch-all" Text Search field. Associated indexes for each of the eight indexed search fields can be opened by clicking on the field name that you wish to search from the right-hand side of the screen. The 12 searchable fields allow you to search on the following criteria:

Foundation Name	Geographic Focus	Total Assets
Foundation State	Trustees, Officers, and	Establishment Year
Foundation City	Donors	Text Search
Fields of Interest	Type of Grantmaker	
Types of Support	Total Giving	

Three of the search fields (Total Giving, Total Assets, and Establishment Year) can be searched using a range entered by the user. Using a drop-down menu, searchers can enter a range (in dollar figures or years) for the appropriate selected field. Search results can be sorted by total giving or alphabetically, both in ascending or descending order.

As an example of a search using the foundations database of *The Foundation Directory Online*, let's assume that a grantseeker wishes to identify grantmakers located in Florida that have a stated interest in funding for AIDS research and that have assets of $50,000 or more. To begin to construct this search, first open the index for the Foundation State field by clicking on it. A corresponding alphabetical index of the 50 states

---

1. Unless otherwise noted, the remaining references in this chapter to *The Foundation Directory Online* refer to the *Platinum* level of service. See Figure 13 for a comparison chart detailing the content and features of each subscription service level.

Figure 13. Comparison Chart: *The Foundation Directory Online* Subscription Plans and *FC Search: The Foundation Center's Database on CD-ROM*

The Foundation Directory Online
Online Subscription Plans

Contents & Features	The Foundation Directory Online			
	Basic	**Plus**	**Premium**	**Platinum**
Grantmaker data	Profiles of the largest **10,000** U.S. foundations based on total annual giving.	Profiles of the largest **10,000** U.S. foundations based on total annual giving.	Profiles of the largest **20,000** U.S. foundations based on total annual giving.	All **75,000+** U.S.-based foundations, grantmaking public charities, and corporate givers. Additional information on defined program areas for 1,500 large funders and expanded application guidelines for 7,200 funders.
Web links	Links to 1,000+ foundation Web sites. Links to 990-PF IRS filings.	Links to 1,000+ foundation Web sites. Links to 990-PF IRS filings.	Links to close to 1,300 foundation Web sites. Links to 990-PF IRS filings.	Links to over 6,000 grantmaker and corporate Web sites. Links to 990-PF IRS filings.
Grants data	No separate grants file. Close to half of the foundation profiles include up to 10 sample grants.	Searchable grants file contains 390,000+ grants awarded by large foundations. One-click link from grant record to funder's record.	Searchable grants file contains 390,000+ grants awarded by large foundations. One-click link from grant record to funder's record.	Searchable file with 390,000+ grants awarded by large foundations. One-click link from grant record to funder's record.
Search fields	**Choose from 12 fields:** foundation name; foundation state; foundation city; fields of interest; types of support; geographic focus; trustees, officers, and donors; total assets; total giving; foundation type; year established; text search.	**Choose from 18 fields:** foundation name; foundation state; foundation city; fields of interest; types of support; geographic focus; trustees, officers, and donors; total assets; total giving; foundation type; year established; text search. Specific to grants database: recipient name; recipient state; recipient city; subjects; year authorized; grant amount.	**Choose from 18 fields:** foundation name; foundation state; foundation city; fields of interest; types of support; geographic focus; trustees, officers, and donors; total assets; total giving; foundation type; year established; text search. Specific to grants database: recipient name; recipient state; recipient city; subjects; year authorized; grant amount.	**Choose from 18 fields:** foundation name; foundation state; foundation city; fields of interest; types of support; geographic focus; trustees, officers, and donors; total assets; total giving; foundation type; year established; text search. Specific to grants database: recipient name; recipient state; recipient city; subjects; year authorized; grant amount.
Sort results	Foundations sort by total giving or alphabetically, in ascending or descending order.	Foundations sort by total giving or alphabetically, in ascending or descending order. Grants sort alphabetically by foundation name or by grant amount.	Foundations sort by total giving or alphabetically, in ascending or descending order. Grants sort alphabetically by foundation name or by grant amount.	Foundations sort by total giving or alphabetically, in ascending or descending order. Grants sort alphabetically by foundation name or by grant amount.
Print options	Print results list up to 100 at a time. For more than 100, go to the next page and print the next 100, etc. Individual records are printed one at a time as they appear in the browser window.			
Save options	Not available. Copy and paste from the browser window.			
Mark records, Save searches, Attach notes	Load last search option available.			
Special features	Subscriber message board; daily news articles and RFPs; book discounts for annual subscribers; e-newsletter.			
Update cycle	Weekly.			
Cost	From $19.95 per month or $195 annually. Multi-user pricing available.	From $29.95 per month or $295 annually. Multi-user pricing available.	From $59.95 per month or $595 annually. Multi-user pricing available.	From $149.95 per month or $995 annually. Multi-user and institution-wide pricing available.

For information on these and other electronic products, visit our Web site at www.fdncenter.org/marketplace, or call our Electronic Products Hotline at 1-800-478-4661.

Figure 13. (continued)

FC Search: The Foundation Center's Database on CD-ROM

Contents & Features	FC Search: The Foundation Center's Database on CD-ROM
Foundation data	Over **76,000** U.S.-based foundations, corporate givers, and grantmaking public charities. Add'l info. on defined program areas for 1,500 top funders and expanded application guidelines for 7,200 funders.
Web links	Links to over 6,000 grantmaker and corporate Web sites. Links to 990-PF IRS filings.
Grants data	Searchable file with over 320,000 grants of $10,000 or more awarded by the top foundations over past four years. Foundation and grants files are linked.
Search fields	**Choose from 21 fields—14 in grantmaker file & 12 in grants file:** grantmaker name; grantmaker state; grantmaker city; grantmaker type; geographic focus; establishment date; fields of interest; trustees, officers, and donors; text search; types of support; total assets; total giving; corporate name; corporate location. Specific to grants database: recipient name; recipient state; recipient city; subjects; grant amount; year authorized; recipient type.
Sort results	Grantmaker search results may be sorted alphabetically or by total annual giving. Grant search results may be sorted alphabetically by grantmaker name or by total grant amount.
Print options	Print search results list up to 1,000 at a time. Print individual records or a group of records with one command (up to 500 at a time). Partial record print is an option.
Save options	Save search results list up to 1,000 at a time. Save individual records or a group of records (up to 500) in ASCII text format. Partial record save is an option.
Mark records	Users have the ability to create and revise multiple marked records lists that can be stored between sessions, revised, printed, and saved to text files.
Attach notes	Affix electronic notes to individual records. Search notes available.
Save searches	Search strategies can be named and saved between sessions.
Update cycle	Semi-annually in March and October.
Cost	$1,195 for the single user disk. Price includes free Fall Update disk and a 100+ page printed manual. Renewal discounts apply. Please inquire for network prices.

For information on these and other electronic products, visit our Web site at www.fdncenter.org/marketplace or call 1-800-478-4661.

Figure 14. Foundation State Index from *The Foundation Directory Online*

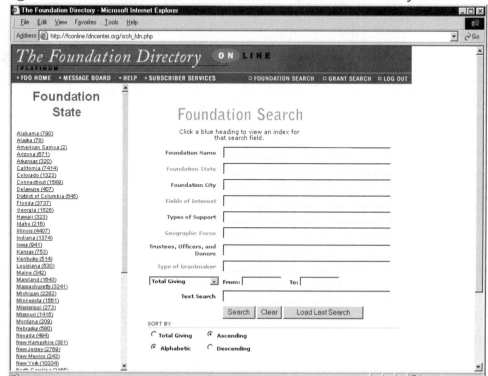

(plus the District of Columbia) will open in a vertical panel on the left-hand side of the screen (see Figure 14). By clicking on Florida, that term will automatically appear in the search entry box adjacent to Foundation State. Next, open the Fields of Interest Index by clicking on it and select the term "AIDS research." Finally, select Total Assets from the drop-down menu and enter "$50,000" in the first box provided. (If you leave the second box empty, your results will include all foundations with assets of $50,000 and up.) To view your search results in descending order by total giving, select the radio buttons "Total Giving" and "Descending" from the sorting options available. The resulting search strategy will look like the one in Figure 15. To execute the search, click on the Search button. Foundations in the search results list are presented with foundation name, foundation city and state, and a total giving figure for the most recent year available. To open the full record of a foundation in your search results, click on the foundation name. Clicking on a record from the search results (the

Figure 15. Foundation Search Screen from *The Foundation Directory Online*

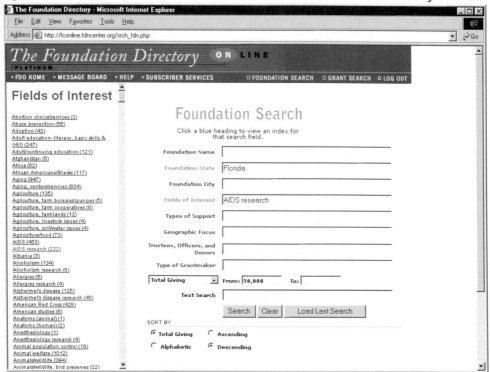

Campbell Foundation of Fort Lauderdale, Florida) will provide an example of what a typical foundation record in *The Foundation Directory Online* looks like (see Figure 16).

While the content of a foundation profile depends largely upon the size and nature of its funding programs and the availability of information on the foundation, most foundation profiles can include any combination of the following: the foundation's name, address, and telephone number; separate application address(es) and contact person(s); fax number and e-mail and/or Web addresses; fields of interest reflected in the foundation's giving program(s); geographic focus; type(s) of support; names of donors, officers, and trustees; financial information, including fiscal year-end date, total assets, gifts received, expenditures, amount and number of grants paid, and separate information on amount and number of employee matching gifts, grants to individuals, or loans; IRS Employer Identification Number (EIN); a link to the foundation's Form 990-PF; type of grantmaker; background information; purpose and

Figure 16. Sample Foundation Record from *The Foundation Directory Online*

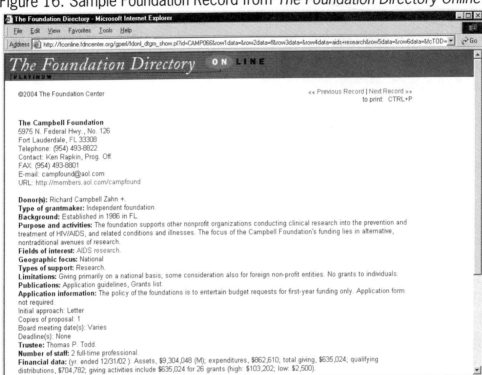

activities; specific limitations on foundation giving by geographic area, subject focus, or types of support; publications and printed material available from the foundation; application information, including preferred initial approach, the number of proposal copies required, deadline(s), board meeting date(s), and final notification date(s); number of full- and half-time professional and support staff; and a selected listing of recently awarded grants designed to provide an overview of a foundation's giving interests.

Grant Search

If you subscribe to the *Plus, Premium,* or *Platinum* service plan, you will have access to the grants file, which contains nearly 400,000 records of grants that have actually been given out in the recent past.

The grants file of *The Foundation Directory Online* has six indexed searchable fields and three non-indexed fields, including a "catch-all" Text Search field. Associated indexes for each of the six indexed search fields can be opened by clicking on the field name that you wish to search on the right-hand side of the screen. The nine searchable fields allow you to search on the following criteria:

Foundation Name	Recipient City	Year Authorized
Recipient Name	Subjects	Grant Amount
Recipient State/Country	Types of Support	Text Search

Two of the search fields (Year Authorized and Grant Amount) can be searched using a range entered by the user. By using a drop-down menu, searchers can enter a range (in dollar figures or years) for the appropriate selected field. Search results can be sorted by grant amount, alphabetically, or by year, all in ascending or descending order.

As an example of a search of the grants database of *The Foundation Directory Online*, let's assume that a grantseeker wishes to identify grants of at least $200,000 awarded to senior centers in California. To begin to construct this search, first open the index for Recipient State/Country by clicking on it. An alphabetical listing of recipient states and countries will then appear on the left-hand side of the screen (see Figure 17). From the Recipient State/Country Index, select the term "California." Next, open the Subjects Index and select the term "Aging, centers/services" from the list of available terms. Finally, select Grant Amount from the drop-down menu and enter "$200,000" in the first box provided. (If you leave the second box empty your results will include all grants of $200,000 and up.) To view your search results in descending order by year authorized, select the radio buttons "Year Authorized" and "Descending" from the sorting options available. The resulting search strategy will look like the one in Figure 18. To execute the search, click on the Search button. Grants in the search results list are presented with foundation name and state, recipient name and state, the year authorized, and the total grant amount. To open a full record of a grant in your search results, click on the recipient name/state or the grant amount. Clicking on a recipient from the search results (a 2003 grant given to the San Mateo County Health Services Agency of San Mateo, California) will provide an example of what a typical grant record in *The Foundation Directory Online* looks like (see Figure 19).

While the content of a grant record varies based on the availability of information from the Form 990-PF, foundation annual reports, and grants lists provided by the foundation, most grant records will include: recipient name and location; a link to the recipient's Web site, if available; type of recipient; grantmaker name; grantmaker geographic focus; grant amount; year authorized; duration (if applicable); grant

Figure 17. Recipient State/Country Index from *The Foundation Directory Online*

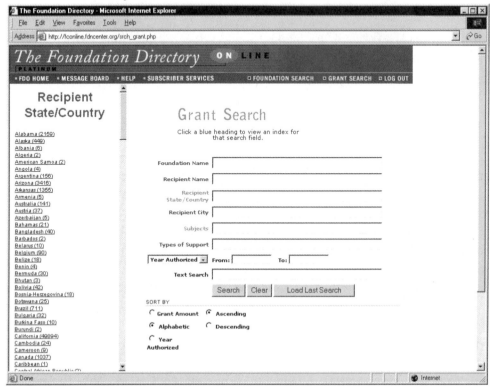

description; type(s) of support; and subject(s). Grant records also include a "Go to Foundation" link to the corresponding foundation profile in the foundations database.

FC SEARCH: THE FOUNDATION CENTER'S DATABASE ON CD-ROM

Shortly after its introduction in 1996, *FC Search: The Foundation Center's Database on CD-ROM* became a popular way to search the grantmaking universe for potential funders. *FC Search* is produced annually in the spring with an update six months later. It includes profiles of more than 75,000 U.S. foundations and corporate givers; the names and foundation affiliations of more than 350,000 trustees, officers, and donors who make the funding decisions at these institutions; and descriptions of close to 325,000 grants reported recently. *FC Search* allows the user to link directly to more than 3,900 grantmaker Web sites, more than 2,200 corporate Web sites, and to the Center's own

Text Search in *The Foundation Directory Online* and *FC Search*

In both *The Foundation Directory Online* and *FC Search*, the Text Search field, which does not have an index, can be used to find information that may or may not be indexed in other fields. When Text Search is used, the program will search all the words in the grantmaker or grants files for the terms you type into the search criteria box next to Text Search. For example, let's assume you want to identify as many grantmakers as possible in New York State that are interested in water conservation issues. If you use *FC Search* and fill in the Grantmaker State box with "New York" and the Fields of Interest box with "Environment, water resources" ("water conservation" is not an indexed term for the Fields of Interest field), you would get ten hits. As an alternative search, or if you simply do not know the specified term used in the Fields of Interest Index, you could delete the term from the Fields of Interest box and enter the term "water" in the Text Search box. This search would yield 31 hits. Upon further examination you will note that several of these hits, such as the Robert and Elaine LeBuhn Foundation and the Frankel Family Foundation, have no documented interest in the environmental issue of water conservation. They were retrieved because their mailing addresses are on Water Street in New York. This is one of the negatives of text searching. However, the search did yield a number of foundations whose selected grants lists or purpose and activities statements do indicate an interest in the subject.

Web site. Either *FC Search* or *The Foundation Dircetory Online* is available in all Foundation Center libraries and at most Cooperating Collections throughout the United States.

FC Search is configured so that you can scroll through the list of grantmakers or grant recipients using the browse feature, or you can adopt one of three search modes (Basic Grantmaker, Advanced Grantmaker, and Advanced Grants) to tailor a search to your specific criteria (see Figure 20).

Figure 18. Grant Search Screen from *The Foundation Directory Online*

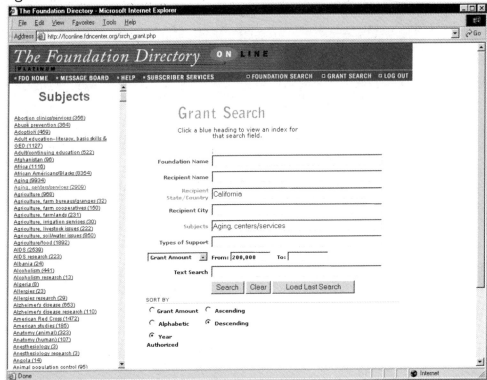

Browsing

The Browse feature is a good introduction to the information in *FC Search*. Browsing the grantmakers file or grants file allows you to:

- become familiar with the contents of the two files comprising the database;

- find a specific grantmaker by name or the grants given to a specific organization (grant recipient);

- browse alphabetically through all grantmakers located in a specific state or browse alphabetically through all grant recipients located in a specific state or country; and

- link to a list of recent grants for a particular foundation, when available, directly from the grantmaker record.

Figure 19. Sample Grant Record from *The Foundation Directory Online*

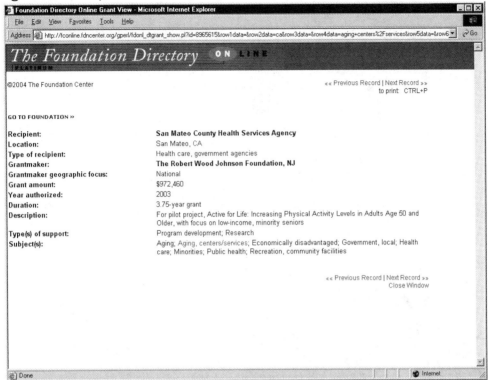

Once familiar with the contents of *FC Search*, you are ready to use its search features to develop a broad list of potential funders that have interests in common with your organization's goals and activities.

Basic Search

The Basic Search mode for the grantmaker file is designed for users new to *FC Search* or for those who wish to use the most common search criteria. Basic Search allows searching on the following five criteria:

- Grantmaker Name

- Grantmaker State

- Fields of Interest

- Trustees, Officers, and Donors

- Text Search

Figure 20. Main Menu Screen from *FC Search: The Foundation Center's Database on CD-ROM*

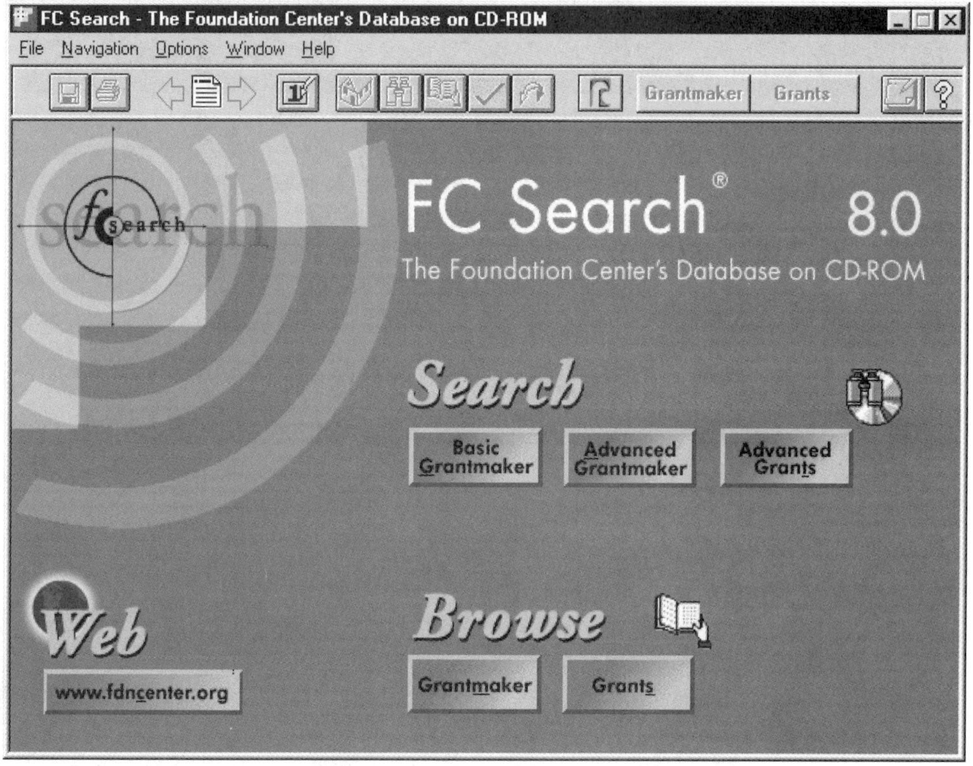

The first four search criteria have associated indexes from which possible search terms can be selected. Searches performed using these criteria result in hits in particular areas (or fields) of the grantmaker records. Text Search searches for words that appear anywhere within the grantmaker records regardless of field.

When designing a Basic Search, you may choose from any one or all five of the default search criteria. An example of a search using two fields of a Basic Search is shown in Figure 21. In this instance, the grantseeker is conducting a search to identify foundations in three Southern states (Alabama, Georgia, or Tennessee) that are interested in environmental programs.

Advanced Search

Advanced Search is available for both the grantmaker and grants files in *FC Search*. The grantmaker file contains profiles of the funders themselves and the grants file contains

Figure 21. Basic Grantmaker Search in *FC Search: The Foundation Center's Database on CD-ROM*

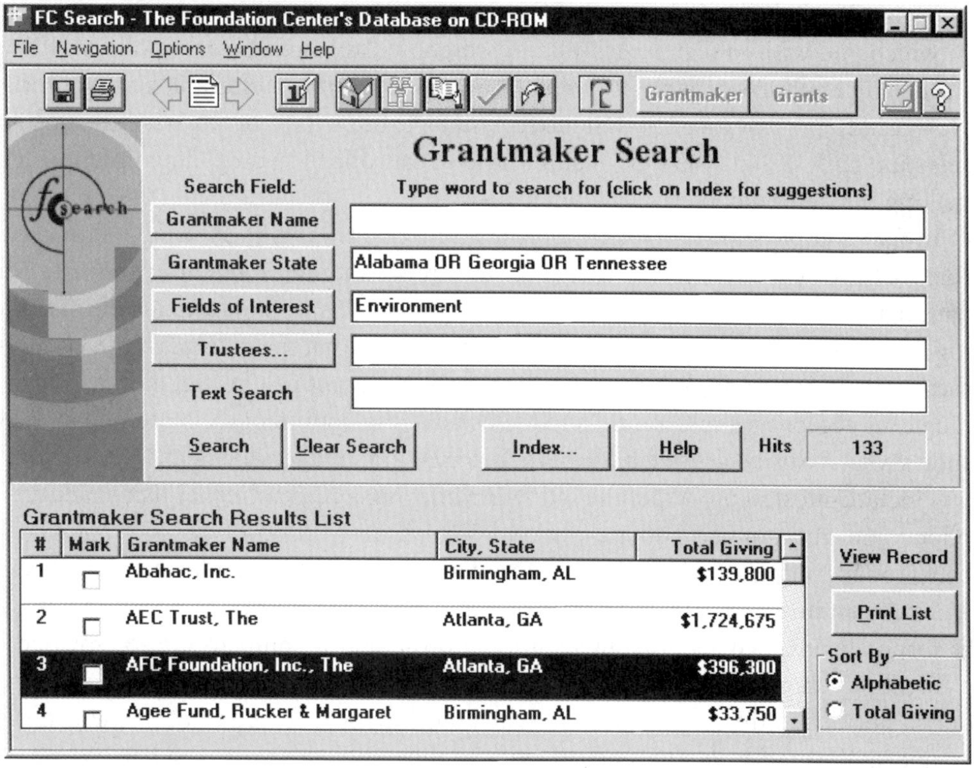

records of actual grants already awarded. The Advanced Search mode for the grantmaker file has additional capabilities beyond those offered in Basic Search mode. It is designed for those with some experience using *FC Search* or for those who wish to search on fields that are not available in the Basic Search mode. In Advanced Grantmaker Search, you have 14 different search criteria to choose from, and you have a choice of Boolean operators that work among different search fields (see Figure 22).

The five default fields in Advanced Search are the same as in Basic Search: Grantmaker Name, Grantmaker State, Fields of Interest, Trustees. . . , and Text Search. However, in Advanced Search, you have nine additional criteria on which to search:

Corporate Location   Geographic Focus   Total Assets
Corporate Name   Grantmaker City   Total Giving
Establishment Date   Grantmaker Type   Types of Support

Five is the maximum number of search criteria you can use in any one search; however, you do not need to utilize all five, and you can organize them in any combination you wish. By clicking on the search criterion drop-down menu, you can select the field in which you wish to search. As in Basic Search, in Advanced Search mode "AND" is the default Boolean operator *between* fields when searching on multiple search criteria. However, in the Advanced Search mode, you have the option of changing the default selection to "OR" or "NOT" by using the Boolean operator drop-down menus and making the desired choice.

In the example shown in Figure 23, the grantseeker wants to identify grantmakers that: (1) provide funds for construction and renovation, (2) give in Minnesota (or nationally), (3) are interested in services to senior citizens, and (4) are capable of making large grants. The grantseeker also wants to be sure that the grantmakers that meet these criteria accept applications. In this case, eight grantmakers met all the criteria, including accepting applications, and are listed at the bottom of the screen. Figure 24 shows what a partial record for one of the selected grantmakers looks like. Each record will include most, if not all, of the following information: grantmaker name, address, phone and fax number, contact person, Web address, donor, type of grantmaker, background, purpose and activities, fields of interest, application information, officers and trustees, financial data, and selected grants. For company-sponsored foundations or corporate direct giving programs, information about the company is also provided.

Figure 25 shows an Advanced Search in the *FC Search* grants file. It is similar to the one performed in the grantmaker file. The grants file is searched in the same general manner as the grantmaker file and provides 12 different fields from which to choose:

Geographic Focus	Recipient City	Subjects
Grant Amount	Recipient Name	Text Search
Grantmaker Name	Recipient State/Country	Types of Support
Grantmaker State	Recipient Type	Year Authorized

The five default search fields that appear when first entering the grants search screen are: Recipient Name, Recipient State/Country, Grantmaker Name, Subjects, and Text Search. Changing the criteria to one of the other seven fields is simple: click on the search criterion drop-down menu and select the new field you wish to search. The Advanced Grants Search function also allows you a choice of Boolean operators ("OR," "AND," "NOT") that work *between* search fields. You can change these by making your selection from the drop-down menu to the left of the search fields.

Figure 22. Advanced Grantmaker Search Screen Showing Boolean Drop-
Down Menu and Field Drop-Down Menu from *FC Search:*
The Foundation Center's Database on CD-ROM

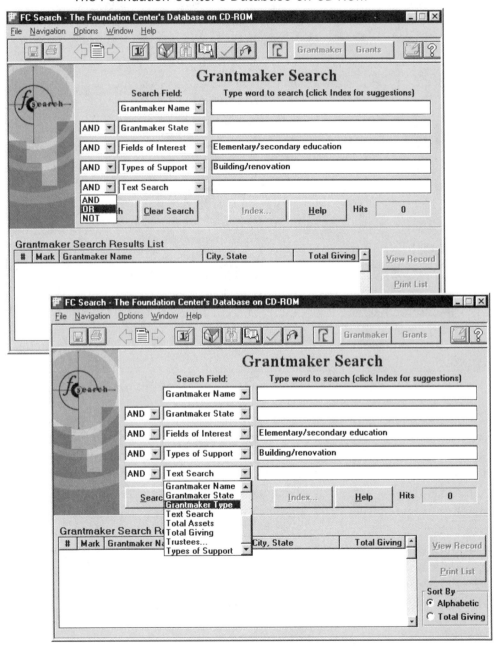

Figure 23. Advanced Grantmaker Search in *FC Search: The Foundation Center's Database on CD-ROM*

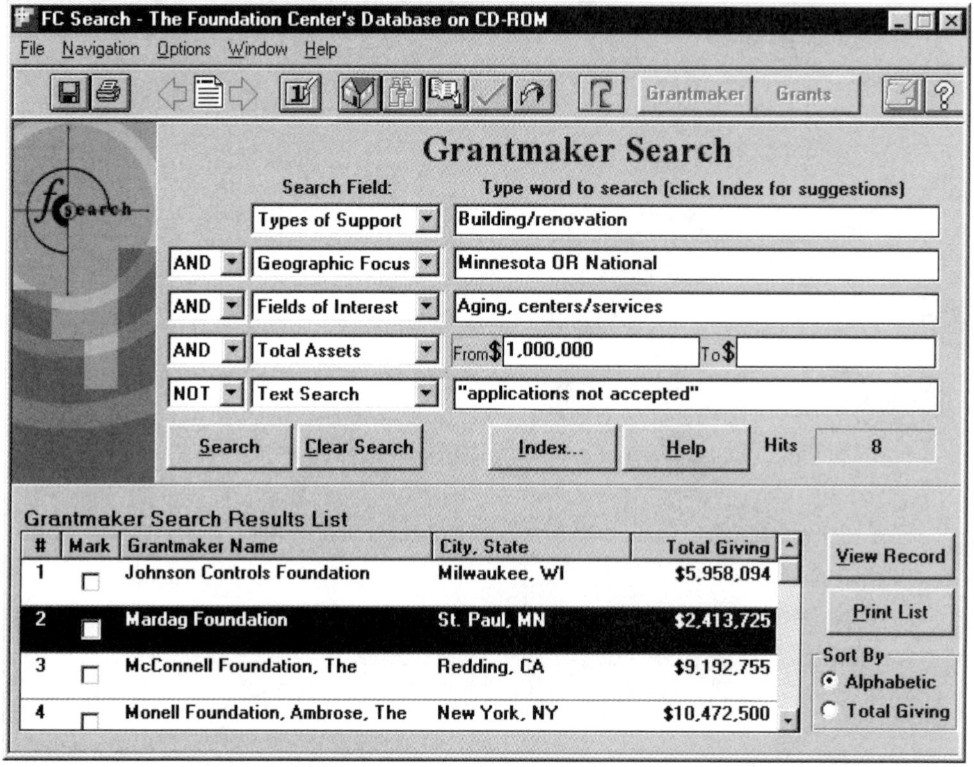

You can develop an initial list of potential funders that have funded organizations or projects similar to your own from the grants file or research the actual grants of funders you have already identified. Reviewing grants that have been given by a foundation or corporation will help you identify funders with a demonstrated interest in your subject or geographic area. All grant records in the grants file provide a link to the profile of the grantmaker in the grantmakers file and some provide links to recipient Web sites.

While *The Foundation Directory Online* and *FC Search* are versatile prospecting tools, grantseekers should further refine the list of potential funders they come up with using these databases by referring to primary and secondary sources, such as Forms 990-PF, grantmaker Web sites, annual reports, grantmaker guidelines, news articles, and so forth.

Figure 24. Sample Grantmaker Record from *FC Search: The Foundation Center's Database on CD-ROM*

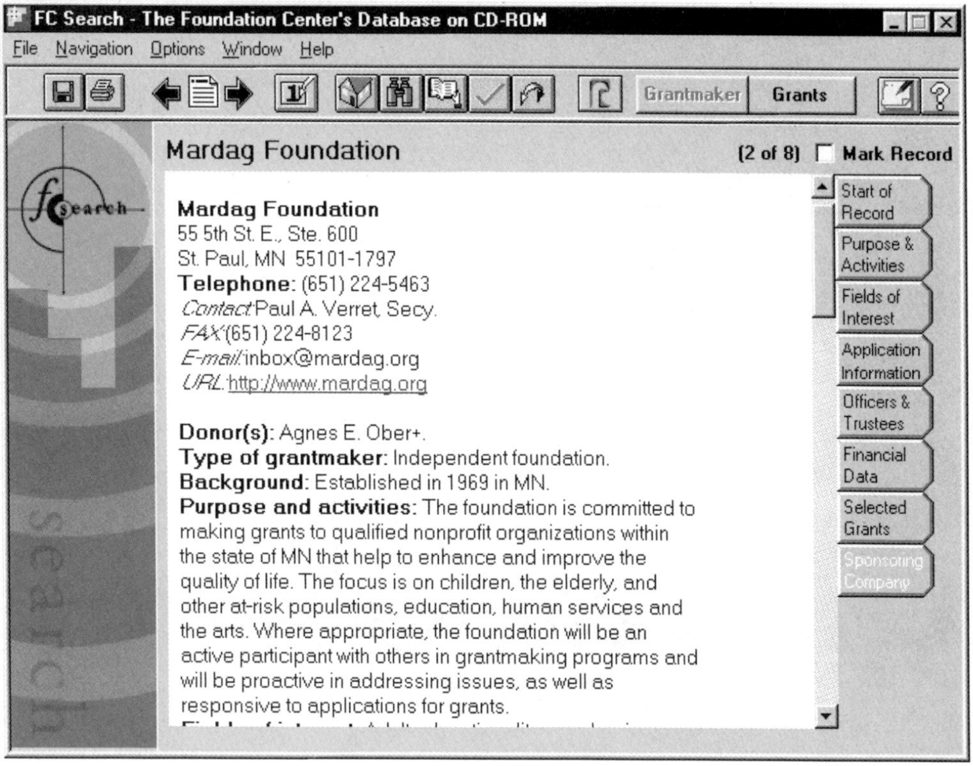

For a comparison chart on *The Foundation Directory Online* and *FC Search*, please see Figure 13.

DIALOG

DIALOG, a commercial service available to the public by subscription or via the Internet, has provided access to the Foundation Center's databases since the 1970s. The Center maintains two databases on DIALOG that are updated on an ongoing basis—one providing information on grantmakers (File 26), and the other on the grants they distribute (File 27).

For further information about online access to the Foundation Center's databases through DIALOG, visit the Dialog Corporation Web site (http://www.dialog.com) or call Dialog at 1-800-334-2564.

Figure 25. Sample Grants Search in *FC Search: The Foundation Center's Database on CD-ROM*

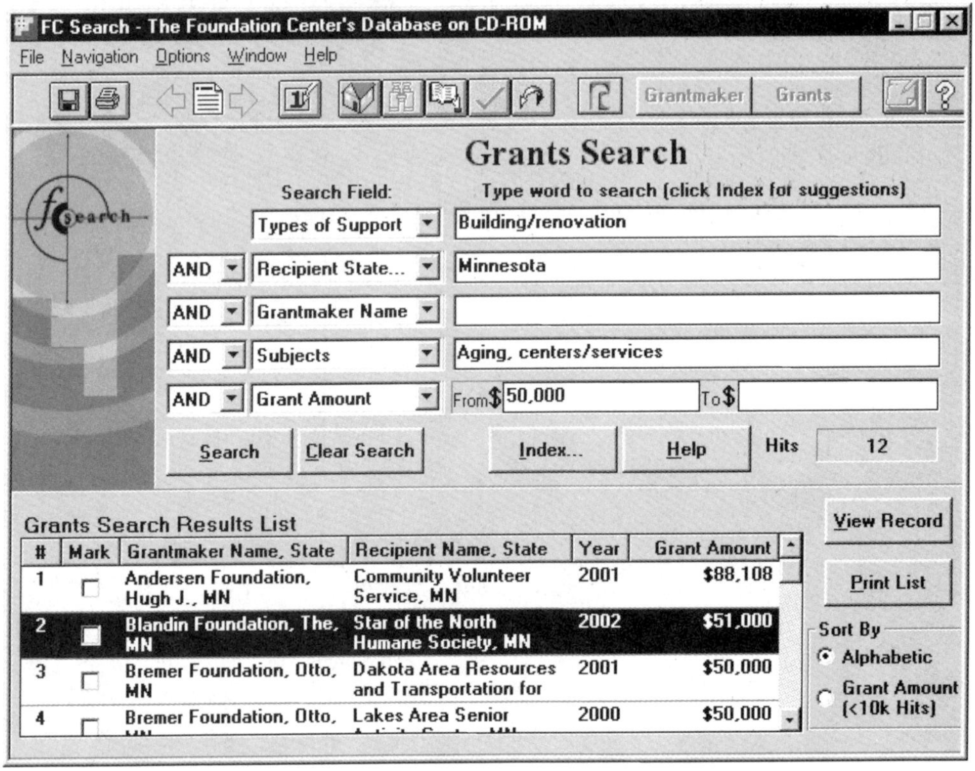

General Grantmaker Directories

General grantmaker print directories, whether national or local, provide information on the broadest possible selection of grantmakers. You may want to begin with general directories and work your way to those with more specific content.

The Foundation Center publishes several major foundation directories that are general in content and well indexed: the *Guide to U.S. Foundations, Their Trustees, Officers, and Donors*, a multivolume annual publication; *The Foundation Directory* and *The Foundation Directory Part 2*, each published annually and updated semiannually by *The Foundation Directory Supplement*; and *The Foundation 1000*, an annual publication in one volume. Please see Appendix A for a listing of general fundraising directories issued by other publishers.

GUIDE TO U.S. FOUNDATIONS, THEIR TRUSTEES, OFFICERS, AND DONORS

In terms of scope, the Foundation Center's most comprehensive grantmaker directory in print is the *Guide to U.S. Foundations, Their Trustees, Officers, and Donors*. This multivolume annual reference book is the only Center print publication that contains all active grantmaking independent, corporate, and community foundations; more than 67,000 in 2004. It includes more than 45,000 grantmakers not covered in other Foundation Center publications. The *Guide to U.S. Foundations* arranges foundations by state and within each state in descending order by total giving. The *Guide* also lists operating foundations by state in descending order by asset amount. The *Guide* contains three indexes: an index of the foundation trustees, officers, and donors included in each edition, a foundation name index, and a community foundation name index.

Entries in the *Guide to U.S. Foundations* may contain any or all of the following: address and contact information; Web site link and e-mail address (if available); establishment date; donors; current financial data, including fiscal year-end date, total grants paid, total assets and asset type, total gifts received, total expenditures, qualifying distributions, loans to organizations, loans to individuals, and program amounts; geographic limitations; publications that the foundation makes available; a listing of officers, trustees, and/or directors; the IRS Employer Identification Number (EIN); and a series of codes that indicate: (1) the type of foundation; (2) its grantmaking status; and (3) other Foundation Center print publications in which an entry for that foundation also appears (see Figure 26).

The Foundation Trustee, Officer, and Donor Index provides a comprehensive list of all the trustees, officers, and donors affiliated with the foundations in the *Guide*. Arranged alphabetically by individual or corporation name, it lists the individual, his/her foundation affiliation (in italics), the foundation's location by state, the foundation's sequence number in the *Guide*, and codes identifying other Center publications in which additional information can be found (see Figure 27). If an individual is both a donor and an officer or trustee of a foundation, his/her name will appear in the index only once for that particular foundation. An individual's name appears as a separate listing for each foundation affiliation, however, thus enabling grantseekers to quickly identify all foundations with which that individual is connected.

The Foundation Name Index and Locator and the Community Foundation Name Index and Locator provide alphabetical listings of the foundations in the *Guide* with their state location and the codes indicating which Center publications contain additional information on that foundation (FD for *The Foundation Directory*, FD2 for *The Foundation Directory Part 2*, FM for *The Foundation 1000*, GTI for *Foundation Grants to Individuals*, and CD for the *National Directory of Corporate Giving*).

The *Guide to U.S. Foundations* is designed for preliminary research on funding sources. It is particularly useful in identifying smaller foundations, which are often good sources of local support.

THE FOUNDATION DIRECTORY, THE FOUNDATION DIRECTORY PART 2, AND THE FOUNDATION DIRECTORY SUPPLEMENT

The Foundation Directory is the most authoritative and widely used print directory of private foundations. It includes descriptions of the largest 10,000 grantmaking foundations in the United States by total giving. The foundations in the 26th edition of the *Directory*, published in 2004, account for approximately 87.5 percent of the total assets owned by foundations and 90.1 percent of the total grant dollars awarded annually by private foundations.

Each *Directory* entry may include the following data elements: foundation name, address, and telephone number; separate application address(es) and contact person(s); fax number and e-mail and/or Web addresses; establishment date; donors; current financial data, including assets, gifts received, expenditures, qualifying distributions, grants to organizations, grants to individuals, matching gifts, loans or program-related investments, and foundation-administered program amounts; purpose and activities; fields of interest; types of support awarded; limitations on its giving program(s), including geographic limitations; application procedures; officers, trustees, and staff; the foundation's IRS Employer Identification Number (EIN); and a list of selected grants, when available (see Figure 28). The volume is arranged by state, then alphabetically within state by foundation name. The 26th edition of *The Foundation Directory* includes the following seven indexes to help you identify foundations of interest:

- an index of donors, officers, and trustees;

- a geographic index to foundation locations by state and city, including cross-references to foundations with identified giving patterns beyond the states in which they are located;

- an international giving index of countries, continents, or regions where foundations have indicated giving interests, broken down by the states in which the foundations are located;

- an index of types of support offered, broken down by the states in which the foundations are located;

Figure 26. Sample Entry and Key from *Guide to U.S. Foundations, Their Trustees, Officers, and Donors*

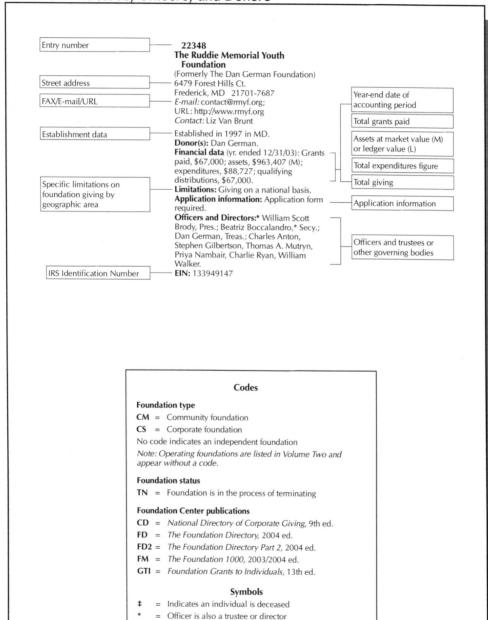

Entry number

22348
The Ruddie Memorial Youth
Foundation
(Formerly The Dan German Foundation)

Street address
6479 Forest Hills Ct.
Frederick, MD 21701-7687

FAX/E-mail/URL
E-mail: contact@rmyf.org;
URL: http://www.rmyf.org
Contact: Liz Van Brunt

Year-end date of accounting period

Establishment data
Established in 1997 in MD.
Donor(s): Dan German.

Total grants paid

Financial data (yr. ended 12/31/03): Grants
paid, $67,000; assets, $963,407 (M);
expenditures, $88,727; qualifying
distributions, $67,000.

Assets at market value (M) or ledger value (L)

Total expenditures figure

Total giving

Specific limitations on foundation giving by geographic area
Limitations: Giving on a national basis.
Application information: Application form required.

Application information

Officers and Directors:* William Scott
Brody, Pres.; Beatriz Boccalandro,* Secy.;
Dan German, Treas.; Charles Anton,
Stephen Gilbertson, Thomas A. Mutryn,
Priya Nambair, Charlie Ryan, William
Walker.

Officers and trustees or other governing bodies

IRS Identification Number
EIN: 133949147

Codes

Foundation type

CM = Community foundation

CS = Corporate foundation

No code indicates an independent foundation

Note: Operating foundations are listed in Volume Two and appear without a code.

Foundation status

TN = Foundation is in the process of terminating

Foundation Center publications

CD = *National Directory of Corporate Giving,* 9th ed.

FD = *The Foundation Directory,* 2004 ed.

FD2 = *The Foundation Directory Part 2,* 2004 ed.

FM = *The Foundation 1000,* 2003/2004 ed.

GTI = *Foundation Grants to Individuals,* 13th ed.

Symbols

‡ = Indicates an individual is deceased

* = Officer is also a trustee or director

Figure 27. Foundation Trustee, Officer, and Donor Index from *Guide to U.S. Foundations, Their Trustees, Officers, and Donors*

FOUNDATION TRUSTEE, OFFICER AND DONOR INDEX

Miller, Arjay, *Arjay R. & Frances F. Miller Foundation,* CA, 1855 (FD)
Miller, Arjay R., *Arjay R. & Frances F. Miller Foundation,* CA, 1855 (FD)
Miller, Arnold, *A. & D. Miller Foundation,* IL, 15685 (FD2)
Miller, Arnold M., *Arnold M. & Sydell L. Miller Foundation,* OH, 44681 (FD2, GTI)
Miller, Arnold M., *The Arnold and Suzanne Miller Foundation,* TX, 53818
Miller, Arnold M., Jr., *The Arnold and Suzanne Miller Foundation,* TX, 53818
Miller, Arthur, *Arthur Miller Foundation,* NY, 40359
Miller, Arthur H., *The Miller Family Fund,* CA, 4418
Miller, Arthur H., *Bernard E. & Edith B. Waterman Charitable Foundation,* MA, 23297 (FD)
Miller, Arthur L., *New Horizons Un-Limited, Inc.,* WI, 66961
Miller, Arthur R., *The Holden Foundation,* IL, 16406
Miller, Asher H., *The Betsy Gordon Foundation,* NY, 38384
Miller, Ashley, *Kare Foundation,* NV, 31016
Miller, Avram, *The Avram Miller Family Foundation,* CA, 2818 (FD2)
Miller, Avrum, *A. & D. Miller Foundation,* IL, 15685 (FD2)
Miller, Avy L., *Avy L. & Roberta L. Miller Foundation,* CA, 4319
Miller, Barbara, *The Barbara and Fred Miller Family Foundation,* CA, 3281 (FD2)
Miller, Barbara K., *The Young Musicians Summer Enrichment Fund,* VA, 57529
Miller, Barbara P., *Pitts Family Scholarship Foundation,* AL, 519
Miller, Barry K., *Noll Foundation, Inc.,* CA, 2646 (FD2)
Miller, Barry L., *The Henry and Ruth Blaustein Rosenberg Foundation, Inc.,* MD, 21890 (FD)
Miller, Beatrice E., *Sam Foundation,* IL, 18012
Miller, Becky, *Maud Nuttall Memorial Greenlake Scholarship Trust,* IL, 17706
Miller, Becky, *Galion Community Foundation,* OH, 44907 (GTI)
Miller, Ben, *The Ben Miller Foundation,* MN, 27997
Miller, Ben, *Sam Miller Foundation,* MN, 28082
Miller, Ben, Hon., *The Agnes B. Hunt Trust,* GA, 13695
Miller, Benjamin A., *Benjamin A. Miller Family Foundation,* MN, 28641
Miller, Bernard, *The Academy of Science and Art of Pittsburgh,* PA, 65822
Miller, Bernard R., *The Nathan & Rosella Sussman Foundation,* NJ, 32181
Miller, Bernard R., *The Miller Family Foundation,* NJ, 32273
Miller, Bertha Gordon, *The Diana and Conrad Weil, Jr. Charitable Foundation,* TX, 53816
Miller, Bertha Gordon, *The Arnold and Suzanne Miller Foundation,* TX, 53818
Miller, Beryl, *Sam Miller Foundation,* MN, 28082
Miller, Bethany, *Alois and Twyla Luhr Foundation,* IL, 17324
Miller, Bette, *Kalman & Ida Wolens Foundation,* TX, 52966 (FD)
Miller, Betty Ann Greenbaum, *The Betty Ann Greenbaum Miller and Daniel L. Miller Family Foundation, Inc.,* MA, 25342
Miller, Betty E., *C. E. Miller Family Foundation,* MI, 26308 (FD2)
Miller, Betty J., *Wayne M. and Betty J. Miller Foundation,* IL, 17317
Miller, Betty Lou, *The Coffey Foundation, Inc.,* NC, 42435 (FD, GTI)
Miller, Betty M., *Miller Charitalble Foundation, Inc.,* FL, 12930
Miller, Beverly, *Beverly and Marvin Miller Foundation,* FL, 11194
Miller, Bill, *Dickinson Area Community Foundation,* MI, 26191 (FD2, GTI)
Miller, Bill, *Associated Charities of Findlay, Ohio,* OH, 44496 (FD2, GTI)
Miller, Blair D., *Joseph J. & Marie P. Schedel Foundation,* OH, 46241
Miller, Bob, *K. L. Smith Scholarship Foundation, Inc.,* OK, 47118
Miller, Bobbie L., *Miller Family Charitable Trust,* MS, 28936
Miller, Boyd J., *Beta Pi Memorial Fund Trust,* MN, 28718
Miller, Brian, *St. Joseph Foundation of Los Angeles,* OH, 65378
Miller, Brian K., *Tyler Foundation,* TX, 54279 (CD)
Miller, Brooke, *Dillon Foundation,* IL, 14750 (FD, FM)
Miller, Bruce, *Milford Chamber of Commerce Trust Fund,* CT, 8810 (GTI)
Miller, Bruce A., *Brener Family Foundation,* LA, 21440
Miller, Bruce H., *Con Amor Foundation,* OR, 47618
Miller, Bruce S., *The Miller Foundation, Inc.,* AL, 572
Miller, Buell A., *Maine Medical Assessment Foundation,* ME, 63231
Miller, Burkett, *Tonya Memorial Foundation, Inc.,* TN, 52137
Miller, C. Davis, *The Miller Foundation,* NC, 42783 (FD2)
Miller, C. John, *C. John and Reva Miller Charitable Foundation, Inc.,* MI, 25972 (FD)
Miller, C. Keith, *Charles J. Miller Family Foundation,* IL, 17047
Miller, C. Richard, *Loats Foundation, Inc.,* MD, 22087 (FD2)
Miller, C. Richard, Jr., *The Community Foundation of Frederick County, Maryland, Inc.,* MD, 21912 (FD, GTI)
Miller, C.E., *C. E. Miller Family Foundation,* MI, 26308 (FD2)
Miller, Calvin L., *The Young Musicians Summer Enrichment Fund,* VA, 57529
Miller, Carey K., *Pendleton and Elisabeth Carey Miller Charitable Foundation,* WA, 57821 (FD)
Miller, Carl Dee, *Miller Family Foundation II,* GA, 13603
Miller, Carl H., Jr., *Carl H. Miller, Jr. Foundation,* AR, 1280
Miller, Carl L., *The Miller Family Foundation, Inc.,* MD, 22506
Miller, Carol, *Goldring Western Foundation,* CA, 5842
Miller, Carol, *The Miller Family Endowment, Inc,* NJ, 31646 (FD)
Miller, Carol, *The Michael Miller Foundation,* NY, 39941
Miller, Carol, *De Beaumont Foundation, Inc.,* VA, 56629 (FD)
Miller, Carol, *Petersburg Methodist Home for Girls,* VA, 56764 (FD2, GTI)
Miller, Carol Ann, *The Meek Foundation,* TX, 54247
Miller, Carol P., *The Miller Family Endowment, Inc,* NJ, 31646 (FD)
Miller, Carole, *The Beltmann-Miller Foundation,* CA, 5974
Miller, Carole, *Balzekas Family Foundation, Ltd.,* IL, 62731

Miller, Carole, *Lithuanian Endowment Fund Ltd.,* IL, 62764
Miller, Carole A., *Gerald M. and Carole A. Miller Family Foundation,* OH, 44776 (FD2)
Miller, Carole R., *The Carole and Mike Miller Foundation,* CA, 3288
Miller, Carolyn, *Allegany County Area Foundation, Inc.,* NY, 37545 (GTI)
Miller, Carolyn C., *The Daniel H. and Carolyn C. Miller Foundation,* CA, 3830
Miller, Carolyn L., *The Carolyn and Chuck Miller Foundation,* CA, 2165 (FD)
Miller, Carson A., *The Orchard House Foundation,* NV, 30841
Miller, Catharine B., *Greater Berkshire Foundation, Inc.,* MA, 23619 (FD2, CD)
Miller, Catherine, *Robert Miller & Catherine Miller Charitable Foundation,* CA, 61144
Miller, Catherine B., *Berkshire Hills Foundation,* MA, 23409 (FD, CD)
Miller, Catherine Derst, *John & Emma Derst Foundation, Inc.,* GA, 13680
Miller, Catherine G., *Irwin-Sweeney-Miller Foundation,* IN, 18412 (FD)
Miller, Catherine M., *The Pietrasiuk Family Foundation,* MI, 26922
Miller, Catherine M., *The Stanley R. Miller Foundation,* NY, 37109 (FD2)
Miller, Catherine McCartney, *The Catherine Terrell McCartney Foundation,* TX, 55198
Miller, Cathy, *Blanche & Irma Weill Foundation,* CA, 3600
Miller, Cathy, *Lakeshore Foundation,* AL, 60794
Miller, Celia G., *Celia G. Miller Scholarship Trust,* IN, 19154
Miller, Charla, *StChar E Charitable Foundation,* NE, 30612
Miller, Charles, *Your Worship Hour, Inc.,* IN, 62956
Miller, Charles, *Sol Y Sombra Foundation,* TX, 66454
Miller, Charles A., Jr., *Charles A. Miller, Jr. Foundation,* AL, 465
Miller, Charles A., Jr., *The Miller Charitable Foundation, Inc.,* MD, 22544
Miller, Charles A. III, *The Miller Charitable Foundation, Inc.,* MD, 22544
Miller, Charles D., *The Amateur Athletic Foundation of Los Angeles,* CA, 1459 (FD, FM)
Miller, Charles D., *The Carolyn and Chuck Miller Foundation,* CA, 2165 (FD)
Miller, Charles D., *Community Foundation of Northwest Georgia, Inc.,* GA, 13131 (FD)
Miller, Charles D., *Heritage Hills Foundation,* VA, 57431
Miller, Charles E., *Gene R. Cohen Charitable Foundation,* ME, 21693
Miller, Charles Wayne, *The Pat and Wayne Miller Family Foundation,* TX, 54159
Miller, Charles Wayne, Jr., *The Pat and Wayne Miller Family Foundation,* TX, 54159
Miller, Charlotte L., *Walter C. and Daisy C. Latham Foundation, Inc.,* NC, 65266 (FD)
Miller, Cherie L., *Francis F. Carnes Education Charitable Trust,* WI, 59517
Miller, Christine, *Gerald M. and Carole A. Miller Family Foundation,* OH, 44776 (FD2)
Miller, Christopher, *Robert Miller & Catherine Miller Charitable Foundation,* CA, 61144
Miller, Christopher D., *The Walt and Lilly Disney Foundation,* CA, 1425 (FD, FM)
Miller, Christopher D., *Walt Disney Family Foundation,* CA, 61027
Miller, Christopher R., *Henry C. Miller Foundation,* PA, 48307 (FD2)
Miller, Claudette T., *Martin and Claudette Miller Foundation,* CA, 6164
Miller, Cleo, *Kappa Alpha Psi Fraternity House of Cleveland, Ohio, Inc.,* OH, 65361
Miller, Clint, *Elizabeth McEachern Foundation,* WA, 58302
Miller, Connie J., *Dutch Neck Community Club,* ME, 63235
Miller, Constance, *Sidney and Constance Miller Foundation, Inc.,* FL, 10909
Miller, Constance A., *Herbert & Gertrude Halverstadt Foundation,* TN, 52125 (FD2)
Miller, Constance H., *Conalin Family Foundation, Inc.,* OH, 46420
Miller, Cynthia, *Library Association of Warehouse Point,* CT, 61924
Miller, Cynthia A., *Lawrence A. Myers Foundation,* IL, 17424
Miller, Cynthia S., *Chip Foundation,* CA, 5729
Miller, Cyril, *The Orion Foundation,* TN, 66101
Miller, Cyrus, *Cy Miller Foundation,* IL, 16699
Miller, D. Byrd III, *William Barnet III Foundation Trust,* SC, 51529 (FD)
Miller, D.B., *The Phileona Foundation,* MN, 27689 (FD2)
Miller, D.F., *Earle M. & Virginia M. Combs Foundation,* IL, 15067 (FD)
Miller, D.J., *The Phileona Foundation,* MN, 27689 (FD)
Miller, Dan, *Harry W. Montague Basketball Memorial Scholarship Committee,* CA, 6322
Miller, Dan, *The DiBianca-Berkman Foundation, Inc.,* NJ, 33127
Miller, Dane A., *The Biomet Foundation, Inc.,* IN, 18528 (FD2, CD, GTI)
Miller, Dane A., Mrs., *The Biomet Foundation, Inc.,* IN, 18528 (FD2, CD, GTI)
Miller, Daniel, *The Miller Family Foundation,* AL, 22506
Miller, Daniel, *Institute for Advanced Therapy, Inc.,* NJ, 31617 (FD)
Miller, Daniel, *The Jim Conner Foundation,* PA, 49676
Miller, Daniel H., *The Daniel H. and Carolyn C. Miller Foundation,* CA, 3830
Miller, Daniel L., *The Betty Ann Greenbaum Miller and Daniel L. Miller Family Foundation, Inc.,* MA, 25342
Miller, Daniel L.R., *Maier Family Foundation,* PA, 49611
Miller, Daniel R., *C. E. Miller Family Foundation,* MI, 26308 (FD2)
Miller, Daniel S., *Alan and Diane Miller Family Foundation,* MN, 28602
Miller, Daniel S., *The Dun & Bradstreet Corporation Foundation,* NJ, 31505 (FD, CD)
Miller, Daphne R., *Telesford Eistrup Miller Family Foundation, Inc.,* NY, 42244
Miller, Darrell, *Mended Wings Foundation,* CA, 61620
Miller, Darrell E., *The More-Blessed-to-Give Corporation,* MO, 30074
Miller, David, *South Madison Community Foundation,* IN, 18724 (GTI)
Miller, David, *The Nussbaum Family Foundation, Inc.,* NY, 37738
Miller, David, *Robert Gladstone Family Foundation, Inc.,* NY, 38585
Miller, David, *Robert J. Alander Scholarship Fund,* NC, 43688 (GTI)
Miller, David, *Ann Norton Sculpture Gardens, Inc.,* FL, 62213
Miller, David, *Kemper Museum Operating Foundation,* MO, 63974

GTI = *Grants to Individuals*   **CD = *National Directory of Corporate Giving***   **1031**

- an index to giving interests in hundreds of subject categories, broken down by the states in which the foundations are located;

- an index listing foundations new to the current edition; and

- an index by foundation name.

In the geographic, subject, and types of support indexes, foundations with national, regional, or international giving patterns are indicated in bold type, while foundations restricted to local giving are listed in regular type. As you define the limits of your funding search, these indexes can help you to focus on locally oriented foundations in your community as well as on national foundations that have an interest in your field of activity.

The Foundation Directory Part 2 is designed as a companion volume to *The Foundation Directory* and provides similar information on the second tier of U.S. foundations—the next-largest 10,000 foundations by total giving. These foundations represent hundreds of millions of grant dollars awarded annually for nonprofits.

The Foundation Directory Supplement provides the latest information on *Foundation Directory* and *Foundation Directory Part 2* grantmakers six months after those volumes are published. The *Supplement* provides complete revised entries for foundations reporting substantial changes in personnel, name, address, program interests, limitations, application procedures, or other areas by the midpoint of the yearly *Directory* publishing cycle.

Each edition of the *Supplement* contains thousands of updated entries. The portions of an entry that have changes are highlighted in bold type to aid you in identifying new information quickly. The *Supplement* entries may also include a section called "Other Changes" that provides additional information about the foundation, including significant growth in its asset base or grants awarded, or to highlight specific changes within the entry, as when a foundation relocates to another state.

THE FOUNDATION 1000

Published annually, *The Foundation 1000* provides detailed descriptions of the nation's 1,000 largest foundations. Although it is confined to a much narrower universe than *The Foundation Directory*, it provides a more thorough description of these foundations' histories, giving programs, application procedures, and grants awarded. Each *Foundation 1000* profile provides the foundation's name, address, and telephone number; separate application address(es) and contact person(s); fax number and e-mail and/or Web addresses; officers, governing board, and principal staff; purpose; current financial data;

Figure 28. Sample Entry and Key from *The Foundation Directory*

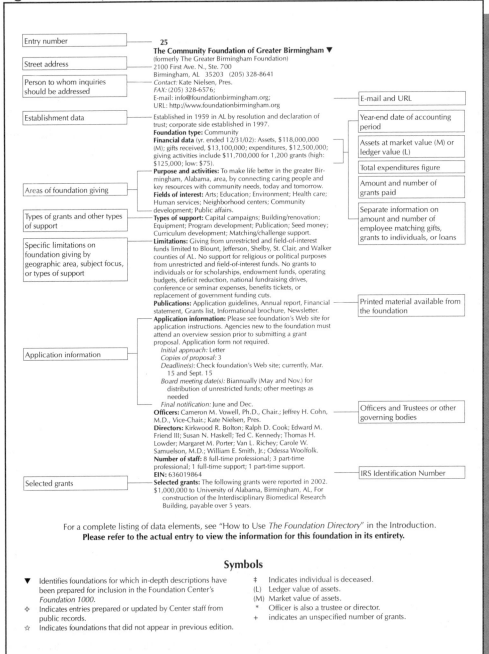

Entry number

25

The Community Foundation of Greater Birmingham ▼
(formerly The Greater Birmingham Foundation)

Street address
2100 First Ave. N., Ste. 700
Birmingham, AL 35203 (205) 328-8641

Person to whom inquiries should be addressed
Contact: Kate Nielsen, Pres.
FAX: (205) 328-6576;
E-mail: info@foundationbirmingham.org;
URL: http://www.foundationbirmingham.org

E-mail and URL

Establishment data
Established in 1959 in AL by resolution and declaration of trust; corporate side established in 1997.

Foundation type: Community

Financial data (yr. ended 12/31/02): Assets, $118,000,000 (M); gifts received, $13,100,000; expenditures, $12,500,000; giving activities include $11,700,000 for 1,200 grants (high: $125,000; low: $75).

Year-end date of accounting period

Assets at market value (M) or ledger value (L)

Total expenditures figure

Amount and number of grants paid

Purpose and activities: To make life better in the greater Birmingham, Alabama, area, by connecting caring people and key resources with community needs, today and tomorrow.

Areas of foundation giving
Fields of interest: Arts; Education; Environment; Health care; Human services; Neighborhood centers; Community development; Public affairs.

Types of grants and other types of support
Types of support: Capital campaigns; Building/renovation; Equipment; Program development; Publication; Seed money; Curriculum development; Matching/challenge support.

Separate information on amount and number of employee matching gifts, grants to individuals, or loans

Limitations: Giving from unrestricted and field-of-interest funds limited to Blount, Jefferson, Shelby, St. Clair, and Walker counties of AL. No support for religious or political purposes from unrestricted and field-of-interest funds. No grants to individuals or for scholarships, endowment funds, operating budgets, deficit reduction, national fundraising drives, conference or seminar expenses, benefits tickets, or replacement of government funding cuts.

Specific limitations on foundation giving by geographic area, subject focus, or types of support

Publications: Application guidelines, Annual report, Financial statement, Grants list, Informational brochure, Newsletter.

Printed material available from the foundation

Application information: Please see foundation's Web site for application instructions. Agencies new to the foundation must attend an overview session prior to submitting a grant proposal. Application form not required.

Application information
Initial approach: Letter
Copies of proposal: 3
Deadline(s): Check foundation's Web site; currently, Mar. 15 and Sept. 15
Board meeting date(s): Biannually (May and Nov.) for distribution of unrestricted funds; other meetings as needed
Final notification: June and Dec.

Officers: Cameron M. Vowell, Ph.D., Chair.; Jeffrey H. Cohn, M.D., Vice-Chair.; Kate Nielsen, Pres.

Officers and Trustees or other governing bodies

Directors: Kirkwood R. Bolton; Ralph D. Cook; Edward M. Friend III; Susan N. Haskell; Ted C. Kennedy; Thomas H. Lowder; Margaret M. Porter; Van L. Richey; Carole W. Samuelson, M.D.; William E. Smith, Jr.; Odessa Woolfolk.

Number of staff: 8 full-time professional; 3 part-time professional; 1 full-time support; 1 part-time support.

EIN: 636019864

IRS Identification Number

Selected grants
Selected grants: The following grants were reported in 2002. $1,000,000 to University of Alabama, Birmingham, AL, For construction of the Interdisciplinary Biomedical Research Building, payable over 5 years.

For a complete listing of data elements, see "How to Use *The Foundation Directory*" in the Introduction.
Please refer to the actual entry to view the information for this foundation in its entirety.

Symbols

▼ Identifies foundations for which in-depth descriptions have been prepared for inclusion in the Foundation Center's *Foundation 1000*.

✧ Indicates entries prepared or updated by Center staff from public records.

☆ Indicates foundations that did not appear in previous edition.

‡ Indicates individual is deceased.

(L) Ledger value of assets.

(M) Market value of assets.

* Officer is also a trustee or director.

+ indicates an unspecified number of grants.

giving limitations; support and program areas; sponsoring company (if applicable); background history; policies and application guidelines; and publications. The "Grants Analysis" section of each profile is what makes this resource unique. It presents statistical charts and analyses of grants awarded in the year of record for the following: subject area, recipient type, type of support, population group, and geographic distribution. A listing of sample grants, selected to best represent the foundation's giving, follows the analyses. For a sample entry from this publication, see Figure 29.

Five indexes in *The Foundation 1000* provide access to the foundations profiled. The indexes include:

- a name index of donors, officers, trustees, and principal staff;

- an index of subject/giving interests, broken down by the states where the foundations are located;

- an index of types of support offered by the foundations, broken down by the states where the foundations are located;

- a geographic index of foundation locations by state and city, with cross-references to foundations with identified giving patterns beyond the states in which they are headquartered; and

- an international giving index of countries, continents, or regions where foundations have indicated giving interests, broken down by the states where the foundations are located.

Like the indexes in *The Foundation Directory*, *The Foundation 1000* subject, types of support, and geographic indexes indicate foundations with a national, regional, or international focus in bold type, while locally oriented foundations are listed in regular type.

The Foundation 1000 is useful for identifying potential funding sources among the nation's 1,000 largest foundations. It is especially helpful in the final stages of your research, when you are gathering detailed information about the carefully selected group of foundations to which you plan to submit a proposal.

Foundation Grants

Indexes to foundation grants help you identify funders with a demonstrated interest in your subject or geographic area by listing the actual grants they have awarded. Studying

Figure 29. Sample Entry from *The Foundation 1000*

321
THE CHARLES ENGELHARD
FOUNDATION

645 5th Ave., Ste. 712
New York, NY 10022 (212) 935-2433
Contact: Mary F. Ogorzaly, Secy.

Purpose: Emphasis on higher and secondary education, and cultural, medical, religious, wildlife, and conservation organizations.

Limitation(s): Giving on a national basis. No support for international organizations. No grants to individuals.

Support area(s): In general, support for general/operating support; continuing support; annual campaigns; capital campaigns; building/renovation; endowments; program development; conferences/seminars; publication; research; and matching/challenge support.

Financial data (yr. ended 12/31/01):
Assets: $106,537,073 (M)
Expenditures: $10,490,884
Grants paid: $9,880,734 for 274 grants (high: $800,000; low: $100; general range: $1,000–$50,000)
Outstanding commitments: $11,189,850

Officers and Trustees:* Charlene B. Engelhard,* Pres.; Mary F. Ogorzaly, Secy.; Edward G. Beimfohr,* Treas. (Partner, Windels, Marx, Lane, and Mittendorf); Sophie Engelhard Craighead, Anne E. de la Renta, Anthony J. Gostkowski, Susan O'Connor, Sally E. Pingree.

Number of staff: 1 full-time professional, 2 part-time professional.

Background: Incorporated in 1940 in NJ. Funds donated by Charles Engelhard (deceased), Engelhard Hanovia, Inc., and others.
Mr. Engelhard's widow, Jane B. Engelhard, is a trustee of the foundation. All of their daughters are also foundation trustees.
At the close of 2001, the market value of the foundation's assets totaled $106.5 million, a 20 percent decrease from the 2000 value ($133.1 million).

Policies and application guidelines: Applications not accepted. Giving only to organizations known to the trustees. Unsolicited requests for funds not considered.
Board meeting date(s): Quarterly

GRANTS ANALYSIS

Although the foundation provided financial information for 2001, the following grants analysis reflects grants paid in 2000. Contributions paid in 2000 totaled $11,401,948. This figure represents a 7 percent increase over giving in 1999.

Subject Analysis:

Subject Area Distribution of Grant Numbers and Grant Dollars Paid in 2000

Subject area	No. of grants	Dollar value	Pct.	General range of grants
Education				
Elementary & secondary	9	$1,887,833	17	
Other	21	1,108,565	10	
SUBTOTAL:	30	2,996,398	27	$10,000–150,000
Arts & culture				
Museums	11	1,750,800	15	
Other	28	913,500	8	
SUBTOTAL:	39	2,664,300	23	10,000–50,000
Medicine—general & rehabilitative				
Advocacy, association & regulation	1	669,000	6	
Nursing care	8	660,000	6	
SUBTOTAL:	9	1,329,000	12	10,000–65,000
Other	32	1,120,000	10	
Environmental protection	19	874,150	8	20,000–50,000
Religion	10	726,250	6	10,000–75,000
Animals & wildlife	14	708,300	6	25,000–75,000

Subject area	No. of grants	Dollar value	Pct.	General range of grants
Human services— multipurpose	10	631,000	6	10,000–30,000
Grants under $10,000	113	352,550	2	
TOTAL:	276	$11,401,948	100%	

High award of the year: $1,328,000, Metropolitan Museum of Art, NYC, NY.

Top subject area by dollars: Education
Largest award in field: $595,000, Potomac School, McLean, VA.
Second largest award: $525,000, Saint Andrews School, Middletown, DE.
Largest single recipient: Potomac School, McLean, VA (2 awards, totaling $695,000).
Second largest subject area by dollars: Arts & culture (also, largest by grant numbers)
Largest award in field: $1,328,000, Metropolitan Museum of Art, NYC, NY.
Second largest award: $185,000, Trisha Brown Dance Company, NYC, NY.
Third largest subject area by dollars: Medicine—general & rehabilitative
Largest award in field: $669,000, Delta Society, Renton, WA.
Second largest award: $250,000, Doctors Without Borders USA, NYC, NY.

Recipient Type Analysis:

Analysis of Grants of $10,000 or More Awarded in 2000*

Recipient type	Dollar value	No. of grants
Schools	$1,937,833	11
Museums/historical societies	1,810,600	14
Environmental agencies	1,154,150	23
Professional societies & associations	1,001,800	9
Public/general health organizations	954,000	4
Colleges & universities	755,000	14
Churches/temples	726,250	10
Animal/wildlife agencies	708,300	14
Human service agencies	701,000	14
Arts/humanities organizations	537,000	17
Hospitals/medical care facilities	465,000	5
Performing arts groups	315,000	7
Graduate schools	295,000	1
Volunteer bureaus	283,333	2
Technical assistance centers	208,232	7
Libraries	197,000	2
Mental health agencies	167,000	3
Research institutes	158,500	6
Philanthropy organizations	150,000	2
Educational support agencies	121,565	6
International organizations	120,000	4
Disease-specific health associations	65,000	4
Civil rights groups	50,000	1
Community improvement organizations	50,000	3
Public policy institutes	50,000	1
Public administration agencies	45,000	2
Science organizations	35,000	2
Recreation organizations	30,000	3
Media organizations	25,000	1
Medical research institutes	25,000	1
Youth development organizations	13,000	1
Federated funds	10,000	1

*Awards may support multiple recipient types, i.e., a university library, and would therefore be counted twice.

Top recipient type by dollars: Schools
Largest award in field: $595,000, Potomac School, McLean, VA.
Second largest award: $525,000, Saint Andrews School, Middletown, DE.
Largest single recipient: Potomac School, McLean, VA (2 awards, totaling $695,000).
Second largest recipient type by dollars: Museums/historical societies
Largest award in field: $1,328,000, Metropolitan Museum of Art, NYC, NY.
Second largest award: $100,000, National Gallery of Art, DC; $100,000, Phillips Collection, DC.

Figure 29. (continued)

321—Engelhard

Third largest recipient type by dollars: Environmental agencies (also, largest by grant numbers)
Largest award in field: $250,000, Ecotrust, Portland, OR.
Second largest award: $130,000, National Fish and Wildlife Foundation, DC.

Type of Support Analysis:
Analysis of Grants of $10,000 or More Awarded in 2000*

Support type	Dollar value	No. of grants
Program support		
Program development	$70,000	3

*Awards may support multiple support types, i.e., seed money for research, and would therefore be counted twice.

Top support type by dollars: Program support (also, largest by grant numbers)
Largest award in field: $50,000.
Second largest award: $10,000.

Multi-year pledges: 162, totaling $11,029,398

Continuing support: 5 grants, totaling $404,000

Population Group Analysis:
Analysis of Grants Over $10,000 Designated for Special Populations*

Group	Dollar value	No. of grants
Children & youth	$122,000	8
Mentally disabled	120,000	2
Economically disadvantaged	100,500	6
Disabled, general	80,000	2
Alcohol or drug abusers	67,000	2
Crime or abuse victims	57,000	1
Women & girls	55,000	3
People with AIDS	50,000	3
Immigrants & refugees	50,000	1
Physically disabled	30,000	2
Minorities, general	22,500	2
Single parents	15,000	1
Blind & vision impaired	12,500	1
Aging	10,000	1
Blacks	10,000	1

*Grants which support no specific population are not included; awards may support multiple populations, i.e., an award for minority youth, and would therefore be counted twice.

Top population group by dollars: Children & youth (also, largest by grant numbers)
Largest award in field: $30,000, Leake and Watts Services, Yonkers, NY.
Second largest award: $25,000, Community Childrens Project, Jackson, WY.

Second largest population group by dollars: Mentally disabled
Largest award in field: $100,000, McLean Hospital, Belmont, MA.
Second largest award: $20,000, National Center for Learning Disabilities, NYC, NY.

Third largest population group by dollars: Economically disadvantaged
Largest award in field: $30,000, Womens Opportunity and Resource Development (WORD), Missoula, MT.
Second largest award: $25,000, Jubilee Jobs, DC.

Geographic Analysis:
The geographic distribution of institutional awards of $10,000 or more is as follows. (Grants to individuals and with unknown locations are excluded. Single grants may be active on more than one continent and would therefore be double-counted.)

U.S. regional breakdown: Middle Atlantic, $2,834,883 (35 awards); New England, $2,455,833 (38 awards); South Atlantic, $1,945,350 (22 awards); Mountain, $1,666,832 (38 awards); Pacific, $1,381,500 (14 awards); West South Central, $125,000 (2 awards); East North Central, $25,000 (1 award); East South Central, $10,000 (1 award).

Dollar value of foreign/international awards: global programs, $320,000; Europe, $235,000; Africa, $50,000; Asia, $10,000.

GRANTS: The following is a partial list of grants paid by the foundation in 2000.

Education
Potomac School, McLean, VA	$695,000
2 grants: $595,000, $100,000.	
Brown University, Providence, RI	150,000
Sussex School, Missoula, MT	32,000
University of Montana Foundation, Missoula, MT	15,300
Trinity College, Hartford, CT	10,000

Arts & culture
Metropolitan Museum of Art, NYC, NY	1,328,000
Boston Ballet, Boston, MA	50,000
San Francisco Museum of Modern Art, San Francisco, CA	35,000
Media Alliance, San Francisco, CA	20,000
Washington Choral Foundation, DC	10,000

Medicine—general & rehabilitative
Delta Society, Renton, WA	669,000
Doctors Without Borders USA, NYC, NY	250,000
Beth Israel Deaconess Medical Center, Boston, MA	100,000
Nantucket Cottage Hospital, Nantucket, MA	65,000
Chalice of Repose Project, Missoula, MT	25,000
United Way of Lee County, Auburn, AL	10,000
For medical care programs.	

Other
Community Foundation of Jackson Hole, Jackson, WY	125,000
Peace Valley Healing Center, Boulder, MT	57,000
French-American Foundation, NYC, NY	50,000
National Organization on Disability, DC	50,000
Community Research Initiative on AIDS (CRIA), NYC, NY	25,000
Jubilee Jobs, DC	25,000
Police Athletic League of Teton County, Jackson, WY	13,000
National Council on Alcoholism and Drug Dependence, NYC, NY	10,000
United Cerebral Palsy Associations, NYC, NY	10,000

Environmental protection
Ecotrust, Portland, OR	250,000
Conservation Law Foundation, Boston, MA	50,000
Idaho Conservation League, Boise, ID	35,000
Island Institute, Sitka, AK	20,000
Montana Land Reliance, Helena, MT	10,000

Religion
Monastery of Christ in the Desert, Abiquiu, NM	333,000
Monastery of Our Lady of the Desert, Abiquiu, NM	75,000
Saint Marys/Our Lady of the Isle, Nantucket, MA	33,000
Saint Bartholomews Episcopal Church, NYC, NY	25,000
Saint Marys Church, Poughkeepsie, NY	10,000

Animals & wildlife
National Fish and Wildlife Foundation, DC	130,000
Peregrine Fund, Boise, ID	75,000
Wild Salmon Center, Portland, OR	50,000
Yankee Golden Retriever Rescue, Hudson, MA	25,000
People Animals Love (PAL), DC	15,000

Human services—multipurpose
Families First Parenting Program, Cambridge, MA	235,000
Leake and Watts Services, Yonkers, NY	30,000
Pregnancy Help, NYC, NY	15,000
American Red Cross, National, DC	10,000

Grants under $10,000
Jesuit Community at Boston College, Newton, MA	8,000
National Outdoor Leadership School, Lander, WY	5,000
Bard College, Annandale on Hudson, NY Graduate Center.	4,000
Municipal Art Society of New York, NYC, NY	2,000
Concord Free Public Library, Concord, MA	1,000
Vietnam Veterans of America Foundation, DC	500

Source(s): 2000 GL

Employer Identification Number (EIN): 226063032

listings of grants a foundation has recently awarded will give you a better understanding of a foundation's giving priorities in terms of the types of programs and organizations it funds, the amount of money it awards for specific programs, the geographic area in which it concentrates its grantmaking activities, the population groups it serves through its grants, and the types of support it typically offers.

The Foundation Center currently maintains computer files on reported grants of $10,000 and more awarded by more than 1,000 major foundations. The Center's database currently contains more than 2.3 million grant records. Some 85,000 new records are added to the database every year. The information included in the database is made available to grantseekers in a variety of electronic and print formats designed to facilitate their individual funding searches.

Each grant record includes the name and state location of the grantmaker as well as that of the recipient organization, the amount of the grant and its duration, the year the grant was awarded, and a brief description of the purpose for which the grant was made. Where applicable, a statement outlining geographic, subject, or other restrictions on the grantmaker's giving program is also provided. Foundation Center editors analyze and index each grant by subject focus, type of recipient organization, population group served, and the type of support awarded (e.g., endowment, research, building/renovation, etc.).

Access to the grants information from the Foundation Center is available in *The Foundation Directory Online*, *FC Search*, *The Foundation Grants Index on CD-ROM*, and the *Grant Guides* series. Each type of publication is designed to offer a different mode of access to the grants information in the database. As you become more skilled at foundation research, you'll be able to determine which of the resources will be most useful. In the beginning it's a good idea to use and become familiar with all of them.

THE FOUNDATION GRANTS INDEX ON CD-ROM

The Foundation Grants Index on CD-ROM offers information on more than 50 percent of all grant dollars awarded annually by private foundations. Because it is searchable electronically, it can help you quickly locate grantmakers that have funded nonprofit organizations that are similar to your own organization; discover foundations that favor your geographic area; and identify funders that demonstrate a strong interest in your subject field.

The Foundation Grants Index on CD-ROM covers the grants of $10,000 or more awarded by more than 1,000 of the largest independent, corporate, and community foundations in the United States, featuring approximately 125,000 grant descriptions in all. *The Foundation Grants Index on CD-ROM* contains 12 search fields to choose from:

Recipient Name	Recipient State	Recipient City
Recipient Type	Grantmaker Name	Grantmaker State
Geographic Focus	Subject	Types of Support
Grant Amount	Year Authorized	Text Search

The Foundation Grants Index on CD-ROM can be used to get a broad overview of a specific foundation's giving priorities, to survey foundation giving within a state, to evaluate giving to a particular recipient or recipient type, and/or to identify the subject areas that currently are most attractive to private foundations.

GRANT GUIDES

Because many grantseekers want to focus their funding search on a particular subject field, the Foundation Center annually publishes a series of books that list grants from the grants database in a more specialized format. Each *Guide* is a subset of the *Grants Index on CD-ROM*, listing grants of $10,000 and up arranged by foundation name and location, as well as by subject. Each grant in the *Grant Guides* may be indexed under a number of headings and subheadings. An illustration will best demonstrate the detail provided by the subject indexes. In Figure 30, you will see that in the subject index for *Grants for Children and Youth*, the subject "Crisis services" has been described by population group (e.g., "Blacks," "Youth," and "Women"), and by type of support (e.g., "Building/renovation," "Hot-lines," and "Income development").

Grant Guides are currently available on the following 12 topics:

Arts, Culture, and the Humanities	Mental Health, Addictions, and
Children and Youth	Crisis Services
Elementary and Secondary Education	Minorities
Environmental Protection and	Physically and Mentally Disabled
Animal Welfare	Religion, Religious Welfare, and
Foreign and International Programs	Religious Education
Higher Education	Women and Girls
Libraries and Information Services	

Specialized Directories

Print and electronic directories that focus on a particular geographic area, type of support, subject area, or a specific type of funder can be extremely useful in identifying foundations that will support your organization or project. These directories may be compiled by commercial publishers, government agencies, libraries, associations of grantmakers, or other nonprofit groups. Many such directories are available, but they vary widely in the type, currency, and amount of information they provide. To identify specialized directories related to your subject or geographic area or some other criteria, look at the bibliographies in the *Guide to U.S. Foundations, Their Trustees, Officers, and Donors* and the various volumes in the Foundation Center's *National Guide* series. The Topical Resource Lists (a resource of bibliographies covering major nonprofit issues, including subject and local, state, and international funding directories) in the Learning Lab directory of the Foundation Center's Web site may also prove useful. The *Literature of the Nonprofit Sector Online* in the Researching Philanthropy directory of the Center's Web site can also be helpful in identifying specialized directories.

STATE AND LOCAL FUNDING DIRECTORIES

State and local funding directories can be a very good source of information, particularly for smaller foundations not covered in depth in major reference works. Those state and regional directories that have a subject index may provide some of the only such access to the giving patterns of smaller foundations. In addition, many of these directories list sample grants, which give you some indication of a local funder's interests. Some directories also include information on corporations that support charitable programs in their geographic area, a very useful complement to foundation information.

The Foundation Center currently publishes five local funding directories: the *Guide to Greater Washington D.C. Grantmakers on CD-ROM*, the *Guide to Ohio Grantmakers on CD-ROM*, the *Michigan Foundation Directory* (also available on CD-ROM), the *Guide to Alabama Grantmakers*, and the *Directory of Missouri Grantmakers*.

The Center's regional funding publications are produced in collaboration with regional associations of grantmakers: the *Guide to Greater Washington D.C. Grantmakers on CD-ROM* is co-produced with Washington Grantmakers; the *Guide to Ohio Grantmakers on CD-ROM* is co-produced with the Ohio Grantmakers Forum and the Ohio Association of Nonprofit Organizations; the *Michigan Foundation Directory* is co-produced with the Council of Michigan Foundations; the *Guide to Alabama Grantmakers* is co-produced with Alabama Giving; and the *Directory of Missouri*

Figure 30. Subject Index from *Grants for Children and Youth*

Subject Index

Crime/violence prevention, seed money 6436
Crime/violence prevention, technical aid 838, 16238
Crime/violence prevention, women 3232, 6389, 6579, 6954, 10746, 12654, 17829, 24468, 27342
Crime/violence prevention, youth 165, 289, 290, 346, 355, 456, 506, 603, 616, 654, 664, 695, 751, 753, 770, 778-780, 796, 808, 828, 836, 838, 857, 897, 899, 952, 1039, 1051, 1055, 1071, 1128, 1194, 1284, 1312, 1351, 1563, 1571, 1593, 1599, 1603, 1625, 1650, 1790, 1924, 2066, 2470, 2537, 2584, 2644, 2672, 2802, 2822, 2998, 3151, 3165, 3195, 3265, 3302, 3381, 3460, 3474, 3549, 3586, 3751, 3863, 4063, 4146, 4212, 4246, 4318, 4347, 4497, 4580, 4617, 4743, 4776, 4950, 5054, 5055, 5067, 5741, 5848, 5959, 6032, 6062, 6128, 6389, 6436, 6548, 6551, 6553, 6569, 6575, 6707, 6718, 6774, 6789, 6802, 6839, 6854, 7179, 7227, 7316, 7434, 7575, 7699, 8281, 8464, 8634, 8955, 9219, 9558, 9626, 9685, 9742, 9763, 9805, 9956, 9977, 10026, 10076, 10086, 10224, 10372, 10515, 10624, 10665, 10682, 10728, 10740, 10770, 10871, 10912, 10962, 11108, 11209, 11228, 11298, 11375, 11458, 11504, 11532, 11617, 11806, 11809, 12121, 12171, 12172, 12193, 12203, 12216, 12222, 12223, 12239, 12245, 12260, 12261, 12353, 12389, 12390, 12550, 12601, 12745, 12755, 12760, 12836, 12853, 12854, 13110, 13187, 13188, 13285, 13286, 13372, 13374, 13388, 13441, 13500, 13501, 13562, 13563, 13676, 13694, 13818, 14066, 14082, 14133, 14204, 14280, 14345, 14398, 14595, 14607, 14610, 15136, 15326, 15870, 15926, 16041, 16042, 16095, 16127, 16134, 16141, 16167, 16168, 16192, 16194, 16227, 16234, 16238, 16271, 16274, 16292, 16332, 17362, 17364, 17671, 17709, 17829, 18185, 18291, 18297, 18299, 18538, 18661, 18697, 18738, 18756, 18904, 19021, 19077, 19081, 19083, 19098, 19121, 19174, 19308, 19321, 19943, 20059, 20192, 20348, 20387, 20427, 20537, 20719, 20769, 20770, 20780, 20788, 20790, 20795, 20796, 20806, 20809, 20811, 20855, 21279, 21289, 21366, 21721, 21781, 22490, 22572, 22574, 22640, 22682, 22734, 22810, 22865, 22900, 22901, 23069, 23108, 23212, 23500, 23585, 23814, 23861, 24058, 24185, 24207, 24248, 24454, 24455, 24619, 24624, 24716, 24744, 24791, 24927, 24942, 24963, 24986, 25033, 25085, 25213, 25679, 26211, 26227, 26272, 26344, 26357, 26385, 26565, 26679, 26681, 26747, 26775, 27104, 27249, 27361, 27374, 27389, 27541, 27572, 27646, 27714, 27738, 27819, 27992, 28106, 28316, 28353, 28394, 28477, 28560
Crisis services, blacks 27905
Crisis services, boys & young men 22831
Crisis services, building/renovation 4351, 5080, 25246, 26272
Crisis services, capital campaigns 4525, 26488
Crisis services, children & youth 196, 683, 756, 1419, 1907, 1919, 2175, 3143, 3469, 4227, 4351, 4525, 4817, 5080, 5272, 6987, 7231, 9224, 9371, 9455, 11966, 12111, 12967, 13935, 16035, 16365, 18584, 21407, 21420, 21542, 22271, 22476, 22644, 22933, 23701, 24942, 25080, 25246, 25430, 25678, 25704, 25743, 25815, 26129, 26334, 26335, 26488, 26489, 26772, 27054, 27068, 27104, 27143, 27905
Crisis services, conferences/seminars 683

Crisis services, crime/abuse victims 196, 756, 1419, 1919, 2175, 3143, 3469, 4227, 4351, 4525, 5080, 6987, 7231, 9224, 9623, 11966, 12111, 12967, 13935, 16365, 17779, 18584, 21420, 22271, 22476, 22643, 22644, 22831, 22933, 23655, 25080, 25246, 25430, 25678, 25704, 25743, 25815, 26129, 26272, 26334, 26335, 26488, 26489, 26772, 27054, 27068, 27143
Crisis services, drug/alcohol abusers 683
Crisis services, economically disadvantaged 683, 756, 21407
Crisis services, electronic media/online services 3146
Crisis services, equipment 756, 16365, 27054
Crisis services, faculty/staff development 13935, 22476, 22933, 24942, 25743
Crisis services, gays/lesbians 683, 4160, 4927
Crisis services, girls & young women 9623, 17779, 22643, 23655
Crisis services, homeless 3146, 9370, 27054
Crisis services, hot-lines 196, 4927, 5272, 6987, 9370, 9371, 9455, 16365, 18584, 20340, 21407, 21542, 22933, 24942, 26129, 26272, 27054, 27104, 27143, 27905
Crisis services, immigrants/refugees 756, 21407
Crisis services, income development 3143, 5272, 26489
Crisis services, management development 3143, 13935
Crisis services, mentally disabled 106, 4817, 16035, 17159, 21420, 22831, 25592, 28002
Crisis services, minorities 13935, 21407
Crisis services, rape victim services 756, 1419, 1919, 2175, 3143, 3469, 4227, 4351, 4525, 5080, 7231, 9224, 9623, 11966, 12111, 12967, 13935, 17779, 21420, 22271, 22476, 22643, 22644, 22831, 23655, 25080, 25246, 25430, 25678, 25704, 25743, 25815, 26334, 26335, 26488, 26489, 26772, 27068
Crisis services, research 10355
Crisis services, suicide 106, 635, 683, 1907, 3146, 4160, 4817, 10355, 16035, 16933, 17159, 20342, 23701, 25592, 28002, 28105
Crisis services, women 756, 1919, 2175, 3143, 3469, 4227, 6987, 7231, 9224, 11966, 12111, 16365, 18584, 22271, 22476, 22644, 22933, 25246, 25430, 26129, 27143
Crisis services, youth 106, 635, 3146, 4160, 4927, 9370, 10355, 16933, 17159, 20340, 20342, 25592, 26272, 28002, 28105
Croatia, international affairs/development 20410, 20444
Croatia, youth development 20410, 20444
Cuba, human services—multipurpose 18762
Cuba, international affairs/development 18759
Cuba, religion 18762
Cuba, youth development 18762
Cystic fibrosis, children & youth 5863, 6692, 17195
Cystic fibrosis, physically disabled 5863, 6692, 17195
Czech Republic, civil rights 5356
Czech Republic, education 5356, 20442, 24006
Czech Republic, human services—multipurpose 18053
Czech Republic, international affairs/development 20442
Czech Republic, mental health/substance abuse 27759, 27760
Czech Republic, recreation/sports/athletics 24006
Czech Republic, religion 27760
Czech Republic, youth development 18053, 20442

Dance, Asians/Pacific Islanders 18265, 20848
Dance, awards/prizes/competitions 24605
Dance, blacks 5126, 17019, 17777, 19839, 20979, 26081
Dance, boys & young men 17019
Dance, building/renovation 9, 6185, 13610, 17460, 24741
Dance, children & youth 9, 38, 370, 564, 565, 685, 1066, 1765, 2222, 2225, 2650, 3260, 3834, 4011, 5126, 5195, 5357, 5514, 5515, 5864, 5870, 5955, 5956, 6044, 6045, 6154, 6185, 6186, 6288, 6449, 7397, 7571, 8488, 12205, 12392, 12551, 12855, 12885, 13610, 14880, 14915, 16904, 16927, 16975, 16977-16979, 17204, 17230, 17460, 17624, 17653, 17777, 18265, 18309, 18420, 18906, 18911, 19263, 19307, 19363, 19705, 19839, 20055, 20056, 20171, 20280, 20309, 20314, 20390, 20438, 20597, 20607, 20644, 20691, 20806, 20938, 20979, 21006, 21021, 21054, 21055, 21221, 21651, 21977, 23180, 24604, 24605, 24741, 26081, 26349, 26402, 27247, 27484, 27485
Dance, conferences/seminars 20938
Dance, curriculum development 370, 20597, 20938
Dance, disabled 564
Dance, economically disadvantaged 370, 685, 2650, 3834, 4011, 5864, 5870, 6044, 6045, 6185, 6186, 6189, 6288, 6449, 7397, 7571, 12205, 12392, 12551, 12855, 12885, 14915, 17204, 17230, 19307, 20171, 20806, 20848, 20979, 21350, 27484, 27485
Dance, endowments 19307
Dance, equipment 14576
Dance, fellowships 2225, 17019, 19839, 20597, 21281
Dance, gays/lesbians 6797
Dance, Hispanics 16975
Dance, income development 2222, 3260
Dance, internships 6189
Dance, management development 38
Dance, minorities 370, 5864, 5870, 6044, 6045, 6185, 6186, 6189, 6288, 6449, 12205, 12392, 12551, 12855, 12885, 17230, 20171, 20607, 20806, 26349, 27484
Dance, Native Americans 14576
Dance, performance/productions 2222, 17230, 20938, 26402, 27247
Dance, program evaluation 2225
Dance, scholarships 16975, 17019, 19307, 20979
Dance, youth 3288, 5395, 6189, 6797, 8266, 8319, 11835, 14576, 17019, 17024, 20848, 21281, 21326, 21332, 21350, 21874
Deaf, arts/culture/humanities 567, 2788, 5546, 16678, 24847, 24869, 24907, 27006
Deaf, crime/courts/legal services 4475, 22734
Deaf, education 3, 80, 90, 199, 412, 413, 726, 934, 1273, 1274, 2095, 2116, 2149, 2263, 2351, 2788, 3175, 3736, 3852, 4652, 5367, 6120, 6415, 7086, 7511, 7966, 7967, 9223, 10130, 10180, 10271, 10296, 10412, 10602, 11840, 12285, 12412, 12433, 12558, 12697, 13609, 13615, 15069, 15100, 15115, 15152, 15175-15177, 15287, 15630, 15664, 15674, 15687, 15701, 15723, 15777, 16380, 16381, 16390, 16662, 16678, 16776, 17556, 17686, 18327, 18610, 18990, 19255, 19301, 19323, 19590, 19898, 20454, 20545, 20766, 21089, 21850, 22025, 22330, 22594, 22734, 23588, 23939, 24208, 24415, 24645, 24672, 24694, 24728, 24802-24808, 24812-24840, 24842-24846, 24848, 24849, 24851-24868, 24870-24911, 25245, 25269, 25297, 25343,

85

Grantmakers is produced in collaboration with the Metropolitan Association for Philanthropy in St. Louis, Missouri. All of these regional directories include corporate direct giving programs and public charities as well as foundations, and list grantmakers outside the specified region if they have identified giving interests in the defined geographic area. All print publications include five indexes: donors, officers, and trustees; types of support; subject; grantmaker name; and geographic. All CD-ROM regional databases contain 12 searchable fields.

The Center's five regional funding publications and many other state and local funding directories are available for public reference in the Center's five libraries. Cooperating Collections generally have directories for their own state or region. In addition, some Cooperating Collections compile bibliographies for their geographic areas.

NATIONAL GUIDE SERIES

The Foundation Center publishes several directories based on subject areas popular with grantseekers. The *National Guide to Funding . . .* series pulls together information from the major grantmaker and grants directories and organizes it by topic for the convenience of the researcher. The *National Guides* are designed to facilitate grantseeking within specific fields of nonprofit activity and are popular with grantseekers because they provide the facts needed to develop a list of funding prospects among foundations, corporate direct giving programs, and grantmaking public charities that have an interest in specific subject areas. Each entry provides address, financial data, giving priorities, application procedures, contact names, lists key officials, and more. Each volume also includes descriptions of recently awarded grants, and provides a range of indexes that will help you target funders by specific program areas.

Volumes in the *National Guide* series are currently available in the following subject areas:

AIDS	Health
Arts and Culture	Libraries and Information Services
Environment and Animal Welfare	Religion

The *Guide to Funding for International and Foreign Programs* is similar in format and content to the titles in the *National Guide* series even though it is international in scope. For detailed information about each book, see Appendix E.

Additional Funding Information Resources

Beyond the resources already described in this chapter, the Foundation Center provides online access to IRS Forms 990-PF and 990, grantmaker Web sites, and more through its Web site. Foundation Center libraries also maintain collections of print resources including annual reports, informational brochures, and newsletters issued by foundations and corporate grantmakers, in addition to files of news clippings, press releases, and historical materials related to philanthropy. Center libraries also provide public access to grantmaker information on the Internet. These supplementary materials are either primary, meaning that they were issued or posted by the foundation itself, or secondary, meaning that they were produced by sources outside the foundation. Such resources can be particularly helpful in the final stages of your research as you gather detailed information about the grantmakers you have identified as the most likely funding sources for your organization or project.

THE WORLD WIDE WEB

The Web is a valuable research tool for the grantseeker because it can provide both primary and secondary resources from a very wide range of sources.

Using a broad-based search engine such as Google or Yahoo! has its drawbacks, the major one being that you will likely find yourself sifting through long lists of search results that contain a lot of irrelevant material. A "gateway" site or a "portal," a Web site offering a variety of services around a specific topic, is usually more helpful to the grantseeker than a general search engine because it can be used as a home base for exploring the Web. The Foundation Center's Web site (http://www.fdncenter.org) is considered a gateway to the Web by many people in the nonprofit and philanthropic communities.

The Center's Web site (see Figure 31) is particularly useful to the grantseeker because it is the most authoritative and information rich source of up-to-date information on private philanthropy in the United States. To help you find your way, we have provided a site map and divided the site into five main directories to assist a variety of audiences with different needs: Finding Funders, Learning Lab, Researching Philanthropy, PND (*Philanthropy News Digest*), and the Marketplace.

The Finding Funders directory provides a range of powerful tools to get you started with your funding research. They include Foundation Finder, a free lookup tool that provides basic information (contact information, assets, total giving, etc.) on more than 70,000 private and community foundations in the United States; Grantmaker Web Sites, an annotated directory of links to the grantmakers that have Web sites,

Figure 31. Home Page of the Foundation Center's Web Site

organized by grantmaker type and searchable by subject and geographic keyword; Sector Search, a specialty philanthropy search engine that regularly "spiders" and indexes every page on every grantmaker Web site on the Internet as well as selected nonprofit organization and government sites; 990-PF Search, a searchable database of Form 990-PF tax returns filed by all domestic private foundations; *Foundation Grants to Individuals Online*, a subscription-based database of more than 6,000 grantmakers that give to individual grantseekers; and *The Foundation Directory Online*, our subscription-based service that allows representatives of nonprofit organizations to search the Foundation Center's own database for funding for their organizations or projects.

If you want to learn about the grantseeking process—or simply brush up on your fundraising skills—the Learning Lab directory should be your first stop. Resources in the Learning Lab include more than 125 frequently asked questions, with well-researched answers to questions on a range of topics, from proposal writing, to the do's and don'ts of starting a nonprofit organization, to the funding research process itself; the Virtual Classroom, which lets you choose from a variety of online training modules, many in a new interactive format, including our basic Orientation to Grantseeking, Demystifying the 990-PF, and the perennially popular Proposal Writing Short Course; Training Opportunities, providing you with descriptions and dates of the Foundation Center's free classes and fee-based seminars; the Online Librarian, which provides customized responses via e-mail within two to three business days to your questions about foundations, philanthropy, fundraising research, and other issues related to nonprofits; User Aids for individuals and nonprofit organizations; Topical Resource Lists on various topics related to philanthropy; and the Online Bookshelf with abridged versions of our most popular monographs.

The Researching Philanthropy directory has many excellent resources for statistical information on foundation giving trends, including FC Stats, which offers free access to a wealth of statistical tables on U.S. private and community foundations drawn from the Center's own research database; Top Funders ranked by assets and by total giving; Funding Trends and Analysis, providing descriptions of and highlights from our *Foundations Today Series* and special reports on particular segments of foundation philanthropy; Philanthropy's Response to 9/11, which brings into focus the role philanthropies and charities played in the relief, recovery, and rebuilding efforts in the aftermath of September 11, 2001, including research reports and a searchable 9/11 Funding Database; the *Literature of the Nonprofit Sector Online* (LNPS), a searchable database of the literature of philanthropy, incorporating the unique contents of the Foundation Center's five libraries and containing more than 23,000 full bibliographic citations, of which more than 15,000 have descriptive abstracts; and PubHub, featuring hundreds of annotated links to grantmaker-issued reports.

PND (*Philanthropy News Digest*), our award-winning digest of philanthropy-related news, is your window on the changing world of philanthropy. In addition to news, PND offers the RFP Bulletin, containing information about new grant opportunities posted by foundations and other grantmaking organizations; the Job Corner, which contains links to job openings at foundations, nonprofit organizations, educational institutions, and corporate grantmaking programs as well as to other sites listing jobs in the nonprofit sector; Connections, a weekly guide to the best the Web has to offer on cutting-edge issues related to philanthropy; the NPO Spotlight, helping nonprofits spread the word about their programs and services; and Newsmakers interviews, book and Web site reviews, a Conference Calendar, and a searchable PND archive. For readers who prefer to have their news and information delivered via e-mail, PND, the RFP Bulletin, and the Job Corner are available as free weekly e-mail newsletters.

The Marketplace can be used to find information on and/or purchase any Center books, CD-ROMs, or online services. It contains a changing roster of special offers, advice for novices, and a browsable catalog of every Foundation Center product. Here you can also register for our fee-based seminars and workshops or join our Associates Program.

The Foundation Center's Web site offers many other unique features and information you may want to know about, including:

- the SearchZone, where we've gathered some of the best general and specialized information retrieval tools from the Foundation Center's Web site;

- our five library/learning centers online—we have offices in Atlanta, Cleveland, New York, San Francisco, and Washington, D.C.—where you can learn more about Foundation Center programs, and philanthropy in general, in your part of the country, and you can sign up for the free weekly e-mail newsletter from the library nearest you;

- our network of Cooperating Collections that puts a core collection of Foundation Center publications and supplementary materials, along with expertise on how to use them, within convenient driving distance of most residents of the continental United States;

- an annotated directory of Links to Nonprofit Resources—a user-friendly gateway to the Web sites of thousands of organizations in the nonprofit sector;

- For Grantmakers, designed specifically for grantmakers to get answers, stay current with the latest news, spread the word about their organizations, and refer their grantees to appropriate resources;

- For Individual Grantseekers, with its own online orientation, information on fiscal sponsorship, and other tools and resources for individual grantseekers;

- For the Media, targeted toward the needs of the print and broadcast media with news, resources, press releases, research findings from the Foundation Center, and free e-mail updates featuring the latest philanthropy news; and

- About the Center, where you can learn more about the Center's mission and our efforts to strengthen the nonprofit sector by advancing knowledge about U.S. philanthropy;

Links to the site map, the Online Librarian, our newsletter subscription page, and a comprehensive set of FAQs, can be found at the bottom of the vertical navigation panel on nearly every page of the Foundation Center's Web site.

For more in-depth information on mining the Foundation Center's Web site and many other Internet resources for grantseekers, see *The Foundation Center's Guide to Grantseeking on the Web*. This guide describes a range of useful sites for grantseekers and provides the important "how-to's" of using the Internet effectively for funding research.

General Search Engines

You can use a general search engine to locate sites that help your grantseeking efforts. You may already be familiar with one or more of such popular search engines as:

- About.com (http://about.com)

- AltaVista (http://www.altavista.com)

- Google (http://www.google.com)

- Hotbot (http://hotbot.com)

- Metacrawler (http://www.metacrawler.com)

- Northern Light (http://www.northernlight.com)

- ProFusion (http://www.profusion.com)

- Yahoo! (http://www.yahoo.com)

And, of course, there are others. Try out each one to see which search engine works best for your needs. You will need to know the parameters of the specific search engine you may be using at the time. For instance, some engines search indiscriminately for every instance of the search term; other search engines utilize a selection process that reviews, classifies, and indexes Web sites for somewhat more focused searching. Also, as with any search, you need to choose the proper wording for your search query. For assistance, consult SearchEngineWatch.com (http://www.searchenginewatch.com), an excellent site that analyzes and recommends general search engines. This site also provides helpful tips to speed your research.

A cautionary note: The information on the Internet and the tools used to search it are constantly changing, and this information is often transitory in nature. That is, material that is available one day may be gone the next, addresses of Web sites may change, and the content of sites may be radically transformed overnight. Furthermore, since anyone can post information on the Internet, and there is no editorial process in place to screen content, you must carefully evaluate the accuracy, scope, and currency of the material yourself. Some questions to ask when visiting a Web site include:

- Who wrote or posted the information?

- Does the author or organization have a good reputation in the field?

- Is there biographical or "about us" information, via a link that allows you to judge the credentials of the author or host?

- Is there a recognizable bias or agenda associated with the author or organization?

- How thorough is the information?

- Is the information appropriate for your needs?

- Are there "last updated" notations to tell you if the information is up-to-date?

- Is research methodology or selection criteria explained?

These and other questions related to your research will help you to critically evaluate the resources you uncover on the Web.

PRIMARY RESOURCES

Most foundations do not issue annual reports, giving guidelines, or other printed matter about themselves; and only a small percentage have as yet established sites on the Web (currently only 5 percent of grantmakers). However, if a foundation has issued such print or electronic resources, the grantseeker should review them carefully for the most up-to-date indication of the funder's giving criteria.

Foundation Information Returns: The Form 990-PF
One of the best and most comprehensive sources of information on a private foundation is its Form 990-PF. Foundations are required to file this tax form annually with the Internal Revenue Service (IRS). Federal law requires that these documents, unlike personal or corporate tax returns, be made available to the public by both the IRS and by

the foundations themselves. This means that for all private foundations, regardless of size, basic facts about their operations and grants are a matter of public record. For many smaller foundations this information return is the *only* complete record of their operations and grantmaking activities. For larger foundations, Forms 990-PF supply key information about assets and investments, as well as a complete list of grants awarded in a particular year. See Figure 32 for a diagram of the Form 990-PF indicating where some of the most important information can be found, including contact information, assets, list of officers, application information, listings of grants paid, and of future planned or committed grants.

Since community foundations generally are classified as public charities and not as private foundations, most are not required to file a Form 990-PF with the IRS. Like other public charities, they file Form 990, which you can acquire from the community foundation itself, the IRS, or other sources. For a complete list of available options for obtaining IRS Forms 990, see the resources in our FAQ "How can I obtain copies of a public charity's 990 tax return?" (http://www.fdncenter.org/learn/faqs/html/990.html). Most community foundations also issue separate annual reports, have Web sites, or otherwise make available information about their activities. Keep in mind that many community foundations are actually engaged in soliciting funds as well as in grantmaking. Hence, it is in their self-interest to make their activities broadly known.

Where to Obtain Copies of IRS Form 990-PF Information Returns

In March 2000, new disclosure regulations went into effect that require foundations to provide, at a "reasonable fee," photocopies of their three most recent tax returns—including Form 990-PF and Form 4720 ("Return of Certain Excise Taxes on Charities and Other Persons Under Chapters 41 and 42 of the Internal Revenue Code")—as well as their original application for tax-exempt status to anyone who requests these documents in person or in writing. As with other tax-exempt organizations, the requirements can be satisfied by private foundations making the documents "widely available" over the Internet. Unlike other tax-exempt organizations, however, private foundations are required to make the names and addresses of their donors available to the public. Foundations will not be required to fulfill requests when they are determined to be part of a campaign of harassment.

The Foundation Center currently offers online access to more than 150,000 Forms 990-PF from approximately 80,000 foundations in Adobe PDF format. (Multiple years are provided where available.) You will need to download Adobe's free Acrobat Reader software—if it is not already installed on your computer—in order to view the returns (http://www.adobe.com/products/acrobat/readstep2.html). Returns can be

Figure 32. 2003 IRS Form 990-PF: Return of Private Foundation

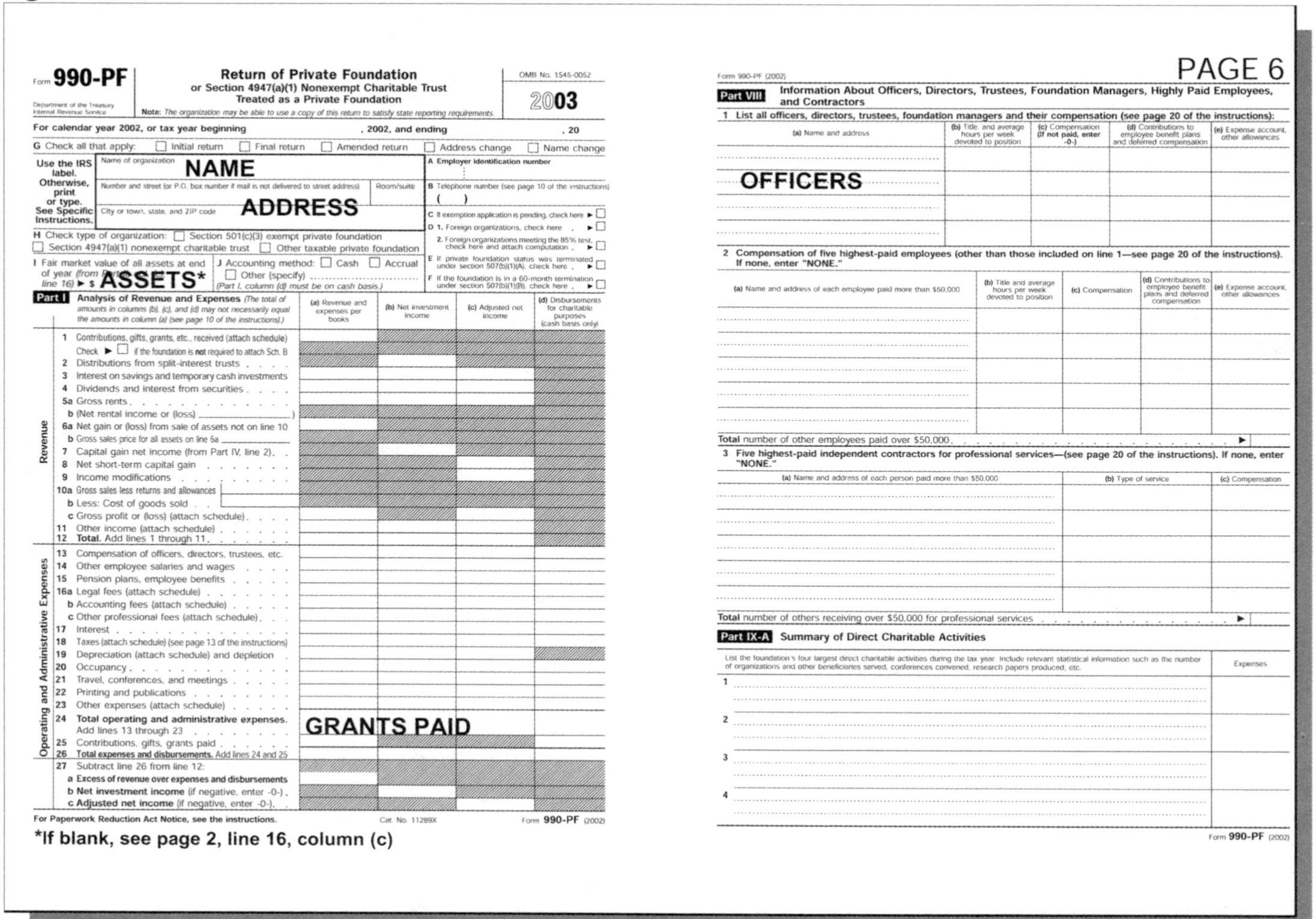

Form **990-PF**

Department of the Treasury
Internal Revenue Service

Return of Private Foundation
or Section 4947(a)(1) Nonexempt Charitable Trust
Treated as a Private Foundation

Note: *The organization may be able to use a copy of this return to satisfy state reporting requirements.*

OMB No. 1545-0052

2003

For calendar year 2002, or tax year beginning , 2002, and ending , 20

G Check all that apply: ☐ Initial return ☐ Final return ☐ Amended return ☐ Address change ☐ Name change

Use the IRS label. Otherwise, print or type. See Specific Instructions.

Name of organization **NAME**

Number and street (or P.O. box number if mail is not delivered to street address) Room/suite

City or town, state, and ZIP code **ADDRESS**

A Employer identification number

B Telephone number (see page 10 of the instructions) ( )

C If exemption application is pending, check here ► ☐

D 1. Foreign organizations, check here ► ☐

2. Foreign organizations meeting the 85% test, check here and attach computation ► ☐

E If private foundation status was terminated under section 507(b)(1)(A), check here ► ☐

F If the foundation is in a 60-month termination under section 507(b)(1)(B), check here ► ☐

H Check type of organization: ☐ Section 501(c)(3) exempt private foundation
☐ Section 4947(a)(1) nonexempt charitable trust ☐ Other taxable private foundation

I Fair market value of all assets at end of year (from Part II, col. (c), line 16) ► $ **ASSETS***

J Accounting method: ☐ Cash ☐ Accrual
☐ Other (specify)
(Part I, column (d) must be on cash basis.)

Part I **Analysis of Revenue and Expenses** *(The total of amounts in columns (b), (c), and (d) may not necessarily equal the amounts in column (a) (see page 10 of the instructions).)*

		(a) Revenue and expenses per books	(b) Net investment income	(c) Adjusted net income	(d) Disbursements for charitable purposes (cash basis only)
Revenue	1 Contributions, gifts, grants, etc., received (attach schedule)				
	2 Check ► ☐ if the foundation is **not** required to attach Sch. B				
	2 Distributions from split-interest trusts				
	3 Interest on savings and temporary cash investments				
	4 Dividends and interest from securities				
	5a Gross rents				
	b (Net rental income or (loss))				
	6a Net gain or (loss) from sale of assets not on line 10				
	b Gross sales price for all assets on line 6a				
	7 Capital gain net income (from Part IV, line 2)				
	8 Net short-term capital gain				
	9 Income modifications				
	10a Gross sales less returns and allowances				
	b Less: Cost of goods sold				
	c Gross profit or (loss) (attach schedule)				
	11 Other income (attach schedule)				
	12 **Total.** Add lines 1 through 11				
Operating and Administrative Expenses	13 Compensation of officers, directors, trustees, etc.				
	14 Other employee salaries and wages				
	15 Pension plans, employee benefits				
	16a Legal fees (attach schedule)				
	b Accounting fees (attach schedule)				
	c Other professional fees (attach schedule)				
	17 Interest				
	18 Taxes (attach schedule) (see page 13 of the instructions)				
	19 Depreciation (attach schedule) and depletion				
	20 Occupancy				
	21 Travel, conferences, and meetings				
	22 Printing and publications				
	23 Other expenses (attach schedule)				
	24 **Total operating and administrative expenses.** Add lines 13 through 23	GRANTS PAID			
	25 Contributions, gifts, grants paid				
	26 **Total expenses and disbursements.** Add lines 24 and 25				
	27 Subtract line 26 from line 12:				
	a **Excess of revenue over expenses and disbursements**				
	b **Net investment income** (if negative, enter -0-)				
	c **Adjusted net income** (if negative, enter -0-)				

For Paperwork Reduction Act Notice, see the instructions. Cat. No. 11289X Form **990-PF** (2002)

***If blank, see page 2, line 16, column (c)**

Form 990-PF (2002) **PAGE 6**

Part VIII **Information About Officers, Directors, Trustees, Foundation Managers, Highly Paid Employees, and Contractors**

1 List all officers, directors, trustees, foundation managers and their compensation (see page 20 of the instructions):

(a) Name and address	(b) Title, and average hours per week devoted to position	(c) Compensation (If not paid, enter -0-)	(d) Contributions to employee benefit plans and deferred compensation	(e) Expense account, other allowances
OFFICERS				

2 Compensation of five highest-paid employees (other than those included on line 1—see page 20 of the instructions). If none, enter "NONE."

(a) Name and address of each employee paid more than $50,000	(b) Title and average hours per week devoted to position	(c) Compensation	(d) Contributions to employee benefit plans and deferred compensation	(e) Expense account, other allowances

Total number of other employees paid over $50,000 ►

3 Five highest-paid independent contractors for professional services—(see page 20 of the instructions). If none, enter "NONE."

(a) Name and address of each person paid more than $50,000	(b) Type of service	(c) Compensation

Total number of others receiving over $50,000 for professional services ►

Part IX-A **Summary of Direct Charitable Activities**

List the foundation's four largest direct charitable activities during the tax year. Include relevant statistical information such as the number of organizations and other beneficiaries served, conferences convened, research papers produced, etc.	Expenses
1	
2	
3	
4	

Form **990-PF** (2002)

Figure 32. (continued)

PAGE 9

Form 990-PF (2002)

Part XIV Private Operating Foundations (see page 25 of the instructions and Part VII-A, question 9)

1a If the foundation has received a ruling or determination letter that it is a private operating foundation, and the ruling is effective for 2002, enter the date of the ruling . . . . ▶

b Check box to indicate whether the organization is a private operating foundation described in section ☐ 4942(j)(3) or ☐ 4942(j)(5)

	Tax year	Prior 3 years			
	(a) 2002	(b) 2001	(c) 2000	(d) 1999	(e) Total
2a Enter the lesser of the adjusted net income from Part I or the minimum investment return from Part X for each year listed					
b 85% of line 2a					
c Qualifying distributions from Part XII, line 4 for each year listed					
d Amounts included in line 2c not used directly for active conduct of exempt activities					
e Qualifying distributions made directly for active conduct of exempt activities. Subtract line 2d from line 2c					
3 Complete 3a, b, or c for the alternative test relied upon:					
a "Assets" alternative test—enter:					
(1) Value of all assets					
(2) Value of assets qualifying under section 4942(j)(3)(B)(i)					
b "Endowment" alternative test— Enter ⅔ of minimum investment return shown in Part X, line 6 for each year listed					
c "Support" alternative test—enter:					
(1) Total support other than gross investment income (interest, dividends, rents, payments on securities loans (section 512(a)(5)), or royalties)					
(2) Support from general public and 5 or more exempt organizations as provided in section 4942(j)(3)(B)(iii)					
(3) Largest amount of support from an exempt organization					
(4) Gross investment income					

Part XV Supplementary Information (Complete this part only if the organization had $5,000 or more in assets at any time during the year—see page 25 of the instructions.)

1 **Information Regarding Foundation Managers:**

a List any managers of the foundation who have contributed more than 2% of the total contributions received by the foundation before the close of any tax year (but only if they have contributed more than $5,000). (See section 507(d)(2).)

b List any managers of the foundation who own 10% or more of the stock of a corporation (or an equally large portion of the ownership of a partnership or other entity) of which the foundation has a 10% or greater interest.

2 **Information Regarding Contribution, Grant, Gift, Loan, Scholarship, etc., Programs:**

* Check here ▶ ☐ if the organization only makes contributions to preselected charitable organizations and does not accept unsolicited requests for funds. If the organization makes gifts, grants, etc. (see page 25 of the instructions) to individuals or organizations under other conditions, complete items 2a, b, c, and d.

a The name, address, and telephone number of the person to whom applications should be addressed:

b The form in which applications should be submitted and information and materials they should include:

APPLICATION INFORMATION

c Any submission deadlines:

d Any restrictions or limitations on awards, such as by geographical areas, charitable fields, kinds of institutions, or other factors:

Form **990-PF** (2002)

***If checked, foundation does not accept unsolicited applications**

PAGE 10

Form 990-PF (2002)

Part XV Supplementary Information (continued)

3 Grants and Contributions Paid During the Year or Approved for Future Payment

Recipient Name and address (home or business)	If recipient is an individual, show any relationship to any foundation manager or substantial contributor	Foundation status of recipient	Purpose of grant or contribution	Amount
a *Paid during the year*				
GRANTS PAID				
Total ▶ 3a				
b *Approved for future payment*				
FUTURE GRANTS				
Total ▶ 3b				

Form **990-PF** (2002)

found using Foundation Finder, 990-PF Search, *The Foundation Directory Online*, and *FC Search*. Forms 990-PF are updated at the Center's Web site with new returns approximately every four to six weeks.

Photocopies of private foundation returns may also be requested from the IRS via the Web (http://www.irs.gov/pub/irs-pdf/f4506a.pdf), by fax (801-620-6671), or by writing to:

Internal Revenue Service
Ogden Service Center
P.O. Box 9941
Mail Stop 6734
Ogden, UT 84409

Include the foundation's full name and the city and state where it is located. The IRS will bill you for the cost of the copies, which will vary depending on the number of pages involved.

State attorneys general (http://www.naag.org/ag/full_ag_table.php) may have copies of Form 990-PF returns for foundations in their states as well. For instance, if the organization you are looking for is in California, the State Attorney General's office of California (http://caag.state.ca.us/charities) posts California charity and foundation tax returns (Forms CT-2, 990, 990-EZ, and 990-PF) on its Web site.

GuideStar (http://www.guidestar.org), an online database of information on the activities and finances of nearly one million nonprofit organizations, run by Philanthropic Research Inc., makes nonprofit tax returns, including foundation Forms 990-PF and 990, accessible via the Internet. To search by EIN on GuideStar, simply click on More Search Options and you will see an EIN search field. Free registration is required in order to view Forms 990-PF and 990 at Guidestar's Web site.

How Soon Will a Foundation's Form 990-PF be Available for Public Scrutiny?

The typical IRS filing deadline for most foundations is approximately six months after the end of the foundation's fiscal year, assuming no filing extension is granted. It then takes another few months for the IRS to process and scan the Forms 990-PF into a digitized format. For example, if a foundation's fiscal year ended on December 31, 2004, you can expect its Form 990-PF to become available sometime in the fall of 2006. Of course, foundations may also request filing extensions from the IRS, which can lead to further delays in the Form 990-PF becoming publicly available. For more information, see our FAQ "What is the lag time between the close of a foundation's fiscal year and the date a copy of its tax return is available in a Foundation Center library or on its Web site?" (http://www.fdncenter.org/learn/faqs/html/lag_time.html).

All five Center libraries and some Cooperating Collections offer assistance to visitors on effective utilization of the 990-PF as part of the funding research process. Center libraries offer a free class, Guide to the Resources on the Foundation Center's Web Site, that includes a segment on finding relevant information on the 990-PF. There is also an online tutorial, Demystifying the 990-PF, in the Virtual Classroom of the Learning Lab directory on the Foundation Center's Web site.

Foundation Publications

Many foundations issue brochures, pamphlets, news releases, or newsletters that provide information on application procedures, specific grant programs or recent grants, and announcements regarding changes at the foundation. Although such publications are most often issued by large, staffed foundations, there are any number of smaller foundations that publish descriptive brochures in lieu of more extensive annual reports. These documents are more than a source of facts about the foundation; they are also a good medium for the grantseeker to determine its "personality."

Foundation Center libraries collect and make available as many foundation-issued documents and news releases as possible. Many of the Center's Cooperating Collections also collect publications issued by area grantmakers and make them available to the public. If you have identified grantmakers active in your subject field or geographic area, you may even be able to have your name added to the foundation's mailing list by writing or calling the foundation directly.

The most common grantmaker-issued publication is the annual report. Approximately 1,400 foundations issue such reports in print and electronic formats. Usually a foundation will mail you an annual report upon request. Although it varies from foundation to foundation, generally a foundation's annual report will provide the most complete and current information available about that foundation. Annual reports usually include detailed financial statements, a comprehensive list of grants awarded or committed for future payment, the names of officers and staff members, and a description of program interests. Most annual reports also indicate the application procedures grantseekers should follow, including any deadlines and particular proposal formats the foundation may prefer. Some annual reports include information on the foundation's donors in addition to essays on the operating philosophy that influences its grantmaking decisions. All of this information is useful to the grantseeker preparing a proposal to a foundation.

Foundations are not required by law to compile a separately printed or electronic annual report. Those that do, tend to be among the community foundations and foundations with assets of $1 million or more. Entries in the general grantmaker directories published by the Foundation Center—*The Foundation Directory Online*, *FC Search*, the *Guide to U.S. Foundations*, *The Foundation Directory*, *The Foundation Directory Part 2*, *The Foundation 1000*, and others—indicate whether a foundation issues an annual report or other publications. Foundation Center libraries maintain collections of annual reports issued by foundations in their local communities and by national foundations located elsewhere. Since few foundations issue annual reports, it is wise to check Foundation Center print and electronic resources in advance about the availability of such documents at your Center library or Cooperating Collection before requesting reports from foundations that don't publish them.

Foundation Web Sites

Relatively few grantmakers, around 4,000 (or about 5 percent) in 2004, currently have a presence on the Internet. Those foundations that do maintain Web sites provide much of the information grantseekers have come to expect from print sources, such as annual reports, grants lists, application guidelines, and so forth. A few foundations provide these publications and other resources *only* on the Web, and this may be a growing trend.

Most grantmakers with a Web presence have established their own Web sites; but close to 120 participate in the Foundation Folder program provided by the Foundation Center. Because most foundations do not have the staff or expertise to set up an independent Web site, the Foundation Center provides its Foundation Folder service, whereby the foundation provides the information and the Center sets up a folder at its site that contains that information. The goals of this service, which is provided without charge, are twofold: to provide individual foundations with an immediate Web presence and to put more foundation information in front of a wider audience by making that information available on the World Wide Web. Any domestic grantmaking private foundation, community foundation, corporate foundation, grantmaking public charity, or grantmaker affinity group that does not already have a Web site is eligible. Public charities wishing to participate in the Foundation Folders program must include information on their grantmaking activities, along with application guidelines to be posted.

Whether a foundation establishes and maintains its own site or asks the Foundation Center to establish a folder on its behalf, the Center helps the grantseeker identify foundations, grantmaking public charities, and corporate giving programs with Web sites by a variety of means. Foundation Center electronic databases such as *The Foundation Directory Online* and *FC Search* allow you to link directly from a grantmaker record to its Web site. (Foundation Center print directories also list the Web addresses of available grantmaker Web sites.) The Center's own Web site (http://www.fdncenter.org) has links to the home pages of private foundations, corporate grantmakers, grantmaking public charities, and community foundations. Since grantmaker Web sites contain the most up-to-date information directly "from the horse's mouth," grantseekers should be sure to explore these resources if available. Grantmaker Web sites are increasingly important information resources.

SECONDARY RESOURCES

Secondary sources include information produced by some source other than the grantmakers themselves. Newspaper and periodical articles are the most-often-referred to secondary sources. Increasingly, you may see articles about individual grantmakers or foundations in general in local and national newspapers and on the Web. You'll note that while a few foundations seem to receive a great deal of press coverage, most are never mentioned. One of the grantseeker's challenges is to locate such articles. The Foundation Center maintains several resources to help identify and access relevant print and electronic articles that are available free to the public at the Center's Web site.

Philanthropy News Digest

Philanthropy News Digest (PND), a news service of the Foundation Center that appears at the Center's Web site, is a compendium, in digest form, of philanthropy-related articles and features culled from print and electronic media outlets nationwide. Articles most likely to be summarized in PND include notices of large grants, profiles of grantmakers, trends in philanthropy, and obituaries of philanthropists.

Each news abstract summarizes the content of the original article with links to relevant organizations mentioned in the article and a citation or link to the original source, which helps you find a copy through a Foundation Center library or Cooperating Collection (see Figure 33).

In addition to searchable news abstracts, PND also provides interviews; reviews of books and Web sites; job listings in the nonprofit sector; and announcements of requests for proposals (RFPs). PND, the RFP Bulletin, and the Job Corner are all available as free weekly e-mail subscription newsletters.

Literature of the Nonprofit Sector

Since 1988, the Foundation Center has sought to increase public access to information on philanthropy and the nonprofit sector by identifying, indexing, and abstracting relevant books, periodical articles, and non-print resources such as audiovisual and CD-ROM materials. To this end, in 1989 the Center established a computerized database and began issuing annual printed volumes of a publication called the *Literature of the Nonprofit Sector*.

In 1997 the Foundation Center launched the *Literature of the Nonprofit Sector Online* (LNPS), a comprehensive searchable database of citations and abstracts of materials collected by the Center's five libraries as well as selected literature from other sources. This authoritative, regularly updated bibliography of works in the field of philanthropy contains more than 23,000 bibliographic entries, of which approximately two-thirds (more than 15,000) have abstracts. Several hundred records also offer links to full-text articles online. "New Acquisitions" contains the latest additions to the database organized by subject category.

The ease with which one can search *Literature of the Nonprofit Sector Online* is its major advantage. LNPS can be searched simultaneously by subject, author, title, publisher, journal title, record type, year of publication, keyword, and library location.

Philanthropic Studies Index

Another resource that helps you locate secondary sources about foundations and fundraising is the Philanthropic Studies Index, compiled and maintained by the Special Collections Department of the Indiana University-Purdue University Indianapolis (IUPUI) University Library. The Index is a reference to literature, primarily academic journals and research reports, on nonprofit organizations and issues concerning the nonprofit sector. It is available on the Internet (http://cheever.ulib.iupui.edu/psipublicsearch) and can be searched in a variety of ways, including by author, title, subject, source, or citation date. While the Index does not include abstracts, it is a useful resource for students and others involved in philanthropy.

Organization Files

Don't overlook the background information in your own organization's fundraising files. As stated in Chapter 4, data gathering and record keeping are essential components of fundraising. All information about donors—past, present, and potential—should be kept in files or electronic databases and organized in a way that facilitates retrieval. If you have received letters from a foundation in the past, such communication should be noted in your records, and the letters should be kept in your fundraising

Figure 33. Sample News Story Abstract from *Philanthropy News Digest*

files. Records of e-mails and phone conversations are also important. Fundraising software can assist you in tracking this information. For further information on software packages, see our FAQ "Where can I find information on fundraising and accounting software packages for my nonprofit organization?" (http://www.fdncenter.org/learn/faqs/html/software.html).

Public Forums

Formal, group information sessions are one possibility for obtaining insights on grantmaking procedures and trends from philanthropic leaders. Some foundations hold periodic forums for the grantseeking public. At these programs, grantmakers present their mission and guidelines and respond to questions from the audience. Foundation Center libraries sponsor such informational programs, usually gathering several grantmakers interested in a particular subject area, type of support, or geographic area for a panel discussion, followed by a question and answer session. Such programs, called "Meet the Grantmakers" or "Dialogue with Donors," are held with varying degrees of frequency. Dates, times, locations, and topics are announced on individual library Web pages at the Center's Web site and in library print and electronic newsletters. Some Cooperating Collections and nonprofit resource centers also sponsor such forums.

Listservs and Message Boards

Listservs and message boards have greatly advanced the ability of grantseekers to share information, advice, and prospecting and other strategies with colleagues. Participants on listservs and message boards can learn efficiently from each other about useful fundraising techniques, directories, books and software, upcoming workshops and meetings, job announcements, and more.

The Foundation Center maintains two message boards in the Philanthropy News Digest directory of its site. The popular PND Talk (http://members4.boardhost.com/PNDtalk) is a very active forum where members of the nonprofit philanthropic community—development professionals, consultants, individual grantseekers, and others—share advice, insights, and questions related to the changing world of philanthropy.

Arts Talk (http://members5.boardhost.com/ARTStalk), another PND message board, is devoted to questions and observations related to funding for the arts.

Summary

In summary, there are many sources of information in a variety of formats to help you find out about the interests, policies, procedures, and funding limitations of grantmakers. You will want to become familiar with as many of them as possible to enable you to sift through the mass of available information in order to compile your prospect list and to narrow that list to the most appropriate potential funders. The next three chapters are devoted to techniques for using these resources to compile and refine your prospect list.

Chapter 6

Finding the Right Funder: The Subject Approach

As indicated in Chapter 4, the first step in finding a funding partner is to develop a broad prospect list. You can do this by identifying foundations that are interested in your subject (subject approach), that give in the geographic area(s) served by your organization (geographic approach), and that award the type(s) of support your organization needs (types of support approach). You may employ all three approaches simultaneously when using an electronic database such as *The Foundation Directory Online* or *FC Search: The Foundation Center's Database on CD-ROM*, or sequentially using the indexes in a variety of print resources.

The subject approach to funding helps a nonprofit organization identify foundations with a common interest in: (1) its field of activity, (2) the population group it serves, and/or (3) the type of agency or organization it represents. A church providing services to children with AIDS, for example, would look for funders with interests in AIDS, children, religious institutions, or all three.

Grantmaker interests generally are indicated in two ways: by the foundation's own description of its purpose and activities and by the giving priorities reflected in the grants it actually awards. Statements of purpose are often left deliberately broad by foundations to allow for future shifts in emphasis. Although they may provide important information about funders' giving priorities, they should not be taken too literally. Instead, you should compare such statements to actual giving records. Purpose statements such as "general charitable giving" and "to promote human welfare" don't really mean to imply that a foundation will support every imaginable type of charitable activity. Since there is no database of grants that are available, your best indication of what a foundation will support is often what it has supported in the recent past. The databases, directories, annual reports, Forms 990-PF, newsletters, Web sites, and other resources described in Chapter 5 will help direct you to both statements of purpose and to records of actual grants awarded.

Step One: Develop a Fields of Interest Prospect List

Before you begin to develop your list of prospective funders with an interest in your subject area, take a few minutes to think about *all* the fields related to your organization's general mission or to the particular program or project you're trying to fund. For example, if you're working for a day care center that is planning a special program for parents on child nutrition, your list of subject terms might include day care, children, food, nutrition, boys, girls, and parental education. Scanning the subject indexes of databases such as *The Foundation Directory Online* or *FC Search* or print publications such as *The Foundation Directory*, the *National Guide to Funding...* series, and others may suggest other applicable terms.

In developing your initial list, keep the focus broad. This is not the time to concentrate your search too narrowly. Remember, it is rare, and not necessarily desirable, to find a recently awarded grant that precisely matches your needs. A funder may not want to make a grant for a project that so closely duplicates one it just funded. If you restrict yourself to looking for exact matches, you'll end up overlooking potential funders interested in activities similar, although not identical, to your own.

As you look into each foundation interested in your subject area, focus on the basic facts outlined in the Prospect Worksheet we've provided (see Figure 11). Check also to see that your organization operates in the geographic area where the foundation makes grants and that the foundation gives the type and amount of support your organization needs. This will save time later. Subsequent chapters discuss in greater detail the geographic and types of support approaches to funding research.

USE REFERENCE SOURCES EFFECTIVELY

You may use several types of online or CD-ROM databases, as well as reference books, to develop your initial prospect list. You should refer to indexes of foundation grants, national and state directories describing foundation giving interests and guidelines, and specialized funding guides in your subject field. Grantseekers tend to develop their own unique research strategies; with experience, you will find the procedures and sequence that work best for you.

To make the best use of your time and to avoid redundancy of information from various reference sources, take time to read the introductory material explaining the coverage of each directory or database. Knowing, for instance, that the *National Guide to Funding...* series contains some of the same information that you will find in *The Foundation Directory* and other print publications, may prevent you from researching the same grants information twice.

GRANTS APPROACH

Listings of actual grants awarded enable you to determine the specific subject interests of a foundation, the type and location of the organizations it has funded in the past, the size of the grants it has awarded, and the types of support it favors. The indexes discussed below derive from the Foundation Center's database, described more fully in Chapter 5. This database tracks grants of $10,000 or more awarded by more than 1,000 major foundations. Because many of these foundations make relatively large grants for programs that have a national focus, the indexes will be most helpful to grantseekers whose projects are of a size and scope to attract the interest of national or regional foundations.

If you have access to the *Plus, Premium,* or *Platinum* service levels of *The Foundation Directory Online*[1] *or FC Search*, their grants files, containing approximately 400,000 and 325,000 grants, respectively, for more than 1,000 of the largest U.S. foundations, are excellent places to start. A foundation's grants for multiple years are usually included to help indicate funding patterns. The subject field is one of multiple criteria that can be searched in the grants files. There are built-in indexes to help you select appropriate terms. You can also search for several subjects simultaneously. You can

---

1. Unless otherwise noted, the remaining references in this chapter to The Foundation Directory Online refer to the *Platinum* level of service. See Figure 13 for a comparison chart detailing the content and features of each subscription service level.

Figure 34. Grants Search Using the Boolean Operator "OR" in *The Foundation Directory Online*

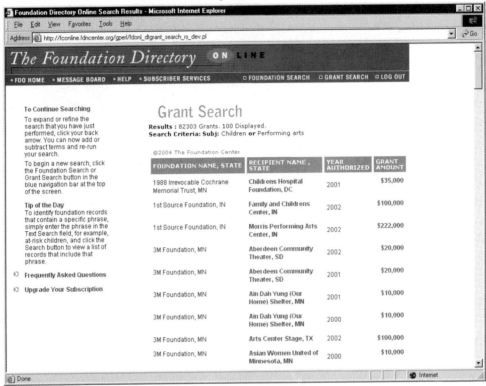

make your search broad by using "OR" as your Boolean operator, or narrow the search by using "AND" as the connector between subjects (see Figures 34 and 35). For instance, if you were trying to raise money for an art museum that produces theatrical productions for children, you would obtain a very broad list by searching for "arts" OR "children," since this would yield all grants covering the subject of arts and all grants covering the subject of children. If you entered your subject search as "arts" AND "children," the resulting much smaller grants list would be composed of only those grants covering *both* arts and children.

Several other search fields will be helpful in locating grants by subject: Recipient Name, Recipient Type (only available on *FC Search*), and Text Search. Foundations that have given grants to organizations that are similar to your own can be searched by organization name (Recipient Name) or by organization type (Recipient Type). If, for

Figure 35. Grants Search Using the Boolean Operator "AND" in *The Foundation Directory Online*

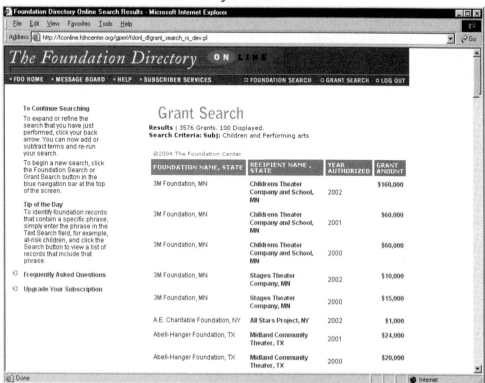

instance, you are interested in starting a club for children ages six to twelve years that emphasizes environmental awareness, you might look at who has been giving grants to the Boy Scouts or Girl Scouts (Recipient Name) or you might search for grants that have been awarded to "Boys & girls clubs" or to "Youth development, centers/clubs" (Recipient Types). To avoid spelling errors or incorrect names, we recommend that you always use the index to select recipient names and recipient types rather than typing them in the box yourself.

Alternatively, you may want to begin your research into foundation grants by looking at the Foundation Center's *Grant Guide* that is most applicable to your program or organization. The 12 print *Grant Guides*, published annually, are arranged alphabetically by foundation state and name. Each includes a list of foundations with their addresses and giving limitations, a subject index, an index of recipients organized by state, and an index of recipients organized by name.

Begin with the alphabetical list of foundations provided in the back of each book. This listing includes the foundation's address and a brief statement of any restrictions on its giving program. This will help you eliminate foundations that do not award grants in your geographic area. To complete your Prospect Worksheet (see Figure 11)—types of grant recipients, types of support awarded, and so on—scan the grants listed under foundations whose restrictions do not seem to prohibit them from funding your proposal.

The *Grant Guides* series will help you locate funders for your specific project, discover the grantmakers that favor your geographic area, and target foundations by looking at grants awarded to other nonprofits, but you should bear in mind that these directories are not comprehensive. They cover recently awarded foundation grants of $10,000 or more, culled from a database of more than 1,000 foundations.

Another path to foundations with a history of making grants in your subject area is *The Foundation Grants Index on CD-ROM*. *The Grants Index on CD-ROM* lists grants of $10,000 or more reported by more than 1,0000 foundations in the preceding year. It is particularly useful if your program or organization falls under a variety of subject fields, or if there is no appropriate *Grant Guide* for your subject area.

The Grants Index on CD-ROM includes grants listings by recipient name, city, state, and type, grantmaker name and city, subject, type of support categories, and geographic focus. You can also search by grant amount and the year the grant was authorized. First, you should scan the grants lists of foundations located in your state. Then, check grants in your specific subject field in the Subject Index. You will find the Subject Index to be very detailed. For example, not only will you find the topic "Civil rights," you will also find "Civil rights, advocacy," "Civil rights, gays/lesbians," "Civil rights, minorities," "Civil rights, race/intergroup relations," "Civil rights, voter education," "Civil rights, women," and many more. You should follow up by looking for grants of a specific kind of funding that is given in your geographic area by using the Types of Support Index and the Geographic Focus Index. Finally, look for grants awarded to organizations similar to your own in the Recipient Name Index and the Recipient Type Index.

Again, you will want to check the size and nature of the grants foundations you uncover typically make in addition to the type and location of the organizations they support. Note any giving-limitation statement provided immediately under a foundation's name. If you don't qualify, you won't want to waste your time applying.

GRANTMAKER DATABASES AND DIRECTORIES

At this point you may have developed a fairly long list of prospects. However, because the grants files in *The Foundation Directory Online* and *FC Search* as well as the Center's grants publications cover only approximately 1,000 of the nation's major foundations, you've really just gotten started. To expand your prospect list, turn to other grantmaker directories and databases. Include local foundation directories as well as national ones, and be especially alert to specialized subject directories in your field. As indicated previously, you'll find that indexes to foundation grants provide far more specific subject references than grantmaker directories, which usually employ a very general terminology to describe foundation program interests; as a result, the terms provided in their subject indexes are relatively non-specific. For instance, the 2003/2004 edition of *Grants for Arts, Culture, and the Humanities* lists more than 59 variations of the subject "Music," whereas the Subject Index for *The Foundation Directory* for the same year list only two variations of "Music" (see Figures 36 and 37).

The grantmaker files of *The Foundation Directory Online* and *FC Search* can help you identify the subject interests of more than 75,000 foundations, grantmaking public charities, and corporate donors. In both databases, the subject field is called Fields of Interest. This field lets you select grantmakers that have a stated interest in a specific subject (art, health, religion, etc.) or who have shown an interest in a particular subject by the grants they have awarded. You can locate the fields of interest terms used and the frequency with which the terms appear in the database by opening the index. (Numbers appear next to each term indicating the number of records in the database with that particular heading.) As with searching the grants file, you can broaden or narrow your subject search of the grantmaker file by using the Boolean "OR" or "AND."

If you prefer to work with books rather than with a computer, or if you do not have easy access to *The Foundation Directory Online* or *FC Search*, we usually recommend that you begin your subject approach with the Foundation Center's flagship publication, *The Foundation Directory*. The 25th edition of the *Directory* covers the largest 10,000 foundations by total giving, with combined assets of more than $420 billion, and includes a subject index subdivided by state to help you identify foundations that have expressed an interest in your subject field. Foundations with national, regional, or international giving patterns appear in bold type under the state in which they are located; foundations that give locally appear in regular type. As you check the references in your subject category, you should add to your prospect list foundations in your own state as well as those foundations in other states indicated in bold type. Make a note of the foundation's state and entry number so that you can refer back to

Figure 36. Subject Index from *Grants for Arts, Culture, and the Humanities*

110

Figure 37. Subject Index from *The Foundation Directory*

Museums (specialized)

California: Bloomfield 280, Booth 285, Broccoli 305, Campbell 337, Greenberg 589, Homer 660, **Schlinger 1052,** Witherbee 1264
Colorado: Chowdry 1316
Florida: Kislak 2036
Georgia: Jones 2350
Illinois: Goldberg 2726, **Harvey 2764,** Madigan 2840
Louisiana: Diboll 3438
Massachusetts: Demoulas 3822, Grantham 3869, Stemberg 4096, Webster 4132
Michigan: **Dogwood 4227,** Ransom 4368
Minnesota: O'Neil 4590
New Jersey: Levitt 5255
New York: Altus 5471, Cohen 5691, Follett 5901, Frohlich 5932, Goldenson 5989, Hemmerdinger 6104, Little 6382, Millard 6500
Ohio: Ferguson 7578
Pennsylvania: Hooper 8236, von Hess 8452
Texas: Levine 9010, McNutt 9056, Mechia 9058, Moncrief 9070, Oshman 9106, Taylor 9241
Virginia: Funger 9437
Washington: Apex 9558, Lockwood 9634, Schultz 9681

Museums (sports/hobby)

Alabama: Scrushy 71
Delaware: Birch 1664
Illinois: Snite 2976
North Carolina: Ebert 7306

Music

Alabama: Hess 41
Alaska: Carr 88
Arizona: Morris 125
California: **Bull 311,** Burnett 317, Capital 341, Cassin 347, **ChevronTexaco 358,** Colburn 370, Community 379, Copley 389, Disney 429, Femino 470, Firks 478, Fitzgerald 482, Fleishhacker 485, Getty 540, Gonda 574, Heller 639, Hewlett 644, Jewett 696, Knapp 738, Lyons 799, Masserini 816, Murdy 883, Oschin 919, Osher 921, **Packard 933,** Plum 970, Samson 1032, San Diego 1035, **Seaver 1067,** Simms 1105, Skaggs 1108, Sonora 1125, Thornton 1182, Wood 1270, Zellerbach 1285, Zimmer 1288
Colorado: Bernstein 1301, Boettcher 1303, El Pomar 1338, Gates 1343, Joy 1363, McCloskey 1378, Schermer 1402, **Staley 1409,** Summit 1415
Connecticut: **Bingham 1451,** Wiener 1649
Delaware: Buckner 1668, Crystal 1676
District of Columbia: Bernstein 1738, Cafritz 1741, Dimick 1751, Kaye 1773, Sprenger 1807
Florida: Appleby 1835, Colen 1891, Darden 1909, Davis 1917, Magill 2069, Thoresen 2206
Georgia: Arnold 2248, Collins 2277, Exposition 2303, Flowers 2305, Morgan 2382, Schwob 2416
Hawaii: Frear 2470
Illinois: Allocation 2527, BANK 2547, Bere 2561, Dunard 2668, Getz 2716, Glossberg 2725, Gray 2738, Kaplan 2794, Kemper 2801, Lederer 2821, Lee 2822, **MacDonald 2838,** Negaunee 2881, OMRON 2899, Rotonda 2940, Seid 2962, Shapiro 2967
Indiana: Clowes 3072, Griffith 3111
Iowa: **Fisher 3260,** Principal 3300
Kentucky: Opera 3411
Maryland: Allfirst 3515, Columbia 3556, Hecht 3609, Meyerhoff 3650, Procter 3670
Massachusetts: Argosy 3738, Babson 3745, Daniels 3819, Dusky 3827, Filene 3844, High 3884, Hoffman 3938, Kingsbury 3920, Leaves 3931, Little 3938, Manitou 3944, Overly 3995, Phillips 4014, Proctor 4022, Shapiro 4071
Michigan: Berrien 4172, Burdick 4183, Community 4199, Eddy 4238, Shapero 4383, Shelden 4384, VanVlack 4427, Westerman 4438, Wolverine 4449
Minnesota: Adams 4455, Bush 4482, Carlson 4488, Duluth 4507, General 4523, Heilmaier 4537, Jerome 4547, O'Shaughnessy 4591
Mississippi: Hearin 4692

Missouri: Bloch 4721, Buder 4729, Gaylord 4760, GenAmerica 4761, Kauffman 4791, Sosland 4860, Stern 4862
Nevada: **Buck 4985,** Fairweather 4997, Wiegand 5033
New Jersey: Bergen 5092, Bulova 5110, Bunbury 5111, Christie 5124, **Colton 5129,** Cowles 5133, Dodge 5142, Holzer 5196, Honeywell 5197, New Jersey 5288, Sunfield 5361
New Mexico: McCune 5420, Santa Fe 5428
New York: A.E. 5436, Ammon 5480, Armstrong 5489, Artzt 5493, **AT&T 5497,** Baird 5518, Barrington 5530, Bayne 5540, Burns 5618, Cary 5639, **Chazen 5663,** Clark 5684, **Copland 5716,** Cypress 5741, Elebash 5844, Ferkauf 5881, **Ford 5906,** Gerry 5957, Gilman 5971, Goldsmith 6002, **Grant 6021,** Greene 6030, **Hauser 6086, Heineman 6097,** Hillman 6118, **Katz 6227,** Kellen 6244, Krimendahl 6300, Liberman 6362, Marcus 6430, **Mercer 6487,** Mercy 6489, **Merlin 6492, MetLife 6495,** Morse 6532, Moses 6537, Moss 6538, **Newhouse 6573, Noble 6583,** O'Malley 6596, Olive 6610, Orvis 6617, **Paul 6645,** Performing 6661, Perkin 6663, Phaedrus 6670, Plant 6684, Pope 6691, Rose 6789, Rosenblum 6803, Samuels 6847, Scherman 6864, **Schwartz 6886,** Schweitzer 6889, Sharp 6903, **Spiegel 6973,** Stiefel 7013, **Trust 7093,** Tuch 7096, Tully 7099, **U.S. 7107,** Ungar 7111, Vidda 7130, Western 7174, Wiener 7188, Wilson 7193, Zesiger 7230
North Carolina: Biddle 7258, Day 7299, **Goodrich 7325,** Halton 7331, Perkins 7388, Smith 7424, Triangle 7438, **Wachovia 7441,** Wells 7444
Ohio: Alms 7467, Baker 7480, Bee 7484, Callahan 7511, DJ 7560, Gale 7600, Gund 7613, Gund 7614, Kacalieff 7660, Kulas 7674, Morley 7726, Muskingum 7733, Nippert 7741, Payne 7757, Peterson 7761, Reinberger 7776, Rieveschl 7783, Robbins 7786, Sage 7792, Schwebel 7810, Van Wert 7854, Wohlgemuth 7874, Youngstown 7882
Oregon: Mentor 8001
Pennsylvania: Arcadia 8045, Arronson 8048, Bristol 8081, Campbell 8094, Cassett 8100, Dietrich 8142, Dolfinger 8143, Eglin 8156, Field 8173, Giop 8193, Greenfield 8200, Hoch 8230, Hooper 8236, Kardon 8258, Kelly 8262, **Pew 8342,** Presser 8354, Roberts 8367, Rockwell 8369, Stabler 8416, Steinman 8421, **Teleflex 8436, Whitaker 8464,** Wyomissing 8477
South Carolina: Central 8555, Montgomery 8578
Texas: Cain 8789, Constantin 8830, Dougherty 8859, Fikes 8889, Haas 8926, Mitchell 9067, Rockwell 9161, **Shell 9191, Starling 9218,** Stemmons 9220, Tobin 9248
Utah: **Huntsman 9343**
Virginia: Delmar 9420, Fralin 9431, Portsmouth 9497
Washington: Allen 9554, Archibald 9559, Bishop 9563, Community 9578, King 9622, **Kongsgaard 9625,** Norcliffe 9653
Wisconsin: Alliant 9745, McQueen 9868, Oshkosh 9886, Pick 9901

Music (choral)

Iowa: Krause 3280
New York: Phaedrus 6670, **Popplestone 6692**
Ohio: Stranahan 7833
Pennsylvania: Ryan 8376

Mutual aid societies

New York: Riggio 6761

Native Americans/American Indians

Alaska: CIRI 89, Doyon 90, Rasmuson 91
Arizona: Ottens 128
California: **American 208,** California 328, Community 379, **LEF 766,** Mental 846, Stern 1144, Wunderkinder 1275
Colorado: **Qwest 1397**
Connecticut: Culpeper 1472, Dibner 1481, **Educational 1488, Ettinger 1489,** Woodward 1653

Delaware: **Raskob 1713**
Florida: **Baker 1845**
Illinois: Burlington 2595
Maryland: **Hughes 3618**
Massachusetts: Community 3803, High 3884, Hyams 3894
Michigan: Grand Rapids 4269
Minnesota: Bell 4470, Bremer 4481, Duluth 4507, General 4523, Grotto 4533, Minneapolis 4574, Phillips 4604
Missouri: **Timmons 4875**
New Jersey: **Carolan 5117,** Johnson 5218, Newcombe 5289
New Mexico: Frost 5412, **Lannan 5417,** McCune 5420, New Mexico 5422, Santa Fe 5428
New York: **Abelard 5437,** Afognak 5450, Bay 5539, Bristol 5598, **Edouard 5834,** Gould 6018, **Macy 6418,** Oestreicher 6601, **Panaphil 6632,** Skadden 6940, Ungar 7111
North Carolina: Cumberland 7294, Meyer 7371, Reynolds 7402, Triangle 7438
North Dakota: Stern 7462
Oregon: Intel 7985
Pennsylvania: **United 8447**
South Dakota: South Dakota 8606
Texas: Dougherty 8859, Edwards 8872, Kempner 8982
Vermont: **Ben 9375**
Virginia: Delmar 9420, Easley 9424, **Gannett 9439**
Washington: Archibald 9559, Norcliffe 9653

Natural resources

Alabama: Barber 11, Brock 17
Alaska: Alaska 86
Arizona: Arizona 93, **Furrow 104, Kieckhefer 116, Schumann 143**
Arkansas: Ross 169
California: Aaroe 182, **American 208,** Barker 247, Bella 261, **Betlach 268,** Braddock 295, Capecchio 340, Chais 352, Chandler 353, Cheeryble 357, **Christensen 361,** Columbia 373, **Compton 382, Conservation 386,** Crawford 399, Crocker 401, **Delano 421, Environment 435,** Epstein 460, Firedoll 475, Flintridge 486, **Foundation 495,** Garen 523, Gateway 527, Gellert 529, Gerhard 536, Gilmore 549, Gold 562, Haas 607, Haynes 633, Hazen 635, Heller 639, Hewlett 644, Hofmann 656, **Homeland 659,** Irvine 680, **JL 698,** JWS 709, King 731, Klein 735, Lee 764, Lipman 779, Ludwick 791, McCaw 829, Mead 842, Mellam 843, **Mohn 862,** Moore 868, Morton 875, Mudd 878, Otter 925, **Packard 933,** Peterson 960, Pfleger 962, Raintree 984, Reid 993, Sacramento 1031, San Francisco 1038, Sapling 1044, **Schlinger 1052,** Schmidt 1054, **Schwab 1060,** Shapiro 1088, Sheinberg 1094, Skaggs 1108, Smith 1111, Sprague 1129, **Stuart 1155,** Ventura 1214, Walris 1225, Windfall 1260, Witter 1266, Wunderkinder 1275, Zilkha 1287
Colorado: **Airport 1290, Benson 1300,** Boettcher 1303, El Pomar 1338, Gates 1343, **Hamilton 1348, Hawley 1351,** Joy 1363, Merlin 1383, Summit 1415, Taylor 1416, True 1419
Connecticut: Baldwin 1441, Beinecke 1447, Community 1468, Connecticut 1469, **Educational 1488,** Flinn 1494, Garden 1501, Grant 1510, **Huisking 1525,** Larsen 1536, **October 1571,** Olin 1572, Patricelli 1577, Schumann 1606, **Scrooby 1608,** Sun 1623, Tsunami 1632, Vanderbilt 1640, Walker 1644
Delaware: Buckner 1668, Cawley 1669, Chichester 1671, Crestlea 1675, Crystal 1676, Ederic 1679, Marmot 1702, Rowland 1717, **Seraph 1721,** Singer 1722, Struthers 1724
District of Columbia: Cafritz 1741, Community 1747, Mazda 1787, McIntosh 1789, **Moriah 1792,** Munson 1794, **Patterson 1799,** Post 1800, Spring 1808, **Summit 1811, Wallace 1816, Winslow 1821**
Florida: Bank 1848, Batchelor 1854, Blank 1869, Community 1892, Community 1896, Darden 1909, Dunn 1933, KBR 2023, Lattner 2050, Marden 2071, Opler 2105, Rayonier 2135, **Regan 2138, Vanneck 2211**

THE FOUNDATION DIRECTORY, 2004 EDITION

the full entry later. Again, the full entry will provide the additional information you need to complete your Prospect Worksheet—that is, program interests, giving limitations, the grant amounts typically awarded, and more.

If your project is regional or national in scope, or of broad enough appeal to attract a major funder, your next stop should be *The Foundation 1000*, an annual publication that provides detailed analyses of the nation's 1,000 largest foundations. *The Foundation 1000* includes a subject index that lists foundations under the subject fields expressed in the "Purpose" section of their entries. Once you have noted foundation names from the appropriate index categories, examine the actual foundation profiles to complete your Prospect Worksheet. Note especially the giving restrictions in the Limitation(s) field found in each foundation entry.

As noted in Chapter 5, state and local online and print grantmaker directories issued by a wide range of publishers are another good resource, although they do vary in content and coverage. When using them, you should examine the most recent update notation for online databases and the most current edition of each relevant print directory. Identify potential funding sources through the subject index, where provided, or by scanning the entries themselves.

NATIONAL GUIDE SERIES

The Foundation Center publishes a number of directories focusing on the major funders and giving trends in a specific subject area or population group. Drawing on information gathered in the Foundation Center's database, the *National Guide to Funding . . .* series combines descriptive financial information with grant records for foundations operating in selected fields. These *Guides* also include introductions, indexes, and specialized reading lists prepared from the Center's bibliographic database. They bring together in one convenient format information from various other Center publications. The subjects covered by the *Guides* are listed in Chapter 5. Appendix E provides annotations for each volume, including coverage, edition, etc.

OTHER SPECIALIZED FUNDING GUIDES

A final step in developing your prospect list by subject is to examine other specialized funding guides and Web sites devoted to your field. For instance, if you need funds for health services for the elderly, you may want to refer to *Grant Funding for Elderly Health Services*, published by Health Resources Publishing of Manasquan, New Jersey. If your interest is in the arts, you may find appropriate funding information on the Arts Over America Web site (http://www.nasaa-arts.org/aoa/aoa_contents.shtml) or the New York

Foundation for the Arts site (http://www.nyfa.org). A listing of some of the major specialized funding guides available in Foundation Center libraries and on Web sites is provided in Appendix A. Professional journals in your field may include information about other guides and Web sites. While these resources vary tremendously in their currency and content, they can be helpful in identifying additional prospects.

Step Two: Refine Your List

You should now have a lengthy list of foundations that possibly might be interested in funding your organization or project. Now is the time to refine the list to a reasonable number of grantmakers that are most likely to look favorably on your program. You should review your subject prospect list to eliminate those foundations that do not give in your geographic area and/or that do not award the type(s) or amount of support your organization needs. If you used *The Foundation Directory Online* or *FC Search* to construct your list, you probably used multiple search criteria, thereby completing this step already. Filling in the Prospect Worksheet (see Figure 11) for each potential funder on your list enables you to quickly rule out the less appropriate candidates.

Now that you have determined that the funders on your list have demonstrated a real commitment to funding in your subject field, in your geographic area, and providing the type(s) of support your organization needs, you are ready to scrutinize your list further to determine those potential funders that are most likely to be interested in your organization or project. You'll want to conduct as much research on all aspects pertaining to these grantmakers as time and resources permit. Posing the questions raised in Chapter 4 is a good place to start:

- Does the funder accept applications?

- Has the funder demonstrated a real commitment to funding in your subject field?

- Does it seem likely that the funder will make grants to organizations in your geographic location?

- Does the amount of money you are requesting fit within the funder's typical grant range?

- Does the funder have a policy prohibiting grants for the type(s) of support you are requesting?

- Does the funder usually make grants to cover the full cost of a project or does it favor projects where other funders have an opportunity to participate?

- Does the funder put limits on the length of time it is willing to support a project?

- What types of organizations does the funder tend to support?

- Does the funder have application deadlines, or does it review proposals continuously?

- Do you or does anyone on your board know someone connected with the funder?

- What are the financial conditions that may affect the foundation's ability to give?

- Do you have the most current and accurate details on the funder?

Most of these questions can be answered by referring to any one of several resources. *The Foundation Directory Online* and *FC Search* will answer many of them. Print directories such as *The Foundation Directory* or *The Foundation 1000* or some of the state and local directories will also provide many of the answers you need. For information such as application deadlines and the names of trustees, officers, or donors, Center databases and directories are excellent sources.

Grantmakers that state that they are interested in a particular subject area may also occasionally award grants to organizations outside their stated subject limitations. Often, you will need to refer to primary sources such as IRS Forms 990-PF and foundation annual reports or application guidelines for a full grants list. This is particularly true for smaller foundations whose grants are not included in online databases and that do not have Web sites. For instance, suppose you are trying to identify funders that would be interested in providing money for staff development to help teachers incorporate math skills in middle school classes. You have identified a funder that gives in your geographic area and that provides funding for staff development. However, there is no indication in any of the databases or directories you consulted that this funder has an interest in elementary and secondary education. On the other hand, there is no limitation statement explicitly saying that the grantmaker will *not* give for this purpose. In this case, it would be in your organization's best interests to seek out a more complete listing of grants awarded than you will find in grants databases and directories. If the grantmaker publishes an annual report, secure a copy and study the grants list if available. Annual reports can be found on many foundation Web sites and in Center libraries and many Cooperating Collections (see Appendix F).

If a full grants listing is not available from these sources, look at the foundation's Form 990-PF. Because the IRS requires a foundation to list all of its grants on the Form 990-PF, the tax return is your best source for comprehensive information about grants awarded for a particular tax year (see Chapter 5 for information on obtaining a foundation's Form 990-PF). When reviewing the Form 990-PF, ask yourself: Has the funder awarded grants for your subject area? Have any grants been awarded to organizations outside the stated subject limitations? Have any grants been awarded to organizations in your geographic area? Have past grants been awarded for the type(s) of support your organization seeks? An examination of a complete grants list can be highly revealing concerning foundation priorities. And if you have the time, comparing several years' worth of grants lists, looking for patterns and/or exceptions, may prove even more instructive.

Don't overlook secondary sources such as articles in newspapers and journals that may provide the most up-to-date information you need. *Philanthropy News Digest* (PND), the Foundation Center's online summary of the news of the world of philanthropy, allows you to keep apprised of recent information about foundations and their philanthropic efforts. PND summaries will also inform you of changes in leadership, very recent large grants, and other such information. You may wish to employ PND's search engine to enter the name of a foundation on your prospect list to see what, if anything, has been reported about this funder's recent gifts. Another source of information on recently awarded grants is the "Guide to Grants" at the *Chronicle of Philanthropy*'s Web site (http://www.philanthropy.com/grants). This is a database of the grants published in the *Chronicle of Philanthropy* since 1995. A listing of other print and electronic nonprofit news and publication resources can be found in the Nonprofit Links section of the Researching Philanthropy directory on the Foundation Center's Web site.

A review of the resources detailed in Chapter 5 will help you to decide which tools (Web sites, databases, directories, annual reports, IRS returns, application guidelines, etc.) will best assist you in answering the specific questions necessary to refine your list to the most likely prospects. When you have answered these questions about the funders on your broad prospect list, you will have narrowed your list to the few that you should approach first.

Summary

A grantmaker's fields of interest are indicated by its own description of its purpose and activities and by the giving priorities reflected in the actual grants it has awarded. There are a variety of materials available to the grantseeker to develop a broad prospect list based on common subject interests. Once you have developed a list of potential funders interested in your subject area, it is very important to find out if those funders give in your geographic area and if they provide the type(s) and amount of support your organization needs. The next two chapters will further explore the geographic and types of support approaches to fundraising research.

Chapter 7

Finding the Right Funder: The Geographic Approach

The phrase "charity begins at home" sums up the most typical pattern of foundation funding. And in fact, philanthropy focused on the funder's home base has been a reality since its earliest days. Of the 20,000 foundations tracked by the Foundation Center in the 2004 editions of *The Foundation Directory* and *The Foundation Directory Part 2*, approximately 88 percent restrict their giving to a specific state or multistate region. Although some of the larger, better known foundations tend to break out of this pattern, most have a strong commitment to funding local nonprofits that serve their communities.

For these reasons, nonprofits interested in attracting foundation funding should learn as much as possible about the funders in their own backyard, both large and small. This is particularly important if you are seeking relatively small grants or funds for projects with purely local impact. Often, it will be possible to build a funding strategy calling upon a variety of components. For example, you might approach local foundations for small grants in the $100 to $5,000 range for continuing operating support, while approaching larger national foundations in your field when introducing a special project.

You are likely to discover that many small foundations give to the same organizations year after year and rarely make grants to new recipients. Don't let this fact deter you from investigating all local sources. Some of your work with potential funders—what professional fundraisers call "cultivation"—can and should be viewed as a learning experience and a valuable investment of your time. Making local grantmakers aware of the services you are providing and the ways in which your organization enhances life in their home community can only benefit you in the long run.

Step One: Develop a Geographic Prospect List

Developing a list of foundations that are either located in or fund projects in your city or state is relatively easy. The resources available include electronic databases, grantmaker directories, and indexes of foundation grants. Keep in mind, however, that simply sharing the same zip code is not reason enough to request funds from a foundation. Once identified, each foundation must be fully researched to see if its grantmaking activities match up in other ways with your organization or project.

GRANTMAKER DATABASES AND DIRECTORIES

If you have access to *The Foundation Directory Online* or *FC Search: The Foundation Center's Database on CD-ROM*, that is the place to begin because you can conduct searches using multiple points of entry, such as geographic focus and fields of interest. If you simply want to identify those foundations located in the state where your organization is based or where your program takes place, use the Grantmaker/Foundation State field. To locate grantmakers in your geographic area, you can also search by zip code by entering the state in the Grantmaker/Foundation State field and the zip code in the Text Search field (see Figure 38). It is also possible to search by telephone area code in the Text Search field (see Figure 39).

Using *The Foundation Directory Online* and *FC Search*, you can additionally search by the city in which the grantmaker is located and/or by the states in which the grantmaker has a stated interest in giving or a history of giving. Searching by Grantmaker/Foundation City can be of great assistance in locating foundations in your hometown. Be aware, however, that a foundation's headquarters may well be located in a suburban municipality of an urban area. For instance, if the organization

Figure 38. Zip Code Search in *The Foundation Directory Online*

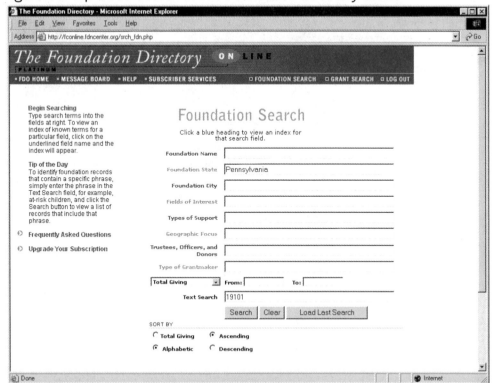

for which you seek funding is located in Atlanta and you conducted a search for grantmakers actually located in Atlanta, you would miss out on some potentially good prospects that give in the greater Atlanta area, but are physically located in the suburbs of Tucker, Norcross, or Roswell, Georgia.

Geographic Focus is the field that notes the states in which the foundation has a record of or indicates it is interested in giving, whether it is based there or not. In addition to the names of all 50 states, the Geographic Focus field has two generic terms that can be helpful—national and international. Grantmakers with "national" as their geographic focus are interested in funding projects in many states. Grantmakers with "international" as their geographic focus give both to U.S.-based nonprofits that are concerned with international issues and/or to nonprofits that provide services outside the United States. Because geographic focus is not available for all foundations, it is a good idea to conduct two geographic searches, one using Grantmaker/Foundation

Figure 39. Telephone Area Code Search in *The Foundation Directory Online*

State or Grantmaker/Foundation City and the other using Geographic Focus (see Figures 40 and 41), and then compare your results.

The print directories—*The Foundation 1000*, *The Foundation Directory*, and *The Foundation Directory Part 2*—have geographic indexes that group foundations by the state and city in which they maintain their principal offices. The names and entry numbers of foundations that make grants on a regional, national, or international basis appear in boldface. For these funders you can adopt an approach based on subject interest rather than geography. Those foundations that give locally or in a few specified states are listed in regular type. Users interested in local giving within their state should check the series of "see also" references at the end of each state section. These cross-references identify foundations that may be located elsewhere but have a history of grantmaking in your state (see Figure 42).

Figure 40. Foundation State Search in *The Foundation Directory Online*

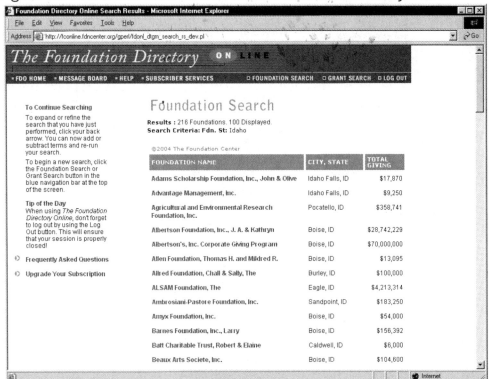

If your search focuses on smaller foundations in your local area, your next stop might be the *Guide to U.S. Foundations, Their Trustees, Officers, and Donors*, the only Center print directory that offers access to the more than 67,000 active grantmaking private and community foundations in the United States. The *Guide to U.S. Foundations* is arranged by state and, in descending order within states, by annual grant totals. Although the information presented in the *Guide to U.S. Foundations* is abbreviated, it does allow you to make some preliminary determinations about each foundation based on its size, location, and principal officer.

The *Guide to U.S. Foundations* also includes all currently active community foundations, which can be valuable resources for funding local projects. In addition to financial support, many community foundations provide technical assistance to nonprofit organizations in areas such as budgeting, public relations, fundraising strategies, and

Figure 41. Geographic Focus Search in *The Foundation Directory Online*

management. Most community foundations maintain Web sites, a valuable source of information on their giving patterns and grantmaking guidelines.

State and Local Directories

Whether you are focusing on large or small foundations, you'll want to search state or local directories. (See the bibliography of state and local directories in the most recent edition of the *Guide to U.S. Foundations, Their Trustees, Officers, and Donors*, also available at the Topical Resource Lists in the Learning Lab directory of the Foundation Center's Web site.) If there are several directories for your area, use them all until you are able to determine through your research which are more current and/or comprehensive.

If your organization is located in Alabama, Michigan, Missouri, Ohio, or Washington, D.C., consult the Foundation Center's state directories covering those five geographic regions. The *Guide to Alabama Grantmakers* (2004), co-produced with the Alabama Giving, features profiles of more than 765 funders in Alabama as well as

Figure 42. Geographic Index from *The Foundation Directory*

GEOGRAPHIC INDEX—RHODE ISLAND

Charlesmead 8494, Charlton 8495, Citizens 8496, Citizens 8497, Citizens 8498, Cuno 8499, **Dorot 8501**, Elms 8502, Ensworth 8503, Fain 8504, Greene 8507, Heydt 8510, Horne 8511, Iorio 8512, Jackson 8513, Koffler 8516, Littlefield 8517, Lord 8518, Mann 8519, McAdams 8520, Moore 8521, Morgan 8522, Palmer 8524, Papitto 8525, Peters 8526, Rapaporte 8527, Rhode Island 8528, Robertson 8529, Roosa 8530, Routhier 8531, Shaw's 8532, Sherman 8533, Wagner 8536, **Watson 8538**
Warren: Narragansett 8523
Warwick: Champlin 8493
Westerly: Kimball 8514, Washington 8537
Woonsocket: CVS 8500

see also 538, 823, 902, 1466, 1516, 1612, 1625, 1632, 1636, 1641, 1653, 1656, 1668, 2050, 2063, 2295, 2918, 3485, 3505, 3722, 3724, 3729, 3777, 3827, 3841, 3842, 3844, 3846, 3848, 3880, 3890, 3900, 3925, 3935, 3938, 3939, 3961, 3976, 3977, 3983, 3984, 3994, 4005, 4018, 4028, 4036, 4044, 4046, 4064, 4078, 4094, 4109, 4120, 5038, 5067, 5466, 5539, 5540, 5569, 5616, 5713, 5725, 6055, 6468, 6686, 6710, 6721, 6807, 6904, 7122, 7170, 7213, 7744, 9137

SOUTH CAROLINA

Anderson: Abney 8540, Foothills 8565, Rainey 8582
Charleston: Addlestone 8541, Ceres 8556, Community 8561, Post 8581
Clinton: Bailey 8545, Bailey 8546
Columbia: Arnold 8543, Central 8555, Christian 8557, Fat 8563, First 8564, Lipscomb 8576
Easley: McKissick 8577
Florence: Bruce 8549
Fort Mill: Springs 8591
Fripp Island: **Wardle 8594**
Gaffney: Fullerton 8566
Greenville: Campbell 8551, Campbell 8552, Campbell 8553, Cline 8558, Community 8559, Daniel 8562, Hipp 8569, Liberty 8575, **Roe 8583**, ScanSource 8584
Greenwood: Self 8586
Greer: Sirrine 8587
Hartsville: Byerly 8550, Sonoco 8589
Hilton Head Island: Community 8560, Kane 8574, **Youths' 8595**
Inman: Inman 8572
Irmo: Mungo 8579
Kershaw: Stevens 8592
Lancaster: TSC 8593
Lexington: Carolina 8554
Myrtle Beach: **AVX 8544**
Orangeburg: Horne 8571
Rock Hill: Hopewell 8570
Seneca: Jayvee 8573
Spartanburg: Arkwright 8542, Barnet 8547, Black 8548, Gibbs 8567, Greenleaf 8568, Montgomery 8578, Phifer 8580, **Security's 8585**, Smith 8588, Spartanburg 8590

see also 141, 489, 1716, 1912, 2069, 2131, 2254, 2256, 2268, 2293, 2394, 2438, 2439, 2660, 3008, 3289, 3587, 3961, 4033, 4240, 4421, 5230, 5286, 7254, 7270, 7280, 7304, 7305, 7310, 7315, 7328, 7349, 7385, 7394, 7415, 7420, 7433, 7439, 7742, 7752, 8052, 8321, 8444, 8682, 9622, 9936

SOUTH DAKOTA

Aberdeen: Aman 8597
Brookings: Larson 8602
Dakota Dunes: Kind 8601
Huron: Griffith 8599
Milbank: Milbank 8603
Mitchell: Hofer 8600
Pierre: South Dakota 8606
Rapid City: Dakota 8598, Stearns 8607
Sioux Falls: Alpha 8596, Rauenhorst 8604, Sioux Falls 8605

see also 527, 1223, 3311, 4231, 4455, 4482, 4527, 4555, 4587, 5421, 7458, 7988

TENNESSEE

Brentwood: EBS 8648, Helping 8666, Israel 8671, Massey 8685, Ware 8715, Zimmerman 8722, Zimmerman 8723
Bristol: **Gatton 8658**, Lazarus 8678, Master's 8686
Chattanooga: Benwood 8620, Caldwell 8624, Chrysalis 8632, Community 8635, Hamico 8662, Hurlbut 8667, Hutcheson 8668, Johnson 8674, Lebovitz 8679, Lyndhurst 8682, **Maclellan 8683**, Osborne 8690, Pattee 8691, Tucker 8709, Wright 8721
Cleveland: Jones 8675
Cookeville: Sawyer 8700
Crump: Brown 8623
Franklin: Ragsdale 8696
Germantown: Cannon 8626
Kingsport: Basler 8616, **Eastman 8647**
Knoxville: 1939 8608, Aslan 8612, Charis 8629, Cole 8634, Dick 8643, East 8646, Fox 8654, Haslam 8664, Pettway 8692, Stokely 8705, Thompson 8708
Maryville: Clayton 8633
Memphis: Assisi 8613, **Behrend 8618**, Belz 8619, Briggs 8622, Children's 8630, Community 8636, Conwood 8638, Day 8642, Durham 8645, First 8652, Goldsmith 8659, Goodlett 8660, Hyde 8669, **Jeniam 8673**, Longleaf 8681, Plough 8694, Rose 8697, Schadt 8701, Shackelford 8702, **Union 8712**, Van Vleet 8713, Wilson 8720
Morristown: Keel 8677
Murfreesboro: Adams 8609, Christy 8631, Jones 8676
Nashville: AMJ 8610, AmSouth 8611, Atticus 8614, B & B 8615, Beasley 8617, **Bridgestone 8621**, Campbell 8625, Carell 8627, Community 8637, Curb 8639, Danner 8640, Davis 8641, Draughon 8644, Eden 8649, Eskind 8650, Ezell 8651, Foster 8653, Frist 8655, Frist 8656, Frist 8657, Gordon 8661, Harnisch 8663, HCA 8665, Ingram 8670, Jeckyl 8672, LifeWorks 8680, Martin 8684, Melkus 8687, Miller 8688, Nelson 8689, Phillips 8693, Potter 8695, Roshan 8698, Shayne 8703, Starfish 8704, SunTrust 8706, Tennessee 8707, Turner 8710, Turner 8711, Wallace 8714, Ware 8716, Washington 8717, Webster 8718, Wilson 8719
Readyville: **Rust 8699**
Sewanee: Cartinhour 8628

see also 6, 1572, 1859, 2063, 2131, 2224, 2239, 2242, 2254, 2268, 2329, 2394, 2743, 3034, 3096, 3289, 3398, 3402, 3746, 4216, 4283, 4314, 4413, 4440, 4705, 4810, 5286, 5328, 5827, 6413, 6417, 6734, 6994, 7025, 7059, 7136, 7242, 7306, 7376, 7953, 8578, 8808, 8855, 9026, 9244, 9456, 9458, 9461, 9474, 9530, 9997

TEXAS

Abilene: Community 8826, Dodge 8857, Greathouse 8916, Owen 9109, Shelton 9192, Taylor 9241
Addison: **Anderson 8737**, Folsom 8893, Haggar 8930, Posey 9129, Staubach 9219, Young 9311
Amarillo: Amarillo 8734, Bivins 8766, Brumley 8779, Gilliland 8906, Mays 9040, Peeler 9118, Read 9145, Ware 9270
Arlington: Fleetwood 8892
Austin: **A Glimmer 8724**, Aragona 8739, Austin 8744, Bentzin 8764, Butler 8783, Cain 8788, Convergence 8831, **Dell 8854**, **Educational 8870**, Fasken 8885, Green 8917, **Hartman 8940**, Hicks 8949, Inman 8965, Jamail 8968, **KLE 8993**, Kodosky 8998, Lindsay 9016, **Link 9017**, Mattsson 9036, **Meredith 9062**, Mitte 9069, Murrell 9082, Papermaster 9113, Reese 9148, Reynolds 9150, **RGK 9152**, **Salzman 9169**, Seriff 9188, **Silverton 9195**, Smith 9202, Still 9222, Sutton 9231, Tapestry 9236, Tocker 9249, Tupfer 9250, Vaughn 9265, Watson 9280, Webber 9283
Avinger: **Simpson 9200**

Beaumont: Dauphin 8848, Dujay 8861, Mechia 9058, Morgan 9074, Reaud 9146, Ward 9275, Wortham 9308
Beeville: Dougherty 8859
Boerne: Branch 8770
Brownwood: Central 8803
Bryan: Astin 8741, RFS 9151
Buda: Johnson 8971
Carrollton: Halliburton 8933
Cleburne: Marti 9035
Corpus Christi: Behmann 8761, Coastal 8817, Durrill 8865, Estill 8878, Haas 8926, Lichtenstein 9013, Moore 9072, Rachal 9141, Sams 9170
Corsicana: Eady 8866, Navarro 9086, Navarro 9087
Dallas: American 8735, Augur 8742, Ayres 8745, Bass 8755, Beal 8759, Beasley 8760, **Bell 8762**, Belo 8763, Boone 8768, Bromley 8776, Buford 8780, Calkins 8791, Chilton 8810, Clements 8816, Collins 8823, **Collins 8824**, Communities 8825, Constantin 8830, **Cornerstone 8835**, Cowden 8837, Cox 8838, Dallas 8846, Dallas 8847, Decherd 8853, **Duda 8860**, Fikes 8889, Flarsheim 8891, Furst 8900, Gaston 8902, Gill 8905, Green 8918, Haggar 8929, Haggerty 8931, Hamon 8937, Hanley 8939, Hawn 8942, Hicks 8950, Hillcrest 8951, Hoak 8952, Hoblitzelle 8954, Hoglund 8955, **Hull 8961**, Hunt 8963, **i2 8964**, Jonsson 8974, Kay 8976, Killson 8984, Kimberly 8987, King 8990, Knox 8997, Kurth 9002, Lantana 9003, Lennox 9008, Lightner 9015, Littauer 9018, Lockheed 9019, Loose 9021, Luse 9025, Lyman 9026, Mankoff 9029, Marcus 9032, Marcus 9033, McDermott 9047, Meadows 9057, Mewhinney 9063, Morning 9075, Moss 9077, Moss 9078, Murchison 9081, Muse 9083, NAH 9084, Nation 9085, Nearburg 9088, New 9089, O'Donnell 9096, Partnership 9115, **Pearle 9117**, **Penney 9120**, Plitt 9126, Pogue 9127, Pollock 9128, Proctor 9134, Prothro 9136, Providence 9137, Rachofsky 9142, Riggs 9155, Roberts 9159, Rosenberg 9164, Rosenberg 9165, Rosewood 9167, Schutte 9180, Seay 9184, Sei 9185, Sevin 9189, Simmons 9197, Simon 9199, Smith 9201, Smith 9204, Smith 9205, Sowell 9211, Speas 9212, Speas 9213, Sturgis 9225, Summerlee 9226, Sumners 9227, Swinney 9229, Swinney 9233, Texas 9245, Thompson 9246, Turner 9252, Vanberg 9261, Vaughan 9262, Waggoner 9268, Wagner 9271, Wal 9272, Wayne 9281, Weaver 9282, Weir 9285, Westcott 9292, Winspear 9296, Wolens 9299, Woodall 9304, Woodward 9307, Young 9312, Zale 9314
DeSoto: Collins 8822
Diboll: Grum 8923, Temple 9243
El Paso: Cimarron 8813, El Paso 8873, Feinberg 8887, Hervey 8947, McKee 9050
Fair Oaks Ranch: **Interdenominational 8966**
Falfurrias: Orth 9105
Fort Worth: **Alcon 8727**, Alexander 8728, Bass 8750, Bass 8751, Bass 8752, Bass 8753, Bass 8754, Bloxom 8767, **Bridge 8771**, Brown 8777, Burnett 8782, Carter 8796, Carter 8797, Community 8827, Deakins 8851, Edwards 8872, Fash 8884, Garvey 8901, Justin 8975, Keith 8978, Kelly 8981, Kimbell 8986, Klabzuba 8992, Lard 9004, McNair 9053, Moncrief 9070, Morris 9076, Once 9100, Paulos 9116, Richardson 9153, Roberts 9158, Rosenthal 9166, Schollmaier 9179, Scott 9181, Snyder 9209, Tandy 9234, Walsh 9274, Weiser 9286, White 9293, Zink 9317
Galveston: Bromberg 8775, Kempner 8982, Mantzel 9030, Moody 9071, Northen 9093, Seibel 9186
Georgetown: Lord 9022, Wright 9310
Graham: Bertha 8765
Hallettsville: Dickson 8856
Harlingen: Gorges 8912
Houston: AIM 8726, Alexander 8729, Alkek 8730, Alkek 8731, **Allbritton 8732**, Allison 8733, Anderson 8736, Ansary 8738, Baker 8748, Barnhart 8749, Bauer 8756, Baugh 8757, Bridgeway 8772, Brockman 8774, Brown 8778, Burlington 8781, Cain 8789, Cameron 8793, Carruth 8795, **Catalyst 8798**, CEMEX 8801, Cemo 8802, CFP 8804, Chaney 8807, **Christian 8811**, Clayton 8814,

107 funders outside the state with a geographic focus that includes Alabama. *The Michigan Foundation Directory* (14th edition, 2004) [also available on CD-ROM], co-produced with the Council of Michigan Foundations, features profiles of over 2,300 foundations that fund in Michigan. The *Directory of Missouri Grantmakers* (5th edition, 2003), co-produced with the Metropolitan Association for Philanthropy, provides information on approximately 1,000 foundations, corporate giving programs, and public charities in Missouri. The *Guide to Ohio Grantmakers on CD-ROM* (2003), produced in collaboration with the Ohio Grantmakers Forum and the Ohio Association of Nonprofit Organizations, features profiles of more than 3,400 foundations in Ohio, plus more than 400 funders outside the state that award grants in Ohio. The *Guide to Greater Washington D.C. Grantmakers on CD-ROM* (2004), co-produced with Washington Grantmakers, provides grantmaker portraits of 2,500 foundations, public charities, and corporate giving programs located in the D.C. region and funders in 40 states that have an interest in D.C.-area nonprofits.

As you add foundation names from state or local directories to your prospect list, be sure to fill in the appropriate information on your Prospect Worksheet (see Figure 11). Note, in particular, any restrictions on a foundation's giving program that would prevent it from funding your project. Some of the smaller foundations are restricted by will or charter to giving to only a few designated or "preselected" organizations. Others may not fund projects in your subject area or may not be able to offer the type or amount of support your organization needs.

GRANTS APPROACH

By this point in time, you may have uncovered a number of foundation prospects through your geographic search. Before you complete this phase of your research, you should check the various indexes of foundation grants to identify foundations (including those that may not be based in your locale) that have actually awarded grants to organizations in your geographic area.

The grants files of *The Foundation Directory Online* (available at the *Plus, Premium,* and *Platinum* service levels)[1] and *FC Search* can be searched quickly to determine which foundations have actually awarded grants in your area. In the Recipient State field, enter your state (see Figure 43). One of the advantages of searching *The*

---

1. Unless otherwise noted, the remaining references in this chapter to *The Foundation Directory Online* refer to the *Platinum* level of service. See Figure 13 for a comparison chart detailing the content and features of each subscription service level.

Figure 43. Grants Search—Recipient State/Country Search in *The Foundation Directory Online*

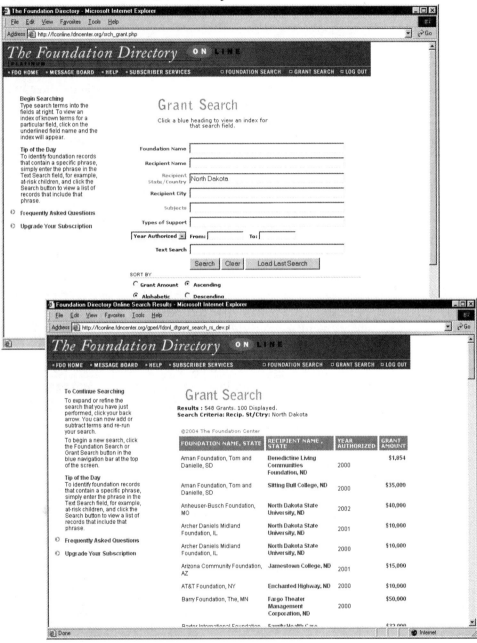

Foundation Directory Online or *FC Search* is that you can search for both geographic limitations and subjects of interest simultaneously. And you can further narrow your search by adding a type(s) of support and/or grant range.

Another alternative is using *FC Search* or *The Foundation Grants Index on CD-ROM*, which include a Geographic Focus Index that helps you identify grants to organizations in your state. Each database also has a Recipient Type Index (see Figure 44) that helps you identify grants to organizations comparable to your own (e.g., hospitals, museums, youth development centers, etc.).

As you scan the grants listings of various funders, look for both patterns and inconsistencies. Try to eliminate foundations that appear to have awarded grants to organizations in your state solely on the basis of their subject focus or because of an affiliation with a specific institution. For instance, suppose you are looking for a foundation to contribute to a medical research program in central Florida. You might uncover two grants to Florida hospitals among the 20 grants made by a foundation located in Massachusetts during the last couple of years, while the other 18 grants were given to organizations in Massachusetts or in other New England states. Further research might indicate that the foundation's two out of pattern grants went to a hospital in West Palm Beach where the donor's mother once received medical attention. That is, these grants were unique, one-time events and not an indication of an ongoing interest in Florida recipients.

Note the types of organizations receiving grants, the subject focus of grant recipients, and the amount and type of support offered by particular foundations. You are looking for repeat patterns of giving. Invariably, you'll find that some foundations limit their giving to specific subject areas or types of institutions. If a foundation's giving pattern does not match your funding needs, it most likely does not belong on your prospect list.

Step Two: Refine Your List

You should now have a lengthy list of foundations that possibly might be interested in funding your organization or project. Now is the time to refine the list to a reasonable number of grantmakers that are most likely to look favorably on your program. You should review your geographic prospect list to eliminate those foundations that are not interested in your subject and/or that do not award the type(s) or amount of support your organization needs. If you used *The Foundation Directory Online* or *FC Search* to construct your list, you probably used multiple search criteria, thereby completing this step already. Filling in the Prospect Worksheet (see Figure 11) for each potential funder on your list enables you to quickly rule out the less appropriate candidates.

Figure 44. Grant Recipient Type Index from *FC Search: The Foundation Center's Database on CD-ROM*

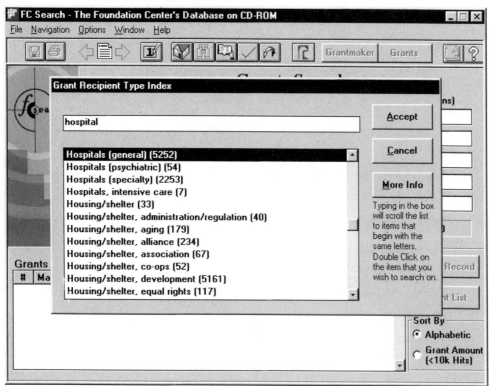

Now that you have determined that the funders on your list have demonstrated a real commitment to funding in your geographic area, providing the type(s) of support your organization needs, and funding in your subject field, you are ready to scrutinize your list further to determine those potential funders that are most likely to be interested in your organization or project. You'll want to conduct as much research on all aspects pertaining to these grantmakers as time and resources permit. Posing the questions raised in Chapter 4 is a good place to start:

- Does the funder accept applications?

- Has the funder demonstrated a real commitment to funding in your subject field?

- Does it seem likely that the funder will make grants to organizations in your geographic location?

- Does the amount of money you are requesting fit within the funder's typical grant range?

- Does the funder have a policy prohibiting grants for the type(s) of support you are requesting?

- Does the funder usually make grants to cover the full cost of a project or does it favor projects where other funders have an opportunity to participate?

- Does the funder put limits on the length of time it is willing to support a project?

- What types of organizations does the funder tend to support?

- Does the funder have application deadlines, or does it review proposals continuously?

- Do you or does anyone on your board know someone connected with the funder?

- What are the financial conditions that may affect the foundation's ability to give?

- Do you have the most current and accurate details on the funder?

Most of these questions can be answered by referring to any one of several resources. *The Foundation Directory Online* and *FC Search* will answer many of them. Print directories such as *The Foundation Directory* or *The Foundation 1000* or some of the state and local directories will also provide many of the answers you need. For information such as application deadlines and the names of trustees, officers, or donors, Center databases and directories are excellent sources.

Grantmakers that state that they are interested in a particular geographic area may also occasionally award grants to organizations outside their stated geographic limits. Often, you will need to refer to primary sources such as IRS Forms 990-PF and foundation annual reports or application guidelines for a full grants list. This is particularly true for smaller foundations whose grants are not included in online databases and that do not have Web sites. For instance, suppose you are trying to identify funders that would be interested in providing support for a capital campaign for a natural history museum. You have identified a funder that has an interest in natural history museums and that provides funding for capital campaigns. However, there is no indication in any of the databases or directories you consulted that this funder gives in your geographic area. On the other hand, there is no limitation statement explicitly saying that the grantmaker will *not* give in your geographic area. In this case, it would be in your organization's best interests to seek out a more complete listing of grants awarded than you will find in grants databases and directories. If the grantmaker publishes an annual report, secure a copy and study the grants list if available. Annual reports can be found on many foundation Web sites and in Center libraries and many Cooperating Collections (see Appendix F).

If a full grants listing is not available from these sources, look at the foundation's Form 990-PF. Because the IRS requires a foundation to list all of its grants on the Form 990-PF, the tax return is your best source for comprehensive information about grants awarded for a particular tax year (see Chapter 5 for information on obtaining a foundation's Form 990-PF). When reviewing the Form 990-PF, ask yourself: Have any grants been awarded to organizations in your geographic area? Have any grants been awarded to organizations located outside the stated geographic limits? Has the funder awarded grants for your subject area? Have past grants been awarded for the type(s) of support your organization seeks? An examination of a complete grants list can be highly revealing concerning foundation priorities. And if you have the time, comparing several years' worth of grants lists, looking for patterns and/or exceptions, may prove even more instructive.

Don't overlook secondary sources such as articles in newspapers and journals that may provide the most up-to-date information you need. *Philanthropy News Digest* (PND), the Foundation Center's online summary of the news of the world of philanthropy, allows you to keep apprised of recent information about foundations and their philanthropic efforts. PND summaries will also inform you of changes in leadership, very recent large grants, and other such information. You may wish to employ PND's search engine to enter the name of a foundation on your prospect list to see what, if anything, has been reported about this funder's recent gifts. Another source of information on recently awarded grants is the "Guide to Grants" at the *Chronicle of Philanthropy's* Web site (http://www.philanthropy.com/grants). This is a database of the grants published in the *Chronicle of Philanthropy* since 1995. A listing of other print and electronic nonprofit news and publications resources can be found in the Nonprofit Links section of the Researching Philanthropy directory on the Foundation Center's Web site.

A review of the resources detailed in Chapter 5 will help you to decide which tools (Web sites, databases, directories, annual reports, IRS returns, application guidelines, etc.) will best assist you in answering the specific questions necessary to refine your list to the most likely prospects. When you have answered these questions about the funders on your broad prospect list, you will have narrowed your list to the few that you should approach first.

Summary

A grantmaker's geographic focus is most likely to be in the city, county, state, or region in which the foundation is located. Corporate givers tend to make contributions where they have employees, operations, and/or plants. (For more information on corporate philanthropy, see Chapter 9.) On the other hand, there are a significant number of foundations that give nationally and internationally. There are a variety of materials available to the grantseeker to develop a broad prospect list based on where a grantmaker gives its grants. Once a list of potential funders based on geography is developed, it is very important to find out if those funders are interested in your subject and if they provide the type(s) and amount of support your organization needs. The previous chapter explored the subject approach, and the next chapter discusses the types of support approach.

Chapter 8

Finding the Right Funder: The Types of Support Approach

As your research progresses you'll notice that grants from foundations usually fall into fairly distinct categories. These may include cash assistance for capital support, operating funds, or seed money, and noncash support such as donations of equipment or supplies, technical assistance, use of facilities, and management advice, the latter types being particularly popular with corporate funders. We call these distinct categories "types of support." The types of support approach helps you identify grantmakers that have expressed an interest in providing the specific type(s) of support your organization needs.

In fact, when considering the type(s) of support your organization needs, it is especially important to investigate avenues other than the traditional dollar grant, or what funders call "in-kind" gifts. For example, a nonprofit that needs a photocopier or computer might look for a local company willing to donate the equipment instead of seeking a cash grant to buy such equipment. Many grantmakers, especially corporate givers, willingly donate office space, computer equipment and time, and facilities; some even lend out executive talent. Securing outright cash donations from these same corporations, on the other hand, can be much more difficult. (For more information about corporate giving, see Chapter 9.) You'll find that many foundations tend to limit their giving to one or, at most, a few types of support. Therefore, in the planning stages that precede a search for funding sources, you should clarify the specific type(s) of support your organization needs and include only those grantmakers on your prospect list that favor those type(s) of support.

COMMON SUPPORT TYPES

The following are some common support types for foundations:

1. *Capital campaigns:* Campaigns to raise funds for a variety of long-term purposes such as building construction or acquisition, endowments, land acquisition, etc.

2. *Conferences and seminars:* Includes workshops.

3. *Emergency funds:* One-time grants to cover immediate short-term funding needs of a recipient organization on an emergency basis.

4. *General/Operating support:* Grants for the day-to-day operating costs of an existing program or organization or to further the general purpose or work of an organization; also called "unrestricted grants."

5. *In-kind gifts:* Contributions of equipment, supplies, or other property as distinct from monetary grants.

6. *Program development:* Grants to support specific projects or programs as opposed to general purpose grants.

7. *Seed money:* Grants to start, establish, or initiate new projects or organizations; may cover salaries and other operating expenses of a new project; also called "start-up funds."

For definitions of other types of support used in Center databases and directories, see Appendix D.

Step One: Develop a Broad Types of Support Prospect List

Once you have determined the type(s) of support your organization needs, you can begin researching foundations that provide that type of support. You will want to review descriptions of grants that have been awarded to organizations similar to your own for the type(s) of support you need. You will also want to use the Types of Support Indexes in various grantmaker and grants databases and directories. If the specific type of support you seek is not included in the index, you might try typing it into the Text Search field.

GRANTS APPROACH

Begin by looking at the types of support foundations have provided nonprofits in the past. Although a foundation's guidelines may express a preference for specific types of support, the type of grants a funder actually provides is a much better indicator of where the real commitment lies. *The Foundation Directory Online* (at the *Plus, Premium,* or *Platinum* service levels)[1] and *FC Search: The Foundation Center's Database on CD-ROM* are good starting points for a search by grants. The grants files can be searched in multiple ways, including by types of support. The index will help you decide on the appropriate terms that describe the type(s) of support your nonprofit needs. A distinct advantage of using *The Foundation Directory Online* or *FC Search* is the fact that you can search for types of support simultaneously with subject and location (Grantmaker/ Foundation State or Recipient State). This approach can significantly speed your research efforts by eliminating a variety of inappropriate prospects all at one time.

You can also use the grants approach with *The Foundation Grants Index on CD-ROM.* As we noted earlier, the *Grants Index on CD-ROM* offers concise descriptions of grants of $10,000 or more reported to the Foundation Center by more than 1,000 of the largest U.S. foundations. Open the Recipient Type Index of the *Grants Index on CD-ROM* (see Figure 45), which provides a breakdown of grants by specific types of support. You can use this index to identify grants of the type in which you are interested that have been made to organizations similar to your own. The index shows grants awarded to more than 850 different types of organizations (e.g., churches/temples, human service agencies, libraries, performing arts groups, schools, and so on).

Each grant record in Foundation Center print and electronic publications includes the names of the grantmaking foundation and recipient organization, along with details—amount, purpose, and so on—about the grant itself. As indicated previously, you should view individual grant records as evidence of a foundation's giving interests. Look for grant records that describe funding for organizations or projects that appear

---

1. Unless otherwise noted, the remaining references in this chapter to *The Foundation Directory Online* refer to the *Platinum* level of service. See Figure 13 for a comparison chart detailing the content and features of each subscription service level.

Figure 45. Grant Recipient Type Index from *The Foundation Grants Index on CD-ROM*

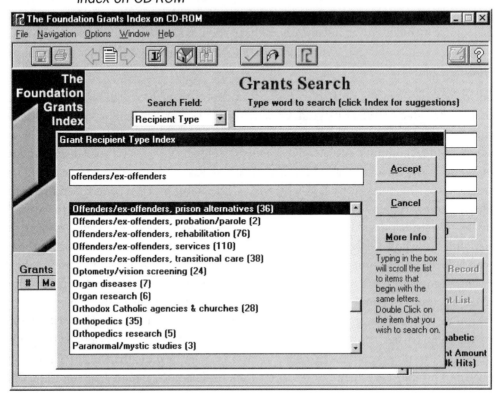

to be similar in several respects to your own or look for grants awarded to recipients in your location with programs similar to yours.

Be sure to note on your Prospect Worksheet (see Figure 11) the name of the foundation awarding the grant, its location, and any geographic limitations on its giving program. You will then want to obtain a full grants listing (either by referring to its Web site, annual report, or Form 990-PF) to determine the foundation's general subject focus, the types of organizations it awards grants to, and the typical size of its grants.

Next you may wish to refer to the Center's *Grant Guides*. Remember, the *Grant Guides* series duplicates the information contained in the grants files in *The Foundation Directory Online*, *FC Search*, and *The Foundation Grants Index on CD-ROM* and repackages it in particular focus areas for your convenience.

Entries in each of the 12 *Grant Guides* are arranged alphabetically by state and, within each state, by foundation name, followed by the actual grant records (see Figure 46). At the back of each *Guide* is an alphabetically arranged list of foundations covered in that volume. For each foundation, the address and a brief statement of type(s) of support, geographic, and subject restrictions on its giving are also included. (See Chapter 5 for a listing of currently available *Grant Guides* titles.)

GRANTMAKER DATABASES AND DIRECTORIES

To search by grantmaker, once again you should begin with *The Foundation Directory Online* or *FC Search*. These databases make available a searchable Types of Support field. The available search terms are indexed in order to help you select the appropriate terminology describing the type(s) of support your organization needs. You can also search by subject and geographic focus, as well as a number of other fields, while you search for type(s) of support, thereby streamlining your research efforts.

Alternatively, if your interest lies with the nation's largest foundations, you might begin with *The Foundation 1000* and its Types of Support Index. This index provides access to the top 1,000 foundations by the types of support they typically provide. Notice that the arrangement is alphabetical by type of support, then by state. You will also notice that certain foundation names are in boldface (see Figure 47). Boldface indicates a foundation with a national, regional, or international focus. Foundations listed in regular type generally limit their giving to the city or state in which they are located. This distinction can speed your research by allowing you to zero in on those foundations whose geographic focus matches that of your organization at the same time that you are identifying those foundations that provide the type(s) of support your organization needs.

To further expand your prospect list, turn to the Types of Support indexes provided in the print products *The Foundation Directory* and *The Foundation Directory Part 2*, which respectively profile the largest 10,000 and next largest 10,000 foundations in the country (by total assets). Keep in mind that, as with other grantmaker databases and directories, these indexes list the types of support funders say they are interested in, rather than the types of support represented by the actual grants they have awarded. While this may seem like a fine distinction, it can be a significant one for the grantseeker.

While a history of grants actually awarded is generally considered to be a better indication of a foundation's willingness to provide a particular type of support than a mere statement to that effect, you should not take such indications too literally. In

Figure 46. Sample Page from *Grants for Women and Girls*

4623. Bethany Christian Services, Grand Rapids, MI. $10,000, 2002. For building fund for North Mississippi Clinic.

4624. Boys and Girls Club of Jackson, Jackson, MS. $10,000, 2002. For computers.

4625. Harbor House of Jackson, Jackson, MS. $16,000, 2002. For building fund.

4626. Resource Center Network for Abused and Battered Women and Children, Pearl, MS. $27,500, 2002. For kitchen equipment.

Mississippi Common Fund Trust

Limitations: Giving primarily in MS. No grants to individuals.

4627. Boys and Girls Club of Jackson, Jackson, MS. $10,000, 2002.

MISSOURI

Anheuser-Busch Foundation

Limitations: Giving primarily in areas of major company operations of its breweries and theme parks: St. Louis, MO, Newark, NJ, Los Angeles, Fairfield, and San Diego, CA, Houston and San Antonio, TX, Jacksonville, Tampa, and Orlando, FL, Merrimack, NH, Baldwinsville, NY, Fort Collins, CO, Cartersville, GA, and Williamsburg, VA. No support for organizations whose activities are primarily religious in nature, social or fraternal groups, or political or athletic organizations. No grants to individuals, or for hospital operating budgets.

4628. Boys Hope Girls Hope, Bridgeton, MO. $200,000, 2002. For general support.

4629. Girl Scouts of the U.S.A., Council of Greater Saint Louis, Saint Louis, MO. $50,000, 2002. For general support.

4630. Girls Inc., Saint Louis, MO. $200,000, 2002. For general support.

4631. Girls Inc., Saint Louis, MO. $200,000, 2002. For general support.

4632. Marguerites Place, Nashua, NH. $10,000, 2002. For general support.

4633. Womens Support and Community Services, Saint Louis, MO. $30,000, 2002. For general support.

Boeing-McDonnell Foundation

Limitations: Giving limited to the St. Louis, MO, region. No support for sectarian, denominational, fraternal, social, religious, or labor organizations, or for university, industry affiliates, or associates programs. No grants to individuals (except for employee-related scholarships), or for advertisements, fundraisers, or sporting events; no loans.

4634. Boys and Girls Club, Herbert Hoover, Saint Louis, MO. $15,000, 2002. For general support.

4635. Girl Scouts of the U.S.A., Council of Greater Saint Louis, Saint Louis, MO. $15,000, 2002. For general support.

The Danforth Foundation

Limitations: Giving limited to the metropolitan St. Louis, MO, area. No grants to individuals.

4636. Policemen and Firemen Fund of Saint Louis, Chesterfield, MO. $500,000, 2002. For challenge grant to raise funds from Saint Louis community to assist families of policemen and firefighters who died in New York City disaster of September 11th through New York Police and Fire Widows' and Children's 9/11 Benefit Fund.

Emerson Charitable Trust

Limitations: Giving primarily in areas of company operations.

4637. Almost Home, Saint Louis, MO. $20,000, 2001.

4638. Big Brothers/Big Sisters of Greater Saint Louis, Saint Louis, MO. $100,000, 2001.

4639. Boys and Girls Club of Collin County, McKinney, TX. $10,500, 2001.

4640. Boys and Girls Club, San Dieguito, Solana Beach, CA. $10,000, 2001.

4641. Boys and Girls Clubs of Marion County, Ocala, FL. $10,000, 2001.

4642. Boys Hope Girls Hope, Bridgeton, MO. $10,000, 2001.

4643. Girl Scouts of the U.S.A., Council of Greater Saint Louis, Saint Louis, MO. $41,500, 2001.

4644. Girls Inc., Saint Louis, MO. $30,000, 2001.

4645. Leadership Foundation, DC. $25,000, 2001.

4646. Womens Support and Community Services, Saint Louis, MO. $10,000, 2001.

Enterprise Rent-A-Car Foundation

Limitations: Giving on a national basis, with some emphasis on MO.

4647. Big Brothers/Big Sisters of Greater Saint Louis, Saint Louis, MO. $10,000, 2002. For unrestricted support.

4648. Big Brothers/Big Sisters of Orange County, Newport Beach, CA. $10,000, 2002. For unrestricted support.

4649. Boys and Girls Club, Herbert Hoover, Saint Louis, MO. $10,000, 2002. For unrestricted support.

4650. Boys Hope Girls Hope of Saint Louis, Saint Louis, MO. $10,000, 2002. For unrestricted support.

4651. Girl Scouts of the U.S.A., Council of Greater Saint Louis, Saint Louis, MO. $10,000, 2002. For unrestricted support.

4652. Girls Inc., Saint Louis, MO. $10,000, 2002. For unrestricted support.

4653. Police Benevolent Association Widows and Childrens Fund, NYC, NY. $50,000, 2002. For unrestricted support.

4654. UFA Widows and Childrens Fund, NYC, NY. $100,000, 2002. For unrestricted support.

4655. Womens Support and Community Services, Saint Louis, MO. $10,000, 2002. For unrestricted support.

The Francis Families Foundation

Limitations: Giving limited to a 60-mile radius of Kansas City, MO, for educational and arts and cultural institutions, and to the U.S. and Canada for pulmonary fellowships.

4656. Boys and Girls Club of Greater Kansas City, Kansas City, KS. $10,000, 2002. To renew sustaining grant for general operating support.

4657. Brigham and Womens Hospital, Boston, MA. $38,000, 2002. For fellowships.

4658. Brigham and Womens Hospital, Pulmonary Division, Boston, MA. $42,000, 2002. For fellowships.

Hall Family Foundation

Limitations: Giving limited to Kansas City, MO. No support for international or religious organizations or for political purposes. No grants to individuals (except for employee-related scholarships), or for travel, operating deficits, conferences, scholarly or medical research, or fundraising campaigns such as telethons.

4659. Amethyst Place, Kansas City, MO. $25,000, 2002. For operating support.

4660. Boys and Girls Club of Eastern Jackson County, Independence, MO. $25,000, 2002. For capital need in transportation.

4661. Boys and Girls Clubs of Greater Kansas City, Kansas City, MO. $3,200,000, 2002. For capital campaign and operating support.

4662. Girl Scouts of the U.S.A., Mid-Continent Council, Kansas City, MO. $1,000,000, 2002. For capital campaign.

4663. Girl Scouts of the U.S.A., Mid-Continent Council, Kansas City, MO. $300,000, 2002. For Urban Scouting operating support.

4664. Metropolitan Organization to Counter Sexual Assault (MOCSA), Kansas City, MO. $75,000, 2002. For Strategic Plan Initiative, volunteer program expansion.

4665. Rose Brooks Center, Kansas City, MO. $125,000, 2002. For Bridge Program.

4666. YWCA of Kansas City, Kansas City, MO. $35,000, 2002. For program support for Girls' Time Out.

Hallmark Corporate Foundation

Limitations: Giving limited to the Kansas City, MO, area, and communities where major Hallmark facilities are located, including Enfield, CT, Columbus, GA, Metamora, IL, Lawrence, Leavenworth, and Topeka, KS, Liberty, MO, and Center, TX. No support for religious, fraternal, political, international or veterans' organizations, athletic or labor groups, social clubs, non-tax-exempt organizations, or disease-specific organizations. No grants to individuals, or for scholarships, endowment funds, past operating deficits, travel, conferences, sponsorships, scholarly or health-

Figure 47. Types of Support Index from *The Foundation 1000*

INDEX OF TYPES OF SUPPORT

Professorships

California: **Avery 60**, Jones 507, Koret 546, Norris 685, Noyce 690, Stauffer 870, Valley 933
Connecticut: **Deloitte 267**
Delaware: Rowland 810
Florida: **Davis 258**, duPont 302
Georgia: Courts 235, Mason 604, Pitts 744, Tull 918
Illinois: Coleman 202, Crown 240, Davee 254, Grainger 414
Indiana: Ball 70, Ball 71, Fairbanks 326
Iowa: Carver 166, Principal 756
Kentucky: Brown 130, **Humana 475**
Massachusetts: Alden 15, Stoddard 878
Michigan: Herrick 453, Towsley 913
New Jersey: **KPMG 547**, Pharmacia 735, Schering 825
New York: Dyson 304, **Ford 350**, Gleason 400, **Johnson 499, Kress 549**, Lang 553, **Luce 582, Macy 591, New York 677**, Oishei 703, **Open 708**, Park 719, **Pforzheimer 734**, Simons 845, **Starr 867, Vetlesen 938, Vivendi 940**
North Carolina: Duke 299, Duke 300
Ohio: **Scripps 831**, Wolfe 987
Oklahoma: Noble 681, Presbyterian 752
Pennsylvania: Eberly 308, Hillman 460, Independence 482, Simmons 843
Rhode Island: **Dorot 289**
Tennessee: Plough 746
Texas: Brown 129, Cain 150, Cain 151, Carter 165, Cockrell 199, Cullen 242, Dunn 301, Fikes 336, Houston 470, McDermott 622, McGovern 624, Rockwell 804, **Shell 836**, Strake 880
Utah: Eccles 309, Stewart 875
Virginia: SunTrust 888
Wisconsin: **Bradley 122, Rockwell 805**

Program development

Alabama: Community 216, Community 220, **Vulcan 941**
Alaska: Rasmuson 769
Arizona: Arizona 48, Flinn 341, **Research 780**
Arkansas: **Frueauff 365**, Rockefeller 802, **Windgate 981**
California: Ahmanson 11, Alliance 21, Amateur 29, Archstone 46, Avery 60, Bechtel 91, California 153, California 155, **ChevronTexaco 182, Christensen 186**, Community 212, Community 221, Community 222, **Compton 224**, Cowell 237, Disney 279, Drown 296, Eisner 313, **Energy 320, Flora 342**, Forest 353, **Foundation 354**, Gap 372, Geffen 380, Gellert 382, Gerbode 391, **Getty 394**, Goldman 404, Haas 429, Haas 430, Haas 431, Hewlett 456, **Homeland 468, Hume 476**, Irvine 488, Johnson 502, **Keck 521**, Koret 546, Marin 600, **Mattel 608**, Moore 658, Murphy 666, Norris 685, Norton 689, Noyce 690, Osher 710, **Packard 715**, Parsons 721, Peninsula 725, **Righteous 794**, Rosenberg 809, San Diego 819, San Francisco 820, Santa Barbara 821, Sierra 840, Soda 857, **Strauss 884**, Stuart 885, Taper 893, **Tenet 900**, Times 908, UniHealth 923, Union 924, Valley 932, Valley 933, Weingart 961, **Wells 964**, Whittier 974, Zellerbach 999
Colorado: Bonfils 115, Colorado 204, Coors 229, **Crowell 239**, Denver 271, El Pomar 315, **General 385, Gill 397, Janus 492**, Johnson 500, **Needmor 673, Qwest 766**
Connecticut: **Aetna 10**, Calder 152, Dibner 275, **Educational 311, GE 378**, Hartford 439, International 486, Tremaine 915
Delaware: **Raskob 768**
District of Columbia: **Arca 43, Banyan 74, Bauman 85**, Cafritz 148, Community 215, **Fannie 329, Ford 351**, Graham 413, **Hitachi 463**, McGowan 625, Meyer 646, **Moriah 662, Public 762**, Stewart 876, **Summit 887, Wallace 947, Wallace 948**
Florida: Bush 142, **Chatlos 180**, Community 213, Dade 246, **Davis 258, DeMoss 270**, duPont 302, **Koch 542**, Lattner 556, **Picower 740**, Publix 763, Scaife 823, Whitehall 972, Winn 982
Georgia: Anderson 36, Blank 107, Community 210, Courts 235, Georgia 388, Georgia 389, Goizueta 403, Mason 604, Murphy 668, **UPS 930**, Woodruff 990

Hawaii: Atherton 52, Castle 171, Hawaii 440
Idaho: Albertson 13
Illinois: **Allstate 23, Baxter 86, Brach 121**, Caterpillar 173, Chicago 183, Coleman 202, Comer 206, Community 223, Crown 240, Dillon 277, Donnelley 287, Driehaus 295, Fry 366, Grainger 414, Grand 416, **Harris 437, Joyce 510**, Lee 561, **MacArthur 588, MacArthur 589, McCormick 618**, Northern 686, Polk 748, Prince 754, Reese 775, Regenstein 776, Retirement 781, Scholl 827, Siragusa 847, Woods 991
Indiana: Anderson 34, Ball 70, Ball 71, Clowes 198, Cummins 245, Dekko 264, Fairbanks 326, Foellinger 345, **Guidant 425**, Indianapolis 483, Lilly 571, Lincoln 572, Noyes 692
Iowa: Carver 166, Principal 756
Kansas: Kansas 515, **Lloyd 574**, Sprint 863
Kentucky: C.E. 146, Community 219, Gheens 395
Louisiana: Baptist 75, Baton Rouge 82
Maine: Libra 568
Maryland: Abell 3, Blaustein 108, **Casey 169**, France 356, Goldseker 406, Lockheed 575, Straus 883, **Town 912**
Massachusetts: Balfour 69, Barr 76, Berkshire 100, Boston 118, Davis 255, Fidelity 334, FleetBoston 340, Hyams 479, Johnson 503, **Kendall 527, Merck 640, Oak 696**, Peabody 724, Riley 795, Shapiro 834, State 869
Michigan: Ave 56, Carls 161, Community 214, **DaimlerChrysler 247**, DeVos 273, **Dow 291**, Dow 292, **Ford 352**, Fremont 361, Frey 362, General 384, **Gerber 390**, Gilmore 399, Grand Rapids 415, Herrick 453, Hudson 473, Kalamazoo 513, **Kellogg 522**, McGregor 626, **Mott 664**, Skillman 848, Steelcase 871, Towsley 913, Wege 958, Whirlpool 969, Wilson 980
Minnesota: Bigelow 102, Blandin 106, Bremer 124, Bush 143, Cargill 160, Deluxe 269, General 383, HRK 471, Jerome 495, McKnight 630, **Medtronic 633**, Minneapolis 651, O'Shaughnessy 695, Phillips 738, **Pillsbury 741**, Saint Paul 816, **St. Paul 864**, Target 894, **3M 904, Thrivent 905**
Missouri: Ameren 30, **Anheuser 38**, Boeing 112, Danforth 252, **Francis 357**, Hall 432, Hallmark 434, Kansas City 514, **Kauffman 519**, Kauffman 520, Kemper 526, **Monsanto 655**
Nebraska: ConAgra 226, Kiewit 531, Omaha 706, **Union 925**
Nevada: Cord 230, **Hilton 462**, Reynolds 785, Wiegand 975
New Hampshire: New Hampshire 674
New Jersey: Dodge 282, Fund 369, Healthcare 442, **Johnson 501**, Kirby 537, Laurie 559, Merck 639, Merrill 643, Prudential 761, Rippel 796, Schering 825, **Schumann 829**, Turrell 921, Victoria 939
New Mexico: Maddox 593, McCune 619, **Thaw 903**
New York: Abrons 6, Altman 27, **Americas 31**, Aron 49, **AT&T 51, AVI 61, Avon 62, Beldon 94**, Bodman 111, Booth 117, Bristol 126, **Bronfman 127, Carnegie 162**, Cary 167, **China 185**, Clark 193, **Clark 194**, Clark 195, **Commonwealth 208**, Community 211, Corning 231, **Cummings 244, Dana 249, DeCamp 261, Deutsche 272, Donner 288, Dreyfus 293**, Dyson 304, Emerson 319, **Engelhard 321, Ford 350**, Freeman 360, **Fuld 367**, Gilman 398, **Grant 417, Greenwall 419, Hartford 438**, Hayden 441, **Hearst 443, Hearst 444**, Heckscher 445, **Heron 452, HKH 464, Johnson 499, Kade 512**, Kaplan 516, **Klingenstein 539, Kohlberg 543**, Lang 553, Lowenstein 579, **Luce 582, Macy 591, Markle 601, Mellon 636, Mertz 644, MetLife 645**, Morgan 660, New York 675, New York 676, **New York 677**, New York 678, **Noble 680, Noyes 691**, Ohrstrom 702, Oishei 703, **Open 708**, Park 719, **Pforzheimer 734**, Pincus 742, Pinkerton 743, Price 753, Prospect 760, Revson 783, Rhodebeck 789, **Rockefeller 800, Rockefeller 801**, Samuels 818, Scherman 826, Slifka 850, **Sloan 851**, Sprague 862, **Surdna 889**, Tinker 910, **United 928**, van Ameringen 934, van Ameringen 935, **Verizon 937, Vetlesen 938, Wallace 946, Warhol 951**, Weill 959

North Carolina: **Babcock 64, Bank 72, Burroughs 141**, Duke 299, Progress 759, Reynolds 784, Reynolds 786, **Wachovia 942**, Winston-Salem 985
Ohio: Bruening 131, Cincinnati 189, Cleveland 197, Columbus 205, Community 217, Eaton 307, Federated 331, Fifth 335, GAR 373, **Generation 386**, Gund 427, H.C.S. 428, Jennings 494, Mathile 607, Morgan 661, Murphy 667, Nationwide 671, NCC 672, Nord 683, Prentiss 751, Reinberger 778, **Scripps 831**, Stranahan 881, **Timken 909**, Wean 956, **Weatherhead 957**
Oklahoma: Presbyterian 752, Southern 859, Warren 952
Oregon: Ford 349, Intel 484, Jeld 493, Meyer 647, Oregon 709, PacifiCorp 714
Pennsylvania: **Alcoa 14, Annenberg 39**, Arcadia 44, Barra 77, Bayer 87, Benedum 97, Buhl 137, CIGNA 188, Connelly 227, Dominion 285, DSF 297, Eberly 308, Eden 310, First 338, Grable 411, Heinz 447, Heinz 448, Heinz 449, Hillman 460, Hillman 461, Jewish 497, McCune 621, McKenna 628, Mellon 637, Penn 726, **Pew 732**, Philadelphia 736, Pittsburgh 745, PPG 750, **Scaife 824**, Simmons 843, Smith 853, **Templeton 899**, Trexler 916, **Whitaker 971**
Rhode Island: **Dorot 289**, Rhode Island 788, **Textron 902**
Tennessee: Benwood 98, **Bridgestone 125**, Community 218, Davis 256, Frist 364, Lyndhurst 585, **Maclellan 590**, Plough 746
Texas: Abell 4, Bivins 105, Brown 129, Burnett 139, Cailloux 149, Carter 165, **Challenge 175**, Cockrell 199, Communities 209, **Cooper 228**, Cullen 242, **ExxonMobil 325**, Farish 330, Feldman 333, Fikes 336, Fondren 347, George 387, Hillcrest 459, Hoblitzelle 466, Houston 470, Kronkosky 550, McDermott 622, McNair 631, Meadows 612, Moody 657, Rapoport 767, **RGK 787**, Richardson 791, Rockwell 804, **SBC 822, Shell 836**, Strake 880, Sturgis 886, Swalm 890, Temple 897
Utah: Eccles 309, Swanson 891
Virginia: Beazley 89, Freddie 358, **Gannett 371, Whitaker 970, WorldCom 992**
Washington: Allen 18, Allen 20, Bishop 104, Bullitt 138, Cheney 181, **Gates 377**, Murdock 665, Russell 814, Samis 817, **Stewardship 874**, Washington 953, **Weyerhaeuser 968**, Wilburforce 977
Wisconsin: Bader 65, **Bradley 122**, Herzfeld 454, Kohler 544, Milwaukee 650, Pettit 731, **Rockwell 805**, Rowland 811, Siebert 838

Program evaluation

Arkansas: Rockefeller 802
California: Alliance 21, Archstone 46, Bechtel 91, California 153, California 154, California 155, **Christensen 186**, Community 222, Haas 431, **Hume 476**, Irvine 488, Koret 546, Marin 600, Noyce 690, **Packard 715**, San Diego 819, Sierra 840, **Strauss 884**, Stuart 885, UniHealth 923, Zellerbach 999
Colorado: Buell 135
District of Columbia: Cohen 200, Community 215, **Summit 887**
Florida: **Davis 258**, duPont 302
Georgia: Community 210
Hawaii: Castle 171
Illinois: Chicago 183, Community 223, Fry 366, Grand 416, **McCormick 618**, Polk 748, Retirement 781
Indiana: Foellinger 345, Indianapolis 483, Lilly 571, Lincoln 572
Iowa: Principal 756
Louisiana: Baptist 75
Maryland: Blaustein 108, Straus 883
Massachusetts: Barr 76, Berkshire 100, Davis 255, FleetBoston 340, **Oak 696**
Michigan: Fremont 361, **Gerber 390**, Gilmore 399, Hudson 473, **Mott 664**
Minnesota: Bremer 124, Phillips 738, Target 894
Missouri: Hall 432, **Monsanto 655**
New Jersey: Dodge 282, **Johnson 501**
New York: Bodman 111, **Carnegie 162, Clark 194, Commonwealth 208**, Community 211, Corning

other words, just because a prospective funder has not offered a particular type of support in the past does not mean it will never do so in the future. Funders that specifically restrict the types of support they provide (e.g., "no grants for endowment funds"), on the other hand, should be taken at their word and eliminated from your prospect list.

SPECIALIZED FUNDING GUIDES

There are a number of specialized guides and handbooks that cover funding geared to a specific type of support. For example, if you are trying to find funds to purchase equipment for a science laboratory in a private secondary school, Richard M. Eckstein's *Directory of Building and Equipment Grants*, published by Research Grant Guides of Lonahatchee, Florida, would be an appropriate resource for you. If you are trying to fund a research project, Phoenix, Arizona-based Oryx Press' annual *Directory of Research Grants* may be helpful. Other particular items of interest to the grantseeker adopting a types of support approach might be guidebooks on capital campaigns as well as those dealing with "bricks and mortar" and equipment grants. Refer to Appendix A for a select listing of these and other specialized guides; and be sure to check with your local library for new titles of publications developed specifically for the type(s) of support you are seeking.

Step Two: Refine Your List

You should now have a lengthy list of foundations that possibly might be interested in funding your organization or project based on the type of support you need and they award. Now is the time to refine the list to a reasonable number of grantmakers that are most likely to look favorably on your program. You should review your types of support prospect list to eliminate those foundations that are not interested in your subject and/ or that do not award grants in your geographic area. If you used *The Foundation Directory Online* or *FC Search* to construct your list, you probably used multiple search criteria, thereby completing this step already. Filling in the Prospect Worksheet (see Figure 11) for each potential funder on your list enables you to quickly rule out the less appropriate candidates.

Now that you have determined that the funders on your list have demonstrated a real commitment to providing the type(s) of support your organization needs, funding in your subject field, and funding in your geographic area, you are ready to scrutinize your list further to determine those potential funders that are most likely to be interested in your organization or project. You'll want to conduct as much research on all aspects pertaining to these grantmakers as time and resources permit. Posing the questions raised in Chapter 4 is a good place to start:

- Does the funder accept applications?

- Has the funder demonstrated a real commitment to funding in your subject field?

- Does it seem likely that the funder will make grants to organizations in your geographic location?

- Does the amount of money you are requesting fit within the funder's typical grant range?

- Does the funder have a policy prohibiting grants for the type(s) of support you are requesting?

- Does the funder usually make grants to cover the full cost of a project or does it favor projects where other funders have an opportunity to participate?

- Does the funder put limits on the length of time it is willing to support a project?

- What types of organizations does the funder tend to support?

- Does the funder have application deadlines, or does it review proposals continuously?

- Do you or does anyone on your board know someone connected with the funder?

- What are the financial conditions that may affect the foundation's ability to give?

- Do you have the most current and accurate details on the funder?

Most of these questions can be answered by referring to any one of several resources. *The Foundation Directory Online* and *FC Search* will answer many of them. Print directories such as *The Foundation Directory* or *The Foundation 1000* or some of the state and local directories will also provide many of the answers you need. For information such as application deadlines and the names of trustees, officers, or donors, Center databases and directories are excellent sources.

Grantmakers that state that they are interested in a particular type of support may also occasionally award grants to organizations outside their stated types of support limitations. Often, you will need to refer to primary sources such as IRS Forms 990-PF and foundation annual reports or application guidelines for a full grants list. This is particularly true for smaller foundations whose grants are not included in online databases and that do not have Web sites. For instance, suppose you are trying to identify funders that would be interested in providing general/operating support for a health care facility. You have identified a funder that has an interest in health care issues and that gives in your geographic area. However, there is no indication in any of the databases or directories you consulted that this funder provides funding for general/operating support. On the other hand, there is no limitation statement explicitly saying that the grantmaker will *not* give for this type of support. In this case, it would be in your organization's best interests to seek out a more complete listing of grants awarded than you will find in grants databases and directories. If the grantmaker publishes an annual report, secure a copy and study the grants list if available. Annual reports can be found on many foundation Web sites and in Center libraries and many Cooperating Collections (see Appendix F).

If a full grants listing is not available from these sources, look at the foundation's Form 990-PF. Because the IRS requires a foundation to list all of its grants on the Form 990-PF, the tax return is your best source for comprehensive information about grants awarded for a particular tax year (see Chapter 5 for information on obtaining a foundation's Form 990-PF). When reviewing the Form 990-PF, ask yourself: Have past grants been awarded for the type(s) of support your organization is seeking? Have any grants been awarded outside the stated type(s) of support limits? Has the funder awarded grants for your subject area? Have any grants been awarded to organizations in your geographic area? An examination of a complete grants list can be highly revealing concerning foundation priorities. And if you have the time, comparing several years' worth of grants lists, looking for patterns and/or exceptions, may prove even more instructive.

Don't overlook secondary sources such as articles in newspapers and journals that may provide the most up-to-date information you need. *Philanthropy News Digest* (PND), the Foundation Center's online summary of the news of the world of philanthropy, allows you to keep apprised of recent information about foundations and their philanthropic efforts. PND summaries will also inform you of changes in leadership, very recent large grants, and other such information. You may wish to employ PND's search engine to enter the name of a foundation on your prospect list to see what, if anything, has been reported about this funder's recent gifts. Another source of information on recently awarded grants is the "Guide to Grants" at the *Chronicle of Philanthropy's* Web site (http://www.philanthropy.com/grants). This is a database of the grants published in the *Chronicle of Philanthropy* since 1995. A listing of other print and electronic nonprofit news and publications resources can be found in the Nonprofit Links section of the Researching Philanthropy directory on the Foundation Center's Web site.

A review of the resources detailed in Chapter 5 will help you to decide which tools (Web sites, databases, directories, annual reports, IRS returns, application guidelines, etc.) will best assist you in answering the specific questions necessary to refine your list to the most likely prospects. When you have answered these questions about the funders on your broad prospect list, you will have narrowed your list to the few that you should approach first.

Summary

Grantmakers offer a wide variety of types of support for nonprofit organizations, from in-kind gifts from corporate donors to multimillion dollar grants for building construction from large private foundations. A nonprofit seeking funds should first determine the type(s) of support the organization needs. The grantseeker must then investigate the type(s) of support each grantmaker provides. You can find out which type(s) of support a specific grantmaker provides in several different ways, including referring to electronic databases, directories, tax returns, annual reports, Web sites, and newspaper articles. A grantmaker's type(s) of support is one of the three cornerstones of funding research, the other two being subject (field of interest) and where a foundation gives its grants (geographic focus). For suggestions on identifying foundations with an interest in your subject field, see Chapter 6; for information on pinpointing the geographic parameters of grantmakers, see Chapter 7. Having followed the recommended procedures for these three funding research approaches, you should have a well-honed prospect list. Now you may be ready to move on to Chapter 10, which will lay the groundwork for presenting your project to a funder. But first, Chapter 9 describes effective utilization of funding resources on a specific type of funder—the corporate giver.

Chapter 9

Resources for Corporate Funding Research

According to *Giving USA*, published by the AAFRC Trust for Philanthropy, U.S. business contributions to nonprofits (including both company-sponsored foundation giving and direct giving by corporations) came to $12.19 billion in 2002, or 5.1 percent of total charitable giving (see Figure 5). It should be noted that nonmonetary support for nonprofits, often called noncash or "in-kind" gifts, is frequently considered an operating expenditure rather than a charitable contribution by the company that incurred the expense, and, hence, is often omitted from corporate contribution statistics such as these. The Conference Board estimates that donations of noncash resources, at tax-valuation rates, surpassed U.S. corporate foundation giving and, for the first time, accounted for the largest portion of U.S. corporate contributions at 35 percent of overall corporate giving in 2002.[1] Although corporate contributions on average are smaller

---

1. Muirhead, Sophia A. "Corporate Contributions in 2002." Report Number R-1343-03-RR (New York: The Conference Board, 2003), pp. 5 and 10.

than grants from independent foundations, nonprofits would be wise to consider corporations as part of their overall funding strategies. As discussed in Chapter 1, the Foundation Center tracks corporate direct giving (when possible), in addition to giving by company-sponsored foundations, because both can be significant potential sources of support for nonprofits.

Unlike foundations and other charitable agencies, of course, corporations do not exist to give money away. Their allegiance, instead, is to their customers, shareholders, employees, and—most of all—to the bottom line. There is no simple answer as to why corporations support nonprofit organizations and their causes. Many, if not most, contribute out of a combination of altruism and self-interest, and it is nearly impossible to determine where one leaves off and the other begins. It is fair to assume, however, that corporate givers will seek some benefit from their charitable activities. Regardless of the motivation behind corporate giving, the attitudes of top management impact the giving philosophies of corporations more than any other factor. Chief executive officers often play a primary role in company giving, with contributions officers usually reporting directly to the CEO or to the chief financial officer.

Company-Sponsored Foundations and Corporate Direct Giving

Corporations may provide support to nonprofit organizations in a variety of ways. Some companies give only through direct giving programs; others choose to channel the majority of their charitable activities through a private foundation; still others use both vehicles to support nonprofit organizations in their communities. Regardless of which method of charitable support the company chooses, it is important for the grantseeker to understand the differences between a company-sponsored foundation and a corporate direct giving program administered within a company.

COMPANY-SPONSORED FOUNDATIONS

Company-sponsored foundations obtain their funds from profit-making companies or corporations, but are legally independent entities whose purpose is to make grants, usually on a broad basis, although not without regard for the business interests of the corporation. In practice, company-sponsored foundations generally maintain close ties to the parent company, and their giving usually is in fields related to corporate activities or in communities where the parent company operates. The governing board of a company-sponsored foundation frequently is composed of officers of the parent company.

Some company-sponsored foundations have substantial endowments from which they make grants. Others maintain small endowments and rely on regular annual contributions (gifts received) from the parent company to support their giving programs. These annual contributions are most often in the form of "pass-through" gifts. They do not increase the company-sponsored foundation's endowment. Rather, they pass through the foundation to the intended beneficiaries in the nonprofit sector. Company-sponsored foundations may be less subject to the ups and downs of the profit cycle or the vagaries of the stock market than corporate direct giving programs. In years of heavy profits, corporations may use their foundations to set aside funds that can be called upon to sustain their charitable giving in years when corporate earnings are lower.

Since company-sponsored foundations must adhere to the same rules, regulations, and reporting requirements that other private foundations follow, including meeting the annual payout rate (currently 5 percent of total assets) and filing a yearly Form 990-PF with the IRS, it is usually much easier for the grantseeker to obtain information about a company-sponsored foundation than it is about a corporate direct giving program. In fact, when approaching corporations, the lack of information about corporate direct giving may be one of the biggest obstacles the grantseeker faces.

CORPORATE DIRECT GIVING PROGRAMS

Corporate direct giving—all non-foundation company giving—is based solely on corporate resources and tends to rise and fall with corporate profits. For federal tax purposes companies can deduct up to 10 percent of their pretax income for charitable contributions. Corporate direct giving is less regulated and less public than that of company-sponsored foundations. Corporations are not required to publicize direct giving programs or to sustain prescribed levels of funding. They can also make various other types of contributions, sometimes treated as business expenses, which are not necessarily included in giving statistics or tracked in any systematic way.

Managers of corporate direct giving programs today increasingly seem to favor nonmonetary, or in-kind, support along with, or in lieu of, cash grants. Such support includes products, supplies, and equipment; facilities and support services (e.g., meeting space, mailings, computer services); and public relations (e.g., printing and duplicating, graphic arts, advertising). As part of noncash support, corporations may also contribute employee expertise in areas such as legal assistance and tax advice, market research, and strategic planning. In addition, many companies encourage and reward employee voluntarism, and some even permit their employees to take time off with pay to perform volunteer work. Corporations tend to support organizations where their employees are involved as volunteers, and some companies donate funds to these organizations exclusively.

Newer forms of corporate activity, including event sponsorship and cause-related marketing—neither of which meet the definition of pure "giving"—have been on the rise in recent years. With event sponsorship, a company provides the money and/or volunteers necessary to promote the nonprofit's program or event to a wide audience. In exchange the company receives favorable publicity for "doing good" in the community. Both the business and the nonprofit increase their incomes and communicate with large numbers of customers and donors. Cause-related marketing is a joint venture between a business and a nonprofit group to market products or services through a public association. For example, such an arrangement may take the form of a credit card company promoting the donation of a percentage of credit card sales to a specified nonprofit organization during a certain time frame. Although some critics feel that a charitable contribution should not provide the donor with a profit, cause-related marketing has proven effective for a variety of causes, including some non-traditional charities, such as those supporting people with AIDS or battered women. Companies find that such marketing-related donations increase sales or help target new markets.

Although company-sponsored foundations and corporate direct giving programs are legally separate entities and are subject to different regulations and reporting requirements, grantseekers often confuse the two giving sources. The confusion is easily understood when you consider that the company-sponsored foundation's grantmaking program and the corporation's direct giving program are often coordinated under the same general policy and may even be administered by the same staff.

Resources

As we have noted, it is far easier for the grantseeker to locate information about company-sponsored foundations than about corporate direct giving programs. Because company-sponsored foundations are private foundations, as defined in the Tax Reform Act of 1969 and its subsequent amendments, the public has access to their Forms 990-PF. On the other hand, there are no public disclosure laws about a company's direct charitable giving program, so the public knows only those activities about which the company chooses to release information. However, with patience and creativity, the grantseeker can locate pertinent information about corporate direct giving programs as well.

THE FOUNDATION DIRECTORY ONLINE AND *FC SEARCH*

The Foundation Directory Online[2] *and FC Search: The Foundation Center's Database on CD-ROM* are good places to begin your quest to identify potential corporate funders that may be interested in your organization or project. *The Foundation Directory Online* and *FC Search* contain a comprehensive database with information on nearly 2,500 company-sponsored foundations and nearly 1,500 corporate direct giving programs. Because direct giving program records are not public information, the Center sends questionnaires to corporations soliciting information about their giving programs. If company personnel complete and return the questionnaire, the information appears in *The Foundation Directory Online*, *FC Search*, and select Center print publications. If there is no response to the questionnaire, the Center has no reliable way to gather or verify the information. Therefore, while there are a significant number of corporate direct giving programs in *The Foundation Directory Online* and *FC Search*, the list should not be viewed as comprehensive.

To concentrate solely on corporate donors, use the Type of Grantmaker/ Grantmaker Type field, respectively, as one of your criteria. Then select either company-sponsored foundation or corporate giving program or both from a list of six types of grantmakers (see Figure 48). The Corporate Name field in *FC Search* (not currently available in *The Foundation Directory Online*) lets you search for a grantmaker, either a company-sponsored foundation or a direct giving program, by specific company affiliation. The Corporate Location field in *FC Search* (not currently available in *The Foundation Directory Online*) allows you to search for grantmakers with company affiliations in particular cities (see Figure 49). Because it accesses plant and subsidiary locations, not just corporate headquarters, the Corporate Location field is useful in identifying local corporate funding in a specific geographic area. As with all records in the Foundation Center's database, if the corporate direct giving program or the company-sponsored foundation has a presence on the Web, *The Foundation Directory Online* and *FC Search* will indicate that by providing the grantmaker's URL, and you can link directly to that grantmaker's Web site (see Figure 50).

---

2. Unless otherwise noted, the remaining references in this chapter to *The Foundation Directory Online* refer to the *Platinum* level of service. See Figure 13 for a comparison chart detailing the content and features of each subscription service level.

Figure 48. Grantmaker Type Index from *FC Search: The Foundation Center's Database on CD-ROM*

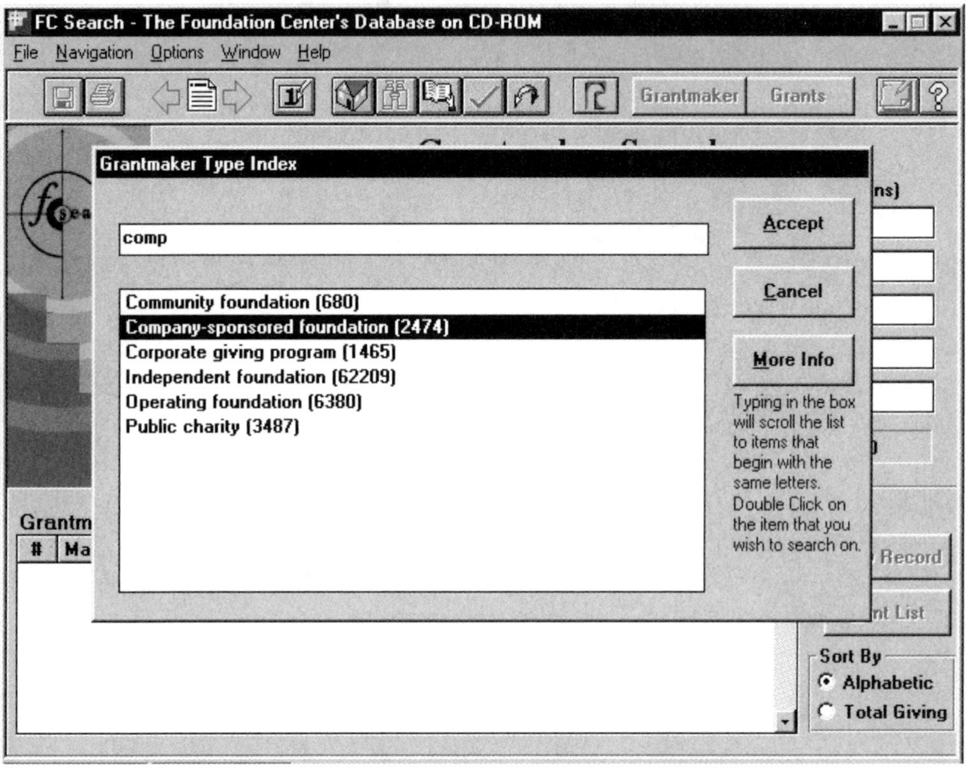

DIRECTORIES

Several print directories can help you locate information about company-sponsored foundations and corporate direct giving. Appendix A lists a number of important resources. The *National Directory of Corporate Giving*, published by the Foundation Center, indexes companies by their trustees, officers, and donors; location; type of business; subject areas of giving; and types of support provided. Entries include plant and subsidiary locations, *Forbes* or *Fortune* rankings, descriptions of business activities, financial data, contact persons, giving interests, application guidelines, and types of support awarded (see Figure 51). All entries are sent first to the corporations for verification, and the information then becomes part of the Foundation Center's database, where it is continually updated.

Figure 49. Grantmaker Corporate Location Index from *FC Search: The Foundation Center's Database on CD-ROM*

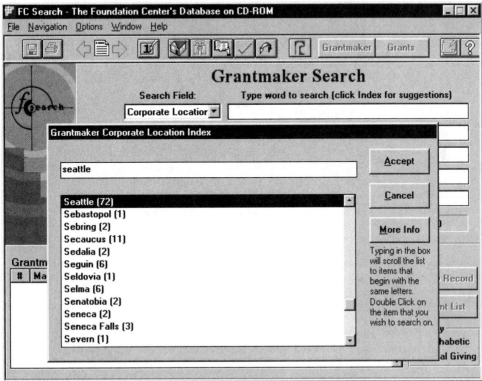

Standard reference works about companies, such as *Standard and Poor's Register of Corporations, Directors and Executives* (New York, NY: Standard & Poor's Corporation, annual), the *D&B Reference Book of Corporate Managements: America's Corporate Leaders* (New York, NY: Dun & Bradstreet, annual), *Corporate Affiliations: Who Owns Whom* (New Providence, NJ: LexisNexis Group, annual), and Chamber of Commerce directories, are typically available in the business reference department of your local public library. Although some of these directories mention company charitable giving, none provides extensive information on this topic. However, you can obtain valuable information about the locations of subsidiaries and the activities and interests of a company by referring to these more general resources. Corporate annual reports, the business section of local newspapers, *The Wall Street Journal*, and business journals, such as *Crain's* (with editions for Cleveland, Detroit, New York, and elsewhere) or

Figure 50. Sample Company-Sponsored Foundation Entry from
The Foundation Directory Online

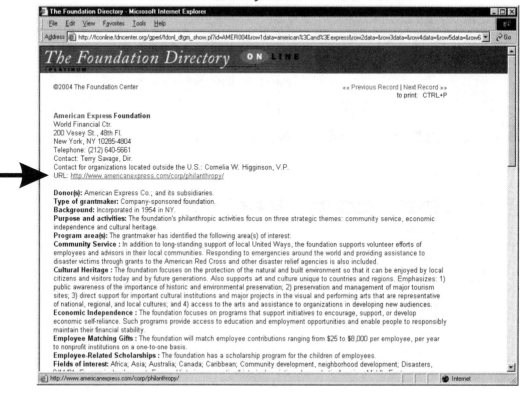

American Cities Business Journals (with editions for Atlanta, Denver, Philadelphia, and elsewhere), are also good sources of information about businesses, their "personalities" and financial health, and other topics of interest to grantseekers.

THE WORLD WIDE WEB AS AN INFORMATION SOURCE

The World Wide Web is an important source of information about corporate community involvement and grantmaking activities. Most of the corporate giving information available on the Web today is about company-sponsored foundations, including specific information concerning grantmaking activities, application procedures, contact names, geographic limitations, fields of interest, types of support, and so forth. Referring to a "portal" or "gateway" site, a comprehensive site offering several services around a specific topic, is probably the easiest way to research corporate grantmaking

Figure 51. Sample Entries from *National Directory of Corporate Giving*

1836
MCCORMICK & COMPANY, INCORPORATED
Sparks, MD

Company URL: http://www.mccormick.com
Business activities: Produces specialty foods, seasonings, and flavorings; manufactures and markets plastic containers.
Financial profile for 2002: Number of employees, 8,700; assets, $1,931,000,000; sales volume, $2,320,000,000
Forbes 500 ranking: 2002—406th in profits
Corporate officer(s): Robert J. Lawless, Chair., Pres., and C.E.O.; Francis A. Contino, C.F.O.; Robert W. Skelton, V.P., Genl. Counsel, and Secy.; Christopher J. Kurtzman, V.P. and Treas.; Joseph A. Anderson, V.P. and Cont.; Mark Timbie, V.P., Mktg.; Allen M. Barrett, Jr., V.P., Corp. Comm.; Karen D. Weatherholtz, V.P., Human Resources
Subsidiaries: Setco, Inc., Anaheim, CA; Tubed Products, Inc., Easthampton, MA
Division(s): Food Service Div., Hunt Valley, MD; Frito Worldwide Div., Hunt Valley, MD; Global Restaurant Div., Hunt Valley, MD; McCormick Flavor Div., Hunt Valley, MD; U.S. Consumer Products Div., Hunt Valley, MD
Joint Venture(s): McCormick Fresh Herbs, LLC, Commerce, CA; Signature Brands, LLC, Ocala, FL; SupHerb Farms, Turlock, CA
Giving statement: Giving through a corporate giving program.

McCormick & Company, Incorporated Corporate Giving Program
18 Loveton Cir.
P.O. Box 6000
Sparks, MD 21152-6000 (410) 771-7301

Contact: Allen M. Barrett, Jr., V.P., Corp. Comm.
Purpose and activities: McCormick makes charitable contributions to nonprofit organizations involved with arts and culture, higher education, health and human services, and to hospitals. Support is given primarily in areas of company operations.
Fields of interest: Arts/cultural programs; higher education; hospitals (general); health care; human services.
Types of support: General/operating support; equipment; scholarship funds; employee volunteer services; sponsorships; employee matching gifts; in-kind gifts; matching/challenge support.
Geographic limitations: Giving primarily in areas of company operations.
Application information: A contributions committee reviews all requests. Application form not required.
  Initial approach: Proposal to headquarters
  Copies of proposal: 1
  Committee meeting date(s): 6 times per year
  Deadline(s): None

1837
MCCRORY CORPORATION
New York, NY

Business activities: Operates variety stores.
Financial profile for 1999: Number of employees, 43,000; sales volume, $200,000,000
Corporate officer(s): Paul Weiner, Sr. V.P., Treas., and C.F.O.
Subsidiaries: McCrory Acquisition Corp., New York, NY; McCrory Stores, York, PA
Giving statement: Giving through a foundation.

McCrory Corporation Needy & Worthy Employees Trust
c/o JPMorgan Chase Bank
P.O. Box 31412
Rochester, NY 14603

Donor(s): McCrory Corp.
Financial data (yr. ended 12/31/01): Assets, $1,235,525 (M); expenditures, $194,621; qualifying distributions, $48,601, including $135,217 for 4 grants to individuals (high: $50,000; low: $16,000).
Purpose and activities: Grants for welfare assistance to needy employees of the McCrory Corporation.
Fields of interest: Economically disadvantaged.
Types of support: Employee-related scholarships; grants to individuals.
Geographic limitations: Giving limted to headquarters city and major operating areas.
Application information: Unsolicited requests for funds not accepted.
Trustee: JPMorgan Chase Bank.
EIN: 136022694

1838
MCDERMOTT INTERNATIONAL, INC.
New Orleans, LA

Company URL: http://www.mcdermott.com
Business activities: Provides marine construction services; manufactures power generation systems.
Financial profile for 2001: Number of employees, 13,300; assets, $2,103,840,000; sales volume, $1,969,806,000; pre-tax income, $91,278,000
Corporate officer(s): Bruce Wilkinson, Chair. and C.E.O.; Frank Kalman, Exec. V.P. and C.F.O.; Louis J. Sannino, Sr. V.P., Human Resources
Giving statement: Giving through a corporate giving program.

McDermott International, Inc. Corporate Giving Program
1450 Poydras St.
New Orleans, LA 70112

Contact: Louis J. Sannino, Sr. V.P., Human Resources, and Corp. Compliance Off.
Financial data (yr. ended 12/31/02): $320,000 for grants.

Purpose and activities: McDermott International makes charitable contributions to nonprofit organizations involved with arts and culture, education, the environment, human services, and civic affairs. Support is given primarily in areas of company operations.
Fields of interest: Arts/cultural programs; education; environment; human services; public affairs.
Types of support: General/operating support; annual campaigns; capital campaigns; program development; scholarship funds; employee volunteer services; loaned talent; employee-related scholarships; scholarships—to individuals.
Geographic limitations: Giving primarily in areas of company operations, with emphasis on Morgan City and New Orleans, LA, West Point, MS, Akron, Alliance, Barberton, Copley, and Lancaster, OH, Houston and Paris, TX, and Lynchburg, VA.
Support limitations: No support for political or religious organizations, secondary schools, or United Way-supported organizations. No grants for advertising.
Publications: Program policy statement.
Application information: The Communications Department handles giving. A contributions committee reviews all requests. Application form not required. Applicants should submit the following:
1) detailed description of project and amount of funding requested
  Initial approach: Proposal to headquarters
  Copies of proposal: 1
  Final notification: Following review
Contributions Committee: Louis J. Sannino, Sr. V.P., Human Resources, and Compliance Off.; Don Washington, Dir., Comm. and Investor Rels.; Bruce Wilkinson, Chair. and C.E.O.
Number of staff: 3 full-time professional.

1839
A. Y. MCDONALD INDUSTRIES, INC.
Dubuque, IA

Company URL: http://www.aymcdonald.com
Business activities: Manufactures brass plumbing equipment, plumbing valves, pumps and water systems, and high pressure gas valves and meter bars.
Financial profile for 2000: Number of employees, 700; sales volume, $150,000,000
Corporate officer(s): John M. McDonald III, Chair., Pres., and C.E.O.; Michael B. McDonald, Sr. V.P. and Corp. Secy.
Giving statement: Giving through a foundation.

A. Y. McDonald Manufacturing Company Charitable Foundation
c/o A.J. Wilherding
P.O. Box 508
Dubuque, IA 52004-0508 (563) 583-7311

Establishment information: Established in 1967 in IA.
Donor(s): A.Y. McDonald Industries, Inc.
Financial data (yr. ended 12/31/01): Assets, $2,613,315 (M); gifts received, $50,000;

on the Web. Several portal sites are good starting points for grantseekers in search of company-sponsored foundations and corporate giving programs. Primary among these are the Foundation Center's Web site, the U.K.-based Charities Aid Foundation's CCInet, and the CSC Non-Profit Resource Center. These sites all have extensive links to company-sponsored foundations and corporate giving programs.

The Foundation Center's Web Sites of Corporate Grantmakers (http://www.fdncenter.org/funders/grantmaker/gws_corp/corp1.html) is a listing of corporate givers that can be browsed alphabetically or searched by subject or geographic keyword (see Figure 52). Abstracts written by Center staff are also provided, giving the grantseeker information about the content of the Web sites themselves as well as the interests of corporate grantmakers.

The Charities Aid Foundation's CCInet (http://www.ccinet.org/search.cfm), a corporate community involvement site, hosts a searchable database of more than 270 companies that offer some form of charitable giving. CCInet is based in the U.K. but includes American companies in its database. You can search alphabetically or by keyword, country, grantmaker type, grant type (or type of support), grant area (or field of interest), online report type, or business type.

The CSC Non-Profit Resource Center's Web site (http://home.comcast.net/~cscunningham/Corporate.htm) has a useful listing of links to corporate givers. Hundreds of links are coded with subject headings to identify funding areas.

Another site for researching corporate information is the Yahoo! Finance Company and Fund Index (http://biz.yahoo.com/i). This site provides a searchable database of information on more than 9,000 public companies in the United States.

One of the most comprehensive sites for corporate information on public and private companies, not only in the United States but abroad, is Hoover's Online (http://www.hoovers.com). Hoover's boasts access to records of millions of companies, although a paid subscription is needed for full access.

Helpful pages for information about businesses on other Web sites include the Internet Prospector's Corporations page (http://www.internet-prospector.org/company.html) and the Companies and Executives section of David Lamb's Prospect Research Page (http://www.lambresearch.com/CorpsExecs.htm). Both sites have links to corporate directories and other sources of business information, and either is a good starting point when looking for corporate information. Those wishing to receive or view corporate annual reports may want to visit the Investor Relations Information Network (http://www.irin.com). Here, annual reports for more than 3,000 companies can be accessed in PDF format.

Figure 52. Web Sites of Corporate Grantmakers from the Foundation Center's Web Site

As another way to uncover information on corporate giving on the Web, try some of the search engines mentioned in Chapter 5, such as Google (http://www.google.com), Yahoo! (http://www.yahoo.com), and others.

When searching for corporate giving information on the Web, the specific keywords or subject descriptors you choose can greatly improve the search results you receive. Try searching initially using phrases like "corporate giving," "community relations," or "corporate contributions." Once you have a sense of what kind of information is available on the Web, you may be able to further narrow your searches by adding words more specific to your own needs (e.g., "arts corporate giving"). You may also want to try the same search using different search engines to see how your results vary. Other keywords to try are "in-kind gifts" if you are looking for product donations, or "community reinvestment act" for those seeking loans.

In the event that you are interested in researching the corporate giving policies of a specific company at the company's Web site, you may be disappointed. Although a corporate Web site may mention the corporation's direct giving program, it usually does not go into great detail about the company's charitable endeavors. Frequently, the corporate giving information is contained on a "page within a page" at a company's Web site. In other words, you have to read through many different sections to get to the information you want. The best way to save time when you visit a corporate Web site is to find the site map (see Figure 53). This is a listing of all of the pages contained within a particular Web site, and is often more reliable than the tedious process of reading through each area of a Web site. Look for items on the site map like "About Us," "History," "Community," "Corporate Relations," and even "News Releases." These headings are the ones most likely to contain information about a company's direct giving program. Even if you are unable to locate specific information about a company's charitable activities, studying the company's Web site, as with reading the company's annual report, can provide you with important clues to its interests.

For more details on corporate giving Web sites, see *The Foundation Center's Guide to Grantseeking on the Web*. This guide has a chapter devoted to corporate giving information on the Web, listing many useful sites and suggesting specific search strategies.

PRIMARY SOURCES

Company-sponsored foundation Forms 990-PF, as with all private foundation information returns, may be accessed at the Foundation Center's Web site, the foundation's own office, from the IRS (see Chapter 5), or through the attorney general and/or charities registration office in the state in which the foundation is chartered.

A company's direct contributions to charitable causes are reported to the IRS on the company's corporate income tax form. This information is private and not available for public scrutiny.

Some company-sponsored foundations and a few corporate direct giving programs issue annual reports, grants lists, brochures, application guidelines, or other publications. Entries in the *National Directory of Corporate Giving* indicate if a company-sponsored foundation or corporate direct giving program issues these publications. If the company in which you have an interest issues such documents, you will want to examine a copy. Foundation Center libraries collect these grantmaker publications and make them available to the public and more and more, corporate grantmakers are making these available online. Some Cooperating Collections (see Appendix F) obtain such reports on companies in their local area. Some companies also issue press

Figure 53. Sample Corporate Web Site Map

releases when they make a significant contribution or participate in a prominent community activity. *Philanthropy News Digest* at the Center's Web site (http://www.fdncenter.org/pnd) is a good source for such announcements, as is the Web site *PR Newswire* (http://www.prnewswire.com).

Local businesses information

Because corporate giving, whether direct or via a foundation, tends to be concentrated in communities where the company operates, geography is a significant factor in fundraising from corporations. For this reason, grantseekers are encouraged to seek support from local businesses and not just from well-known multinational corporations. However, ferreting out information about these smaller, often intensely private, companies can be time-consuming and challenging.

Research by Subject, Geographic Focus, and Types of Support

When looking for corporate funders, grantseekers should employ the same strategies as with other potential donors. Ask yourself the following questions: (1) Is the corporate funder interested in the same subject as my organization or project? (2) Does the funder give in the geographic area served by my organization or project? (3) Does the company provide the types of support needed by my organization? Detailed descriptions of three approaches—subject, geographic focus, types of support—are provided in Chapters 6, 7, and 8. The subject approach and the geographic approach are significant in the corporate giving arena, since, whether by means of a company-sponsored foundation or by direct giving, corporate contributions tend to be concentrated in fields related to corporate interests, and/or in communities where the company operates. The types of support approach permits the grantseeker to expand the search for in-kind and other noncash gifts.

You can develop a broad prospect list of corporations by employing the three basic research approaches simultaneously using *The Foundation Directory Online* or *FC Search*, or sequentially using a variety of print resources. First, choose Type of Grantmaker/Grantmaker Type as one of your search fields and select either company-sponsored foundation or corporate giving program, or both. Your other search fields might include Fields of Interest, Types of Support, and an appropriate field to designate geographic giving preferences (see Figure 54).

SUBJECT APPROACH

To make the best use of the subject approach, consider how a grant or in-kind gift to your nonprofit would actually benefit the company making the contribution. For instance, ask yourself: could a partnership between your organization and a specific company help that company sell more products, reach new customers, and/or improve its image in the community? Does your nonprofit organization offer programs or services that could be used by or otherwise benefit the company or its employees?

A good place to start is the Fields of Interest field in *The Foundation Directory Online* or *FC Search*, or the Subject and Types of Business indexes in the *National Directory of Corporate Giving*. The Types of Business Index (see Figure 55) is unique to the *National Directory of Corporate Giving* and can be particularly helpful in discovering a common bond between a nonprofit organization and corporate interests and activities. Some shared nonprofit/corporate interests will be rather obvious. A sporting goods manufacturer might subsidize an athletic program for disadvantaged youth; a manufacturer

Figure 54. Type of Grantmaker Search in *The Foundation Directory Online*

of musical instruments may support a school's music appreciation program; a pharmaceutical company or alcoholic beverage distributor could be a likely candidate to fund a drug-education program. Other common fields of interest may be less obvious. For instance, textile manufacturers predominantly employ women, and child care is frequently an issue for working women. Therefore, an after-school day care center may be able to secure a gift from a local clothing manufacturer whose employees utilize the day care center's services for their children.

GEOGRAPHIC APPROACH

The grantseeker should pay particular attention to the geographic location of potential corporate donors, and not just the company's headquarters. Find out where plants, field offices, and subsidiary operations are located, since companies tend to spread charitable dollars in these locations as well. You may be able to obtain the names of businesses and

Figure 55. Types of Business Index from *National Directory of Corporate Giving*

TYPES OF BUSINESS INDEX

This index is an alphabetical listing of the products and services provided or the types of businesses conducted by the corporations in this edition of the *Directory*. Corporations are identified by abbreviated versions of their names and referenced by the sequence numbers assigned in the Descriptive Directory.

Abrasive, asbestos, and nonmetallic mineral products, American 129, Armstrong 202, CertainTeed 570, Erie 991, Global 1224, Johns 1557, Martin 1814, Norton 2103, Owens 2180, SGL 2622, 3M 2867, Transco 2907, USG 3013, Walter 3079

Accounting, auditing, and bookkeeping services, Altschuler 89, Associated 213, Cohn 669, Deloitte 839, Ernst 992, Goodman 1237, Grant 1255, Havey 1349, KPMG 1665, Kupferberg 1670, Levy 1715, Paychex 2217, Plante 2295, PricewaterhouseCoopers 2341, Stauffer 2760

Administration/environmental quality program, Burns 478

Advertising, Ackerley 17, Berry 349, Burnett 477, Catalina 541, Clear 646, DDB 827, DoubleClick 903, Fallon 1017, Haan 1308, Keller 1604, Landmark 1684, Lefton 1708, Liberty 1724, Midcontinent 1902, Morris 1964, Ogilvy 2131, Omnicom 2149, Rainbow 2391, Ruder 2511, Saatchi 2525, Thompson 2859, TMP 2881, Tulsa 2930, Valassis 3019, Young 3199

Agricultural production crops, Cargill 517, Chiquita 607, North 2082, Pony 2311

Agricultural production livestock and animal specialties, Simplot 2662

Aircraft and parts, Allegheny 69, AMETEK 153, Ball 258, Barnes 292, Bell 326, Boeing 411, Boston 426, Brunswick 461, Cessna 571, Deutsch 861, Goodrich 1239, Grimes 1281, Guardian 1296, Honeywell 1413, Hughes 1437, Interlake 1502, Kaman 1585, Learjet 1700, McDonnell 1842, New 2041, Northrop 2093, Parker 2211, Raytheon 2404, Remmele 2442, Rockwell 2483, Sequa 2613, SIFCO 2655, Teleflex 2835, Textron 2853, United 2995, Vesper 3044, Woodward 3172

Airports, AAROTEC 3, Aviall 238, Kimberly 1629, Ryder 2517

Ammunition, ordinance, and accessories, Beretta 336, Browning 458, Duchossois 921, FMC 1109, ICI 1459, Northrop 2093, Olin 2144, Pentair 2236

Amusement and recreation services/miscellaneous, American 120, Anheuser 172, Bally 260, Baltimore 264, Caesars 496, Chicago 597, Colorado 682, Detroit 859, Disney 885, Feld 1039, Grand 1253, GTECH 1292, Harrah's 1336, InterActiveCorp 1497, Jacksonville 1537, Kansas 1588, Marlborough 1805, Meadowlands 1858, Mirage 1931, Natural 2016, New York 2043, New York 2044, New York 2045, Old 2142, Pacers 2188, Sacramento 2528, Silver 2659, Sports 2722, Turf 2932, Universal 3005

Animal services, except veterinary, Charles 580, PETsMART 2260

Apparel and accessories/miscellaneous, Kimberly 1629, LaCrosse 1675, Standard 2746

Apparel and accessory stores, American 133, Bauer 303, Bean 314, Men's 1864, Stage 2738

Apparel and accessory stores/miscellaneous, Angelica 170, Fall 1016, Hartmarx 1344

Apparel and other finished products made from fabrics and similar materials, Bally 259, Gymboree 1307, IdentityNow 1464, Jordache 1569, NIKE 2062, Patagonia 2214, Reebok 2422, Timberland 2872

Apparel—girls' and children's outerwear, Candlesticks 507, Kahn 1581, Kleinert's 1646, Lee 1704, Mamiye 1783, Oshkosh 2169, Oxford 2183, Wrangler 3180

Apparel—men's and boys' coats and suits, Belleville 327, Genesco 1204, Wrangler 3180

Apparel—men's and boys' outerwear, Adidas 25, Cintas 625, Descente 855, Guess 1299, Haggar 1312, Hartmarx 1344, Hilfiger 1383, Hudson 1433, Jones 1567, Kahn 1581, Klein 1643, Lee 1704, New 2034, Oshkosh 2169, Oxford 2183, Phillips 2275, Polo 2309, Rawlings 2398, Russell 2514, V.F. 3018, Wrangler 3180

Apparel—women's outerwear, Capezio 510, Claiborne 641, Descente 855, Fisher 1092, Genesco 1204, Guess 1299, Haggar 1312, Hartmarx 1344, Hilfiger 1383, Jones 1567, Kahn 1581, Kellwood 1607, Klein 1643, Lee 1704, Oxford 2183, Paddy 2196, Tanner 2821, V.F. 3018, Wrangler 3180

Apparel—women's, girls', and children's undergarments, Candlesticks 507, Guess 1299

Apparel, piece goods, and notions—wholesale, Adidas 25, Brown 455, Claiborne 641, Descente 855, Dollar 893, Exclusively 1004, Genesco 1204, Heritage 1369, Jim's 1554, Myers 1987, Nomura 2069, Parthenon 2213, Phillips 2275, Strauss 2778, Stride 2779, Wolff 3169

Appliance stores/household, Best 355, Circuit 626, Conn 714, Lowe's 1756, Nashville 1995, Richard 2457, Smulekoff 2684

Appliances/household, Allegheny 69, Bemis 332, Berkshire 344, Conair 708, Dollar 893, Eliason 966, Eureka 998, Fetzer 1046, Maytag 1830, National 2010, Philips 2271, Snap-On 2737, Sub 2781, Thermos 2854, Tomkins 2887, Whirlpool 3133

Asphalt and roofing materials, Elcor 958, Harsco 1340, Koch 1653, Middlesex 1903, Monarch 1946, Russell 2515, Three 2865, United 2987

Audio and video equipment/household, AOL 177, Bertelsmann 353, BOSE 421, Capitol 513, Crown 786, Kaman 1585, Koss 1662, Philips 2271, Reader's 2409, Righteous 2462, SANYO 2549,

Sharp 2627, Sony 2697, Sparrow 2718, Thomson 2862, Ufer 2952, Yamaha 3193, Zenith 3205

Auto and home supplies—retail, AutoZone 233, Dart 822, Fairmount 1015, Jeg's 1548, MFA 1890, Pep 2244

Bakeries, Dunkin' 924

Bakery products, Campbell 505, Dillon 879, Fleming 1098, Frito 1156, General 1201, Kellogg 1606, Lance 1682, McKee 1845, Pepperidge 2246, Ralcorp 2393, Rich 2456, Seaboard 2590, Spunkmeyer 2725, Sunshine 2799, Tasty 2824, White 3134, World 3173

Bands, orchestras, and entertainers, Creative 772, Solo 2692

Banks/commercial, Abbotsford 7, Allfirst 76, AMCORE 98, American 136, AmSouth 162, Androscoggin 169, Associated 211, Audubon 227, BancorpSouth 266, Bangor 268, Bank 269, Bank 270, Bank 271, Bank 272, Bank 274, Bank 275, Bank 276, Bank 277, Bank 278, Bank 279, Bank 280, Bank 282, Banknorth 285, Bay 310, BB&T 313, Beneficial 334, Berkshire 343, Boston 425, Brown 454, Bryn 463, Cape 509, Carolina 524, Central 558, Chase 583, Chemical 588, Chevy 595, Citigroup 629, Citizens 630, Citizens 631, Citizens 633, Citizens 634, Citizens 636, Citizens 637, Citizens 638, City 639, City 640, Colonial 677, Colorado 683, Comerica 692, Commerce 693, Commerce 694, Commerce 695, Commercial 696, Community 700, Community 701, Compass 702, County 759, Delaware 835, Dubois 920, Edgar 944, Equimark 988, Everett 1001, Exchange 1002, Exchange 1003, Fairfax 1013, Fairfield 1014, Farmers 1022, Farmers 1024, Fifth 1055, First 1065, First 1066, First 1067, First 1068, First 1071, First 1072, First 1073, First 1074, First 1075, First 1076, First 1077, First 1078, First 1080, 1st 1084, First 1085, First 1086, Fleet 1097, Framingham 1138, Franklin 1139, Fremont 1149, Frost 1158, Fulton 1165, GAB 1171, Gardiner 1179, Goldome 1234, Greater 1265, Guaranty 1293, Harris 1339, Hawaii 1350, Hibernia 1378, Home 1408, Hopkins 1418, HSBC 1427, Huntington 1449, Hyde 1454, ING 1487, INTRUST 1516, Iowa 1522, Iowa 1523, Irwin 1527, Isabella 1528, KeyBank 1618, LaSalle 1692, Long 1747, Longview 1750, Manufacturers 1788, Mascoma 1816, Mason 1817, MASSBANK 1819, MBNA 1833, Mellon 1863, Merchants 1869, Mid 1899, Midway 1907, Milford 1912, Milwaukee 1923, Minnesota 1926, Morgan 1959, National 1996, National 1998, National 1999, National 2000, Net.Bank 2030, New Bethlehem 2035, North 2081, North 2083, Northern 2091, Old 2141, Ozaukee 2184, Palos 2200, Park 2207, Park corporations in your area simply by consulting the local yellow pages or the local Chamber of Commerce. Company executives can be convinced to support a program because it provides direct service to employees and other community residents, because it brings public recognition and/or prestige to a company and its management, and/or because it will improve customer relations and help build a future customer base in an important market.

If you are using *The Foundation Directory Online* or *FC Search*, you will find that you have several fields from which to choose when designating geographic search parameters: (1) Foundation/Grantmaker State, (2) Foundation/Grantmaker City, (3) Corporate Location (not currently available in *The Foundation Directory Online*), or (4) Geographic Focus. You will find that using Foundation/Grantmaker City as your search field will yield a different result than a search by Corporate Location (see Figure 56). A Foundation/Grantmaker State or Foundation/Grantmaker City search will yield hits for only those states or cities where the company-sponsored foundation or corporate direct giving program is headquartered. When concentrating on a city, it is wise to use both state and city, since a city's name may appear in more than one state. For example, there is Portland, Maine, and Portland, Oregon. A Corporate Location search will include not only the headquarters city of the foundation or direct giving program, but also any cities where the company has plants, offices, or subsidiaries. The results of a Geographic Focus search will show whether the corporate funder gives in particular states, nationally, or internationally. Since many foundations and companies do not indicate a geographic focus, it is wise to conduct at least one of the other geographic searches mentioned above.

Another good starting point is the Geographic Index in the *National Directory of Corporate Giving* (see Figure 57), which refers back to the main entries. Entries include plant and subsidiary locations.

TYPES OF SUPPORT APPROACH

Companies provide many types of support, including funds for operating budgets, employee matching gifts, and program development, as well as a variety of noncash contributions such as in-house printing, loaned executives, and donations of company products. *The Foundation Directory Online* and *FC Search* will be valuable sources for types of support information. Use the Types of Support Index and consult the definitions provided in the Help files (see Appendix D). The *National Directory of Corporate Giving* is a useful print source for a types of support approach as well. Refer to the definitions at the beginning of the Types of Support Index in the print edition.

Figure 56. Grantmaker City and Corporate Location Search in *FC Search: The Foundation Center's Database on CD-ROM*

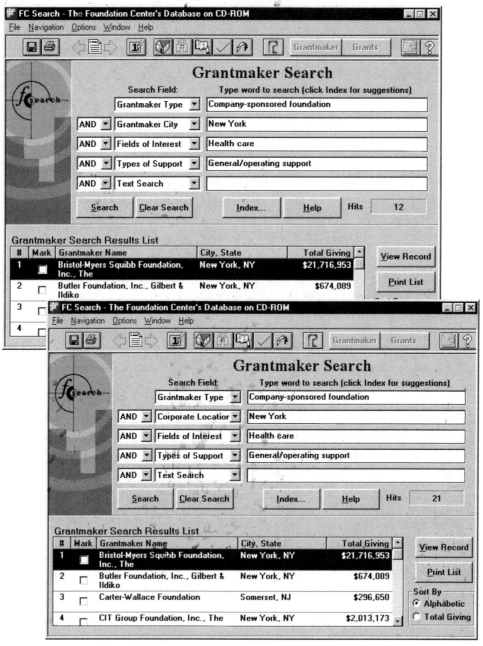

Figure 57. Geographic Index from *National Directory of Corporate Giving*

784, Fulton 1165, Global 1224, HCA 1356, Hughes 1438, ICI 1459, Jones 1567, National 2010, Pep 2244, Philips 2271, Rohm 2489, U.S. 2944, Verizon 3040, WSFS 3182, XTRA 3191
Office(s): Liberty 1725, Pulte 2369, Skadden 2670
Plant(s): Alliant 78, First 1086, Georgia 1212, Quaker 2373

Yorklyn
Corporate Headquarters: NVF 2113
Subsidiaries: NVF 2113, Sharon 2626

DISTRICT OF COLUMBIA
Washington
Corporate Giving Program(s): Giant 1214, Kiplinger 1641, Marriott 1807, Potomac 2319, Riggs 2461, Washington 3086, Washington 3089
Foundation(s): Arnold 203, Cassidy 537, Covington 761, Dart 822, Federal 1032, Giant 1214, Hitachi 1391, Mazda 1831, S.B.E. 2523, Washington 3089, Wilkes 3142
Corporate Headquarters: Baker 249, Beitzell 321, Cassidy 537, Covington 761, Danaher 817, Federal 1032, Ferris 1044, GEICO 1189, Kiplinger 1641, Nasdaq 1992, Potomac 2319, Riggs 2461, S.B.E. 2523, Washington 3086, Washington 3089, Wilkes 3142
Subsidiaries: ABC 9, BB&T 313, Berkshire 344, CCH 544, GEICO 1189, Grant 1255, Kiplinger 1641, Marriott 1807, May 1828, Potomac 2319, Riggs 2461, Scripps 2588, Tribune 2914, US 3010, Verizon 3040, WorldCom 3176
Office(s): Ashland 209, Chadbourne 575, Dickinson 871, Grant 1255, Hale 1314, Hewitt 1374, Jones 1568, Korn 1661, Marasco 1791, Mazda 1831, Miller 1919, Natsource 2015, Robins 2476, Salomon 2537, SBC 2560, Skadden 2670, Skidmore 2671, Sullivan 2785, Toyota 2899, Turner 2933, Vinson 3054, Weil 3106, Weyerhaeuser 3129, Whiting 3136, Willis 3145, Winston 3156
Plant(s): ChevronTexaco 594, Edison 947, Enron 978, Florida 1104, Interface 1500, Katten 1595, McDonnell 1842, Mitsui 1942, Northrop 2093, Raytheon 2404, TJX 2880, United 2995, Vulcan 3069, Williams 3144

FLORIDA
Altamonte Springs
Corporate Headquarters: Greater 1266
Subsidiaries: Vilter 3053

Apopka
Division(s): Eclipse 941
Office(s): BankAtlantic 284
Plant(s): Scotts 2586

Aventura
Office(s): Northern 2091

Bartow
Joint Venture(s): HCA 1356
Plant(s): Ashland 209

Boca Raton
Foundation(s): Globe 1226, Sanders 2545, Tyco 2939
Corporate Headquarters: Implantation 1477, Palm 2199, Sanders 2545, St. 2731
Subsidiaries: Kimberly 1629, Lennar 1712, St. 2730, Tribune 2914
Office(s): BankAtlantic 284, Northern 2091, Whirlpool 3133
Plant(s): GTECH 1292, Intel 1496, Symbol 2811

Bonita Springs
Foundation(s): York 3196
Office(s): Cummings 796

Boynton Beach
Office(s): BankAtlantic 284
Plant(s): Motorola 1970, Teleflex 2835

Bradenton
Subsidiaries: Galileo 1174, HCA 1356, Knight 1649, PepsiCo 2251
Division(s): ETCO 995
Office(s): BankAtlantic 284
Plant(s): Oshkosh 2170

Brandon
Office(s): BankAtlantic 284

Brooksville
Office(s): BankAtlantic 284

Cantonment
Plant(s): International 1510

Cape Canaveral
Plant(s): McDonnell 1842

Cape Coral
Office(s): BankAtlantic 284

Charlotte
Office(s): BankAtlantic 284

Clearwater
Foundation(s): Eckerd 940, Metal 1881, St. 2731
Corporate Headquarters: Isaly 1529, Metal 1881
Office(s): BankAtlantic 284, Regis 2431, State 2758
Plant(s): Alliant 78, Carpenter 526, Honeywell 1413, U.S. 2947, West 3120

Clewiston
Foundation(s): Kelly 1609, United 2990
Corporate Headquarters: United 2990
Subsidiaries: United 2990

Cocoa
Plant(s): PerkinElmer 2255

Cocoa Beach
Subsidiaries: Boeing 411

Coconut Creek
Foundation(s): Minto 1929
Corporate Headquarters: Minto 1929
Office(s): BankAtlantic 284

Coral Gables
Subsidiaries: Phelps 2268
Office(s): BankAtlantic 284, Northern 2091

Coral Springs
Office(s): BankAtlantic 284
Plant(s): CHEMCENTRAL 587

Dania
Office(s): BankAtlantic 284, Hitachi 1392

Daytona Beach
Plant(s): Coca 666

Deefield Beach
Corporate Headquarters: JM 1555

Deerfield Beach
Corporate Giving Program(s): JM 1555
Foundation(s): JM 1555
Subsidiaries: Roto 2503
Office(s): BankAtlantic 284
Plant(s): Eckerd 940

Deland
Office(s): Fishel 1089

Delray Beach
Corporate Headquarters: Globe 1226
Office(s): BankAtlantic 284

Destin
Office(s): AmSouth 162

Elgin
Subsidiaries: Safety 2531

Estero
Plant(s): Florida 1103

Fernandina Beach
Subsidiaries: Synovus 2815

Fort Lauderdale
Corporate Giving Program(s): AutoNation 232, Republic 2443
Foundation(s): Arby's 190, BankAtlantic 284
Corporate Headquarters: Arby's 190, AutoNation 232, BankAtlantic 284, Republic 2443
Subsidiaries: Centex 554, Franklin 1142, Johnson 1562, Tribune 2914, Tweeter 2936

Office(s): American 111, Grant 1255, Kimley 1631, Northern 2091, Pulte 2369, United 2993, Whiting 3136
Plant(s): Gibraltar 1217, Guardian 1297, Novell 2106, Owens 2179, York 3197

Fort Myers
Foundation(s): Implantation 1477
Subsidiaries: Hilb 1382
Office(s): BankAtlantic 284, KeyBank 1618, Kimley 1631, Northern 2091, Pulte 2369, Sony 2697
Plant(s): Lennar 1712

Fort Pierce
Subsidiaries: HCA 1356
Office(s): BankAtlantic 284
Plant(s): Freedom 1146

Fort Walton Beach
Plant(s): Gulf 1304

Gainesville
Subsidiaries: Hilb 1382, Nestle 2027
Plant(s): Anheuser 172, Florida 1103, Florida 1104, Fuller 1163

Hallandale
Office(s): BankAtlantic 284

Hallandale Beach
Foundation(s): NVF 2113

Hialeah
Office(s): BankAtlantic 284
Plant(s): International 1507

Hillsborough City
Office(s): BankAtlantic 284

Holiday
Plant(s): Florida 1103

Hollywood
Office(s): BankAtlantic 284, Clark 643

Immokalee
Subsidiaries: Plains 2294

Jacksonville
Corporate Giving Program(s): CSX 792, St. 2730, Winn 3153
Foundation(s): Florida 1103, Florida 1104, Jacksonville 1537, Rayonier 2402, Winn 3153
Corporate Headquarters: CSX 792, Florida 1103, Florida 1104, Jacksonville 1537, St. 2730, Winn 3153
Subsidiaries: Allen 73, Allied 81, American 102, Biomet 378, Florida 1104, Leggett 1709, Praxair 2328, Raymond 2401, St. 2730, Walter 3079
Office(s): AmSouth 162, Hitachi 1392, Kimley 1631, Mazda 1831, Merrill 1877, State 2756, State 2758, United 2993, Wachovia 3071
Plant(s): Anheuser 172, Commercial 698, Georgia 1212, Goodrich 1239, Lydall 1761, Owens 2179, Owens 2180, Pactiv 2195, Williams 3144

Juno Beach
Corporate Giving Program(s): Florida 1102
Foundation(s): Florida 1102
Corporate Headquarters: Florida 1102
Office(s): BankAtlantic 284

Jupiter
Subsidiaries: Philips 2271
Office(s): BankAtlantic 284

Kennedy Space Center
Subsidiaries: PerkinElmer 2255
Plant(s): McDonnell 1842

Key Biscayne
Subsidiaries: Sonesta 2695
Office(s): Northern 2091

Kissimmee
Office(s): BankAtlantic 284
Plant(s): Quaker 2374

Lake Buena Vista
Corporate Giving Program(s): Disney 886
Corporate Headquarters: Disney 886
Subsidiaries: Disney 885

Lake City
Office(s): GATX 1183

Refine Your List

Once you have developed a list of possible corporate prospects, you should review it to eliminate those that are not interested in your subject area, that do not give in your geographic area, and/or that do not award the type(s) of support your organization needs. If you used *The Foundation Directory Online* or *FC Search* to construct your list, you probably used multiple search criteria, thereby completing this step already. Filling in the Prospect Worksheet (see Figure 11) for each potential funder on your list enables you to quickly rule out the less appropriate candidates.

You are now ready to scrutinize your list further to determine those corporate funders that are most likely to be interested in your organization or project. You'll want to conduct as much research on all aspects pertaining to these corporate grantmakers as time and resources permit. Posing the questions raised in Chapter 4 is a good place to start:

- Does the funder accept applications?

- Has the funder demonstrated a real commitment to funding in your subject field?

- Does it seem likely that the funder will make grants to organizations in your geographic location?

- Does the amount of money you are requesting fit within the funder's typical grant range?

- Does the funder have a policy prohibiting grants for the type(s) of support you are requesting?

- Does the funder usually make grants to cover the full cost of a project or does it favor projects where other funders have an opportunity to participate?

- Does the funder put limits on the length of time it is willing to support a project?

- What types of organizations does the funder tend to support?

- Does the funder have application deadlines, or does it review proposals continuously?

- Do you or does anyone on your board know someone connected with the funder?

- What are the financial conditions that may affect the corporate funder's ability to give?

- Do you have the most current and accurate details on the funder?

Most of these questions can be answered by referring to any one of several resources already covered. *The Foundation Directory Online* and *FC Search* will answer many of them. The print directory, the *National Directory of Corporate Giving*, will also provide many of the answers you need. For instance, note that in each entry for a company-sponsored foundation in the *National Directory*, you will find an indication of the largest grant paid (high) and the smallest grant paid (low) during the most recent fiscal year. In addition, up to ten grants reported during a given fiscal year will be listed for those foundations with annual giving of at least $50,000. Other print sources on corporate giving will be found in Appendix A. For application deadlines and the names of trustees, officers, or donors and other such information about corporate funders, Center directories and databases are excellent sources.

As with all prospective funders, you will want to learn all you can about a corporate giver *before* submitting a request.

If the company you are researching is a public company, that is, one whose stock is publicly traded, the Securities and Exchange Commission's (SEC) database (http://www.sec.gov/edgar.shtml) is a good place to locate information. Called EDGAR, this database contains an archive of all the financial documents filed with the SEC since 1993. There are many different types of material about the company and its operation. The 10-K report is the company's annual report and will probably be one of the most useful documents for you.

During the course of your research you may need to consult primary sources, such as the IRS Form 990-PF, annual reports, or application guidelines. Keep in mind that Forms 990-PF are not available for corporate direct givers, only for company-sponsored foundations. The *National Guide to Corporate Giving* will indicate whether or not a company-sponsored foundation or corporate direct giving program issues an annual report, informational brochure, or other publications. If not, ask for an annual business report. While corporate annual reports usually do not contain actual information on charitable activities, they can aid you in shaping an appeal. Business reports often present a company's philosophy and its plans for the future, which in turn may prove helpful when it comes to linking a funding request to the corporation's interests.

Secondary sources such as articles in newspapers and journals may also prove informative. *Philanthropy News Digest* (PND), the Foundation Center's online summary of the news of the world of philanthropy, has a search engine that allows you to seek recent information about companies and their philanthropic efforts. PND summaries will also inform you of recent major grants, funding initiatives, and other such information. You may wish to use PND's search engine to enter the name of a foundation or company and see what, if anything, has been reported about this funder's recent gifts. PND also offers requests for proposals issued by corporate givers through the RFP Bulletin. Another source of information on recently awarded grants is *PR Newswire* on the Web (http://www.prnewswire.com). *PR Newswire* provides access to news releases issued by corporations. You should also stay abreast of economic conditions and the local business news. A company that is laying off employees or running a deficit may not be the best one to ask for a donation.

Some companies prefer to receive a preliminary letter of inquiry; others have application forms, and still others require multiple copies of formal proposals. If at all possible, find out the preferred means of approach in advance of submitting a proposal. If you are applying to a company-sponsored foundation, the application procedures will most likely appear in *The Foundation Directory Online, FC Search,* and in print directories, such as the *National Directory of Corporate Giving.*

For direct giving programs of privately held companies, you will probably need to place a telephone call to the company to ask for application information. If you are unable to identify the correct person to call, ask to be connected to the department of "community affairs," "public affairs," "public relations," "communications," or some other term that connotes a relationship to the larger community. In large cities, the correct contact person might be in the department of "urban affairs." If corporate giving is not operated out of that office, the person you talk with will probably be able to put you in touch with the correct individual. If the company is large enough to appear in the standard business directories, such as *Standard & Poor's Register of Corporations, Directors and Executives* or the *Corporate Affiliations* directory, you may want to refer to one of those books at your local public library to identify a vice president or director responsible for corporate giving.

Personal Contacts

In fundraising, personal contacts help—if for no other reason than to get information—but their impact varies. It makes sense that company-sponsored foundations and corporate direct giving programs with separate staff and explicit guidelines or formal procedures are unlikely to require personal contacts, while companies with informal giving programs and no specific guidelines are more likely to be amenable to personal contacts. The grantseeker who "knows someone" will want to utilize that relationship but to do so judiciously. Grantseekers without personal contacts may want to develop them in order to facilitate receipt of corporate gifts. Establishing a rapport with a corporate funder can be difficult. Such cultivation requires long-term effort.

Summary

Companies make charitable donations of money, products, services, and staff time in the communities in which they do business. These gifts make the community a better place to live and to work, and they enhance the companies' standing among customers and employees. Companies may make their gifts through a private foundation or a direct giving program or both. Finding information about a company-sponsored foundation is relatively easy because of the public disclosure laws governing private foundations. Finding information about corporate direct giving programs is more difficult, since the only public information about such programs is that which the company chooses to release. Although company donations, whether from a company-sponsored foundation or from a corporate direct giving program, are usually smaller than contributions by independent foundations to similar causes, corporate funding is a significant part of a strategic fundraising plan for many nonprofits.

Remember not to limit your thinking about corporations to asking only for money or in-kind support. Look to local businesses as sources for board members and volunteer assistance. Keep in mind as well that a good relationship with one company may pave the way to good relationships with others.

The next chapter is devoted to putting together a proposal that will present your organization and cause in the best light to a prospective funder, be it a corporate or other funder.

Chapter 10

Presenting Your Idea to a Funder

By now you should have a short list of grantmakers that seem likely to fund your project on the basis of a match you've established between the funders' interests and your nonprofit organization's subject focus, the geographic area and population groups you serve, and the type and amount of support you require for your project. And you have thoroughly researched each funder on your list to uncover as much current information as possible about these grantmakers. It is time to present your idea to those funders on your list and convince them to support it.

While some foundations are quite flexible about the format and timing of grant applications, many have developed specific guidelines and procedures to facilitate the decision-making process. In an effort to save time for the grantmaker and the grantseeker, some regional groups of grantmakers have adopted a common grant application format so that grant applicants can produce a standard proposal for participating grantmakers. Common grant application forms can be downloaded from the Finding Funders directory of the Foundation Center's Web site. Before applying to a funder that accepts a common grant application form, you must, of course, ascertain whether your project matches the funder's stated interests and determine if the funder would prefer a letter of inquiry in advance of receiving a proposal, when is the funder's deadline for proposals, and how many copies of the proposal are required.

Whether the grantmaker uses a common grant application form or has its own individual format, follow the stated procedures to the letter. You'll want to review the notes you made during the course of your research about a potential funder, including items from Web sites, funder-issued annual reports, application guidelines, or informational brochures. Knowing whom to contact and how to submit your application can be critical in ensuring that your request receives serious consideration.

If no guidelines are provided by the grantmaker, use the format described in this chapter. The Proposal Writing Short Course in the Finding Funders directory at the Foundation Center's Web site provides a useful framework as well. *The Foundation Center's Guide to Proposal Writing, The Foundation Center's Guide to Winning Proposals,* and other books, listed in Appendix A, are available at Center libraries and many Cooperating Collections (see Appendix F) to assist you in crafting a compelling grant proposal.

Timing and Deadlines

Timing is an essential element of the grant-application process. Grant decisions are often tied to board meetings, which can be held as infrequently as once or twice a year. Many foundations need to receive grant applications at least two to three months in advance of board meetings to allow time for review and investigation, and some require an even longer lead time. If the foundation you have targeted has no specified application deadline, try to determine when its board meets and submit your request as far in advance of its next board meeting as possible. Then be prepared to wait three to six months, or even longer, for the proposal-review process to run its course.

Initial Inquiries

Many foundations, both large and small, prefer to have grant applicants send a letter of inquiry before, or even in place of, a formal proposal. Some grantmakers may be willing to offer advice and/or assistance in preparing the final proposal for applicants whose ideas seem particularly relevant to their funding programs. If the foundation cannot provide funding because of prior commitments or a change in its program focus, this can also save you a lot of time in preparing a full proposal application. Some grantmakers will even make their funding decisions based solely on a letter of inquiry.

Unless the funder specifies otherwise, your letter of inquiry should be brief, no more than two to three pages. It should describe in clear, concise prose both the purpose of your organization and the parameters of the project for which you are seeking funds. You should be specific about the scope of your project, how it fits into the grantmaker's own program, the type and amount of support you are seeking, and other funders, if any, being approached. Your opening paragraph should summarize the essential ingredients of your request, including the amount of money and type of support you are seeking. All too often grant applicants bury these important facts in long descriptions of their organization or project. Most grantmakers will also want to see a copy of the IRS letter determining your organization's tax-exempt status. Depending on what you have learned about the funder, offer to send a full proposal for their consideration or ask about the possibility of a meeting with foundation staff or officials to discuss your project. Sample letters of inquiry will be found in *The Foundation Center's Guide to Winning Proposals* and in the Center's FAQ "Where can I find examples of letters of inquiry?" (http://www.fdncenter.org/learn/faqs/html/loi.html).

You may need to be somewhat assertive in your approach to foundations. Give the funder adequate time to respond to your inquiry, but don't be afraid to follow up with a phone call or e-mail about two weeks after you've sent your letter to confirm that it was received, and if not, to offer to send another copy. The call also provides the opportunity to ask whether you can supply additional information and to inquire about the timing of the review process. Remember, there's a fine line between behaving in a proactive manner and being perceived as "pushy" by prospective funders. You'll want to take care not to cross that line.

The Proposal

The full grant proposal may be your *only* opportunity to convince a grantmaker that your program is worthy of its support. Depending on what you've uncovered about a funder's application procedures, it will either be your first direct contact with the funder or will follow an initial exchange of letters, e-mails, or conversations with staff and/or trustees. The proposal should make a clear and concise case for your organization and its programs. Grantmakers receive and review hundreds, sometimes thousands, of proposals every year. In reviewing your proposal, they need to be able to identify quickly and efficiently how you intend to put the requested grant funds to work to benefit the community or to further the cause(s) in which the grantmaker has an interest.

At this stage your board may feel it's time to turn to outside help and hire a consultant to develop a proposal. Although bringing in a professional proposal writer can bolster your confidence, it is rarely necessary and may even prove inadvisable, since no one knows your project better than a representative of your own organization. Grantmakers aren't impressed by slick prose and fancy packaging. They want the facts, presented clearly and concisely, and they want to get a feeling for the organization and the people who run it.

As we have noted, there are a number of excellent books on the proposal-writing process, and you may find it useful to review several of them before you get started. Many of these titles, listed in Appendix A, can be found at Foundation Center libraries or Cooperating Collections. Some may be found in your local public library. *The Foundation Center's Guide to Proposal Writing* takes you step-by-step through the proposal-writing process, supplementing advice from the author, an experienced fundraiser, with excerpts from actual proposals, and offering helpful hints from grantmakers interviewed in the preparation of the *Guide*. There is also help available in the form of educational courses. The *Guide* serves as the basis for the Center's Proposal Writing Seminar, held each spring and fall in various locations throughout the country. Announcements of upcoming seminars appear on the Center's Web site and in newsletters issued by Center libraries. Also at the Center's Web site, you may wish to consult the Center's Proposal Writing Short Course, an abbreviated version of the aforementioned proposal writing guide and the FAQs on proposal writing found in the Learning Lab directory of the Foundation Center's Web site.

While application criteria and proposal formats vary, most funders expect to see the following components in a grant proposal:

TABLE OF CONTENTS

If your proposal is quite lengthy, you may wish to include a table of contents at the beginning. The table of contents makes it easier for the prospective funder to find specific components of the proposal. While your proposal should be brief (most funders recommend limiting it to ten pages or less), a table of contents helps you organize your presentation and outline the information therein.

EXECUTIVE SUMMARY

The summary briefly describes the problem or need your project hopes to address; your plan of action, including how and where the program will operate, its duration, and how it will be staffed; a reference to the budget for the project, including the specific amount requested from the funder and your plans for long-term funding; the anticipated results; and a brief statement of the name, history, purpose, and activities of your agency and its capacity to carry out this proposal. The summary should be presented as the first section of your proposal and can be as short as one or two paragraphs; it should never be longer than a page.

Even though the executive summary is the first item in the proposal, it should be the last thing you actually write. By that point you will have thought through and thoroughly documented the need you plan to address, your plan of action, and the projected outcomes for your project, making it easier to pull out the most important facts for the summary.

STATEMENT OF NEED

Here's where you state as simply and clearly as possible the problem, need, or opportunity your project will address. Be sure to narrow the issue to a definable problem that is solvable within the scope of your project. A broad picture of the many problems that exist within your community will only detract from your presentation. You want to paint a compelling picture of a pressing need, which might inspire a funder to support you. You should avoid describing a problem that is overwhelming in its size and/or complexity, which might make addressing it seem hopeless to the prospective funder.

Be sure to document your description of the problem you've identified with citations from recent studies and current statistics pertaining to your geographic area, statements by public officials and/or professionals, and previous studies by your agency and/or other agencies. Your object is to convince the funder that the problem or need is real and that your approach builds upon the lessons others have learned. Show the funder that you have researched the problem carefully and that you have a new or unique contribution to offer toward its resolution. And remember, no matter how well you document a specific need, you are unlikely to convert a grantmaker who has no interest in your specific subject area.

PROJECT DESCRIPTION

Now that you've presented the problem, you need to clarify exactly what it is you hope to accomplish. Here's where you state the goals and objectives of the project, the methods you plan to use to accomplish these objectives, a time frame in which the project will take place, and how you will determine the success or effectiveness of your project or program. If you are seeking basic operating support for your organization rather than project support, you will want to refer to your agency's mission, the activities engaged in to accomplish that mission, and the audiences served.

OBJECTIVES AND GOALS

Goals are abstract and subject to conditions. As such, they may not always be fully attainable. Objectives, on the other hand, are based on realistic expectations and therefore are more specific. Since clearly stated objectives also provide the basis for evaluating your program, be sure to make them measurable and time-limited. The realization of each stated objective will be another step toward achieving your goal. For example, if the problem you've identified is high unemployment among teenagers in your area, your objective might be to provide 100 new jobs for teenagers over the next two years. The goal of the project would be a significant reduction in or even the elimination of teenage unemployment in your community.

Don't confuse the objective of a program with the means to be used in achieving that end. You might achieve your objective of providing 100 new jobs for teenagers through a variety of methods, including working with local businesses to create jobs, running a job placement or employment information center, or providing jobs within a program operated by your agency. But your measurable objective remains the same: to provide 100 new jobs for teenagers over the next two years.

IMPLEMENTATION METHODS AND SCHEDULE

The methods section of your proposal should describe the plan of action for achieving your goals and objectives, as well as how long it will take. Why have you chosen this particular approach? Who will actually implement the plan? If you're involving staff or volunteers already active in your program or consultants from outside your organization, note their qualifications and include abbreviated versions of their resumes in the appendix to your proposal. If you'll need to hire new staff, include job descriptions and describe your plans for recruitment and training. You should also provide a timetable for the project, making sure to indicate the projected starting and completion dates for each phase of the program. Be sure to allow ample time for each stage, bearing in mind the possibility of delays while you await funding.

EVALUATION CRITERIA AND PROCEDURES

Evaluation criteria provide a measure for determining how effective your project has been in achieving its stated objectives. If your objectives are specific and measurable, it will be easier to evaluate your success. Although evaluating the outcome and end results of a project is a primary concern, don't overlook the need to evaluate the process or procedures as well. A good evaluation plan will enable you and others to learn from your efforts.

Most grantmakers today require an evaluation component as part of your proposal. Crafting the evaluation component of a proposal often presents a major stumbling block to the inexperienced grantseeker. Try to remember that evaluation is nothing more than an objective means by which both you and the funder determine whether or not you have accomplished what you set out to do. It is an important part of your proposal because, among other things, it demonstrates that you are aware of the responsibility implicit in receiving a grant. Evaluation should *not* be an after-thought. It should be built into the design of your procedures as a continuous monitoring system.

An effective evaluation procedure will attempt to answer the following questions:

- Did you operate as intended, following the methods outlined in your procedures section?

- What beneficial changes have been brought about that are directly attributable to your project?

- Is your project the only variable responsible for these changes?

- What conclusions may be drawn from this evaluation?

- What future directions may be projected for your organization as a result of your accomplishments under this grant?

BUDGET

Developing a budget requires both candor and common sense. For example, if your proposal involves hiring staff, don't forget that Social Security payments, worker's compensation, and benefits have to be included. Try to anticipate your full expenses in advance. It's unrealistic to expect grantmakers to provide additional funding at a later date to cover needs overlooked in your initial request.

Remember, too, that foundation and corporate donors are experienced in evaluating costs. Don't pad your budget, but don't underestimate the amount you need, either. If other funders have contributed to your project, be sure to say so. The fact that others have confidence in your organization is a plus. If you expect to receive in-kind donations of equipment, office space, or volunteer time, be sure to mention these as well. Many funders want your budget (or your budget narrative) to reflect any staff time, resources, or overhead costs your organization will contribute to the cost of the project.

When seeking funds for a specific project, be sure to supply both the budget for your project and, in the appendix, the overall operating budget of your organization. Typically, the budget for a nonprofit organization includes two sections: personnel and nonpersonnel costs (see Figure 58). When in doubt, seek professional assistance from an accountant or someone with financial expertise in compiling a budget.

In addition to lists of current institutional donors to your organization, most funders will want to know your future funding plans, and how you plan to sustain your project after their grant money has run out. Even with requests for one-time support (e.g., the purchase of equipment), you should describe how you'll handle related expenditures, such as ongoing maintenance. Vague references to alternative funding sources are not enough. Grant decision makers want *specifics*. Do you plan to solicit additional support from the public or other grantmakers? Do you expect the program ultimately to become self-supporting through client fees or sales of products or services? Is there a local institution or government agency that will support your program once it has demonstrated its value? Show the funder that you have thought through the question of sustainability by listing other potential funding sources (government grants and private grantmakers) and income-producing activities (direct mail, fees for services, sale of products, etc.).

BACKGROUND ON YOUR ORGANIZATION

Even if your organization is large and relatively well known, you shouldn't assume that the grant decision makers reading your proposal will be familiar with your programs or accomplishments. In fact, they may not be aware of your existence. Therefore, you need to provide them with enough background information to build confidence in your group and its ability to carry out the program you are proposing. State the mission of your organization succinctly and provide a brief history of your activities, stressing relevant accomplishments and recognition as well as your present sources of support. You should include a list of your board of directors in the appendix to the proposal, and you may also want to call attention to well-known individuals on your board or staff who have played a major role in your organization. Remember, your purpose is to convince the prospective funder that you are capable of producing the proposed program results and are deserving of support.

Figure 58. Sample Budget Format for a Nonprofit Organization's Grant Project

Pleasant Valley Community Center
Knowledge Exchange Project Expense Budget Fiscal 2004

Costs:

Personnel Costs (1):	Annual Salary	Project %		
Salaries:				
Sally Smith, Executive Director	$75,000	10%	$	7,500
Ben Jones, Project Director/				
Instructor	40,000	50%		20,000
Ruth Givens, Instructor	40,000	25%		10,000
Two teaching assistants				18,000 (2)
			$	55,500
Payroll taxes and fringe benefits		25%		13,875
Total Personnel costs			$	69,375

Other than Personnel costs:		
Consultant—evaluation	$	5,000 (3)
Books and other reading materials		2,400 (4)
Rent		5,200 (5)
In-kind rent (donated)		5,200
Van		1,800 (6)
Nutritious Snacks		4,000 (7)
Supplies		300
Total Direct Costs	$	93,275
Administrative Costs/Overhead		18,655 (8)
Total Costs	$	111,930

Budget Narrative:

(1) Personnel costs include a portion of the salaries plus fringe benefits of an additional 25% of salaries for the 5 employees directly involved in the project as itemized above.

(2) Two teaching assistants at $15/hr. for 3 hours per day.

(3) A consultant will be hired to conduct pre-program and post-program testing of each participating student and an overall evaluation of the entire program at the end of the year.

(4) This represents the cost of books and other reading materials that will be given to each of the estimated 160 students participating in the program at an estimated cost of $15 per student.

(5) This represents the cost of renting space on the south side of town.

(6) This represents the program's share of a contract with a local transportation service.

(7) This represents the cost of nutritious snacks at 50¢ per student, per day.

(8) This represents a proportionate share of PVCC's organizational overhead, which is 20% of direct costs.

You can begin to do the groundwork for this section by keeping a "credibility file" that documents your progress and activities. Save letters of encouragement and praise, newspaper articles, and studies that support your work. Soliciting letters of endorsement from individuals and organizations that have benefited from your organization's activities is perfectly acceptable, and you may want to include some in the appendix.

Keep it short and to the point. The background statement should be no longer than a page.

CONCLUSION

Close your proposal with a paragraph or two that summarize the proposal's main points. Reiterate what your organization seeks to accomplish and why it is important. Since it is your final appeal, at this juncture, you are justified in employing language intended to be persuasive. But remember, a little emotion goes a long way; you do not want to overdo it.

APPENDIX

The appendix to your proposal should include all appropriate supporting documents for your request, including a copy of your agency's tax-exempt determination letter from the IRS, a list of your board of directors (with affiliations), your current operating budget and an audited financial statement, a list of recent and current funding sources (both cash and in-kind), and resumes of key staff members and consultants. Include letters of endorsement and news clippings only if essential to the review of the request. Remember, appendices may not be read that carefully by grant decision makers. If something is essential, include it in the body of the text. Not every proposal requires an appendix.

Cover Letter

A cover letter should accompany every proposal. The cover letter, which should be on your organization's letterhead and signed by your board chairman, president, or chief executive officer, highlights the features of your proposal most likely to be of interest to the grantmaker. It should point out how you selected the funder and why you believe that particular grantmaker will be interested in your proposal, thus establishing an immediate link between the two organizations. It should also include the amount of money and type of support you are seeking and refer to any prior conversations with the funder about the proposal/request.

Presenting Your Ideas to a Corporate Giver

There are a few tips that are particularly applicable to corporate funders. First, make an effort to understand the corporate infrastructure. At some companies, nonmonetary support and sponsorships may be handled by the marketing department, while employee voluntarism may be coordinated in the human resources department. Second, draw up a realistic budget and be prepared to divulge your sources of income. Corporate grant decision makers are likely to scrutinize the bottom line, and many will ask for evidence of your nonprofit's fiscal responsibility and of efficient management. And, third, and possibly most important, focus on company self-interest more than benevolence by considering what a business stands to gain by giving your organization a grant, now or in the future, directly or indirectly. For example, a corporate giver may want to develop a trained pool of potential employees, support research for future products, expand its markets, respond to related social issues, ward off criticism of company policies, and, of course, increase sales. Address these concerns clearly in the proposal. If your program is innovative, if it tackles an emerging issue of importance to the company or its customer base, or if it addresses a need that few other agencies are addressing, emphasize that fact, without undue self-promotion and in as noncontroversial a fashion as possible.

Writing Style and Format

Make your proposal as readable as possible by using active language and by being specific about what it is you hope to accomplish. Keep your proposal succinct and to the point.

It is a good idea to use the group approach to generate ideas, but let one writer draft the proposal. Writing by committee doesn't work when you need a concise and well-organized final product (see Figure 59). Ask colleagues who have been successful in securing foundation grants to review the proposal. You may also want to have someone unfamiliar with your project read the proposal to be sure its meaning is clear and that it avoids specialized jargon.

Prior to submission, review the application procedures issued by the grantmaker, if any. Have you fulfilled the requirements and addressed any concerns that might crop up? Do your proposal and cover letter establish strong connections between your project and their interests? Grantseekers often ask whether they should tailor proposals to individual funders. Unfortunately, the answer to this question is "yes and no." While it is generally not a good idea to develop a proposal or make major adjustments in your operations to conform to the interests of a particular funding source, you should be sure that your proposal reflects any connections that exist between you and the grantmaker you have targeted. Establishing links is what fundraising is all about.

What Happens Next?

Submitting your proposal is nowhere near the end of your involvement in the grantseeking process. About two weeks after you have submitted your proposal, follow up with a phone call or e-mail to make sure your materials were received, if this has not been acknowledged. If the grantmaker seems open to the idea, you may want to arrange a meeting with foundation representatives to discuss your program or project.

Grant review procedures vary widely, and the decision-making process can take anywhere from a few weeks to six months or longer. During the review process, the funder may ask for professional references or for additional information either directly from you or from outside consultants. This is a difficult time for the grantseeker. You need to be patient but persistent. Some foundations outline their review procedures on their Web site, in annual reports, or in application guidelines. If you are unclear about the process or timetable, don't hesitate to ask.

REJECTION IS NOT THE END

Most grantmakers receive many more worthwhile proposals than they can possibly fund in a given year. In its grant proposal guidelines, the M.J. Murdock Charitable Trust described the situation as follows:

"It is seldom that the Trust is faced with having to decline a poor proposal. Rather, it is a matter of having to decide among a great many worthy proposals. A denial, therefore, is hardly ever a rejection on the merits of a proposal, but it is simply the result of a highly competitive system and the limitation of financial resources."

Figure 59. Stylistic Hints for Proposal Writers

1. Use the active rather than the passive voice.

2. Avoid jargon; use acronyms only when absolutely necessary.

3. Stick to simple declarative sentences.

4. Keep your paragraphs short; employ headings and subheadings.

5. Address yourself to a human being: Picture the grant decision maker across the desk from you as you write. Always address your cover letter to an individual. Never begin with "Dear Sir" or "To Whom It May Concern."

6. Write with the needs of the people you hope to help in mind, making sure to demonstrate how your program will be of benefit to them.

7. Unless you have evidence to the contrary, assume that the reader is unfamiliar with your organization.

8. Do not resort to emotional appeals; base your arguments on documented facts.

Just because a grantmaker is unable to fund a particular proposal in a given grantmaking cycle does not mean the door is closed forever. An increasing number of funders are willing to discuss with you why your proposal was declined. You can ask whether the funder needed additional information. Would they be interested in considering the proposal at a future date? Could they suggest other sources of support you should pursue? Such follow-up discussions may be particularly helpful if the grantmaker has demonstrated a commitment to funding projects in your geographic area and subject field.

Rejection is not necessarily the end of the process. In fact, it may be worthwhile to cultivate the funder's interest for the future. Put grants decision makers on your mailing list so that they can become further acquainted with your organization. Remember, there's always next year.

WHEN YOU GET THE GRANT

Congratulations! You have received formal notification of your grant award and are ready to implement your program. Before you begin to hire staff or purchase supplies however, take a few moments to acknowledge the funder's support with a letter of thanks. You also need to pay careful attention to the wording of the grant letter to determine if the funder has specific forms, procedures, and deadlines for reporting the progress of your project under the grant. Clarifying your responsibilities as a grantee at the outset, particularly with respect to financial reporting, will prevent misunderstandings and serious problems at a later date. So be sure you understand all the qualifications attached to your grant before you start to spend the money.

While you must respect the wishes of grantmakers that request anonymity, you will find that many appreciate acknowledgment of their support in press releases, publications, and other products resulting from or concerning grant-related activities. A few of the larger, staffed corporate and other foundations offer assistance to grantees in developing press releases and other publicity materials. Again, if you are unsure about the grantmaker's expectations, be sure to ask.

Keep detailed records of all grant-related activities, including contacts with and payments from the funder. Prepare a schedule of deadlines for reports and follow-up phone calls. Communicate with funders selectively. Don't inundate them with mail or invitations, but don't forget to keep them "in the loop" regarding important events or developments relating to your project. This is the beginning of what you hope will be a long and fruitful relationship. Treat it with the care and attention it deserves. And good luck with all your foundation fundraising endeavors!

Appendix A

Additional Readings

World of Foundations

Avery, Caroline D. *The Guide to Successful Small Grants Programs: When a Little Goes a Long Way*. Washington, D.C.: Council on Foundations, 2003.

    A practical guidebook with case studies and foundation profiles covering traditional funding and also international grants and grants to individuals and for-profits.

Beggs, Sarah, Erica C. Johnson, and Jack Thomas, eds. *The New Foundation Guidebook: Building a Strong Foundation*. Bethesda, MD: Association of Small Foundations, 2003.

    Experts and representatives from various philanthropies provide advice on starting a foundation. Topics covered include vision and mission statements, board members, tax and legal issues, financial management, grantmaking, and grantmaker associations.

Edie, John A. *First Steps in Starting a Foundation*. 5th ed. Washington, D.C.:
Council on Foundations, 2001.
   Discusses in nontechnical language the various types of organizations
   that are generally labeled as foundations by the public and the
   requirements for establishing, and regulations governing, each type.

Esposito, Virginia, ed. *Splendid Legacy: The Guide to Creating Your Family Foundation*.
Washington, D.C.: National Center for Family Philanthropy, 2002.
   Composed of contributions by various specialists on topics ranging from
   start-up to grantmaking. It is illustrated throughout with examples and
   lessons from those involved with family philanthropies.

Freeman, David F. *The Handbook on Private Foundations*. Revised ed. New York, NY:
The Foundation Center, 1991.
   Provides practical information on most aspects of foundations, including
   history, reasons for creating a foundation, the grantmaking process,
   governance and administration, tax regulations and legal issues, and
   management of assets.

Foundations Today Series. New York, NY: The Foundation Center, annual.
   Provides comprehensive statistical analysis of foundation growth and
   giving trends.

Indiana University Center on Philanthropy and Brown, Melissa S., ed. *Giving USA*.
New York, NY: AAFRC Trust for Philanthropy, annual.
   Statistical analysis of charitable contributions by corporations,
   foundations, individuals, and through bequests. Also provides data about
   charitable recipients.

Kibbe, Barbara D., Fred Setterberg, and Colburn S. Wilbur. *Grantmaking Basics:
A Field Guide for Funders*. Washington, D.C.: Council on Foundations, 1999.
   Written for staff from any type of foundation, the authors cover the
   typical work and workday of a grantmaker, how to review grant
   proposals, how to say no, how to assess nonprofit budgets,
   communications with the board and others, and how to develop
   professionally. Worksheets and sample forms are provided.

McIlnay, Dennis P. *How Foundations Work.* San Francisco, CA: Jossey-Bass, 1998.
  Postulates that there are six identities of foundations: judges, editors,
  citizens, activists, entrepreneurs, and partners. Understanding these roles
  provides a new way to comprehend foundations' complex and sometimes
  contradictory nature.

Weitzman, Murray S., Nadine T. Jalandoni, Linda M. Lampkin, and Thomas H.
Pollak. *The New Nonprofit Almanac and Desk Reference: The Essential Facts and Figures
for Managers, Researchers, and Volunteers.* 6th ed. Washington, D.C.: Independent
Sector. 2002.
  Sixth in a series of statistical profiles of the size and scope of the U.S.
  nonprofit sector. Provides an overview of the independent sector's place
  in the national economy, trends in private sources of support for
  nonprofit organizations, employment trends, an overview of the financial
  condition of nonprofit organizations, and a national summary of
  organizations in the sector. Data covered is up to 1998.

Internet resources:

Association of Small Foundations (http://www.smallfoundations.org)
  This Web site offers program information, a calendar of events, links
  to philanthropy organizations, a listing of members by state, links to
  members' sites, an online version of the association's newsletter, and
  more.

AAFRC Trust for Philanthropy (http://www.aafrc.org)
  Contains information about philanthropy, including charts on
  distribution of funds to private nonprofit organizations.

Council on Foundations (http://www.cof.org)
  This national nonprofit membership organization for grantmakers offers
  information useful for grantseekers as well and is organized into broad
  subject categories.

Forum of Regional Associations of Grantmakers (http://www.givingforum.org)
  The Forum of Regional Associations of Grantmakers (RAGs) is a
  membership association of the nation's largest RAGs across the country.

The forum's Web site includes the Regional Association Locator, which lists contact information for each individual RAG in the United States.

Foundation Center's Grantmaker Information on the Internet (http://www.fdncenter.org/funders)
Information about private, community, and corporate foundations, corporate giving programs, and grantmaking public charities. Links to thousands of grantmaker Web sites.

Foundation Center's Funding Trends and Analysis (http://www.fdncenter.org/research/trends_analysis/index.html)
Excerpts from recent Foundation Center research reports on foundation giving trends.

National Center for Family Philanthropy (http://www.ncfp.org)
The center's Web site includes a set of links to family foundations' Web sites, links to resources on foundations and nonprofit organizations, and NCFP publications that can be ordered online.

Corporate Foundations and Corporate Giving

Corporate Affiliations: Who Owns Whom. New Providence, NJ: LexisNexis Group, annual.
Eight volumes cover the affiliations of U.S. public companies, U.S. private companies, and international public and private companies. Includes two-volume master index to all volumes.

Corporate Contributions. New York, NY: Conference Board, annual.
This survey of major U.S. corporations provides a detailed overview, complete with charts and tables on their contributions.

Corporate Giving Directory. Farmington Hills, MI: The Taft Group, annual.
Contains profiles of more than 1,000 corporate giving programs making contributions of at least $200,000 annually.

Dun and Bradstreet. *D&B Reference Book of Corporate Managements: America's Corporate Leaders.* New York, NY: Dun & Bradstreet, annual.

Provides information on the officers and directors of approximately 12,000 companies with the highest revenues in the United States. Entries are indexed by state, by industry classification, and by principal officers and directors. Principal officers and directors are indexed by college or university attended and military affiliation.

Giving by Industry: A Reference Guide to the New Corporate Philanthropy. Gaithersburg, MD: Aspen Publishers, 2002.

Details the primary corporate givers within 20 industry categories and provides short profiles of leading companies in each industry.

Matching Gift Details: Profiles of More Than 7,500 Companies with Matching Gift Programs. Washington, D.C.: Council for Advancement and Support of Education, annual.

Lists corporations that match employee gifts to nonprofit institutions.

National Directory of Corporate Giving. New York, NY: The Foundation Center, annual.

A directory of more than 3,600 corporations that make contributions to nonprofit organizations through corporate foundations or direct-giving programs.

National Directory of Corporate Public Affairs. Washington, D.C.: Columbia Books, annual.

Provides profiles of nearly 1,900 companies identified as having public affairs programs and lists approximately 13,000 corporate officers engaged in the informational, political, and philanthropic aspects of public affairs.

Standard and Poor's Register of Corporations, Directors and Executives. New York, NY: Standard and Poor's Corp., annual.

Contains a Corporation Directory, listing more than 55,000 corporations, and the Register of Directors and Executives, listing biographical information of more than 70,000 individuals serving as officers, directors, trustees, partners, etc.

Internet resources:

Charity Aid Foundation's CCInet (http://www.ccinet.org)
   Searchable database of hundreds of corporate Web sites focusing on
   giving and community relations.

Corporate Information (http://www.corporateinformation.com)
   One of the most comprehensive sites for links to corporate information
   on public and private companies in the U.S. and abroad.

Foundation Center's Corporate Grantmakers on the Internet
(http://www.fdncenter.org/funders/grantmaker/gws_corp/corp1.html)
   Links to Web sites of corporate grantmakers.

PR Newswire (http://www.prnewswire.com)
   News releases from corporations worldwide; frequently contains
   information on major corporate gifts.

Laws Regulating Foundations and Nonprofits

Bromberger, Allen R., Richard S. Hobish, and Barbara A. Schatz, eds. *Getting
Organized.* 5th ed. New York, NY: Lawyers Alliance for New York, 1999.
   Introductory manual for organizations that wish to incorporate and
   secure recognition of federal and state tax-exempt status.

Colvin, Gregory L. *Fiscal Sponsorship: Six Ways to Do It Right.* San Francisco, CA:
Study Center Press. 1993.
   Describes the six forms of fiscal sponsorship recognized by the Internal
   Revenue Service (IRS), with examples, charts and diagrams. Includes
   hypothetical scenarios, a sample sponsorship agreement, IRS Revenue
   Rulings, criticism and commentary.

Edie, John A. *Corporate Giving and the Law: Steering Clear of Trouble.* 3rd ed.
Washington, D.C.: Council on Foundations, 2002.
   Written primarily for corporate giving officers, this handbook identifies
   legal and regulatory problem areas. Provides a brief explanation of basic

rules and recommends additional sources for more in-depth examination. Includes chapters on company foundations versus corporate giving programs, rules for charitable deductions, state and federal requirements, self-dealing, domestic grants, international grants, and the use of legal counsel.

Edie, John A. *Expenditure Responsibility Step by Step.* 3rd ed. Washington, D.C.: Council on Foundations, 2002.
   Outlines and discusses the five steps to fulfilling the Internal Revenue Service requirements for expenditure responsibility, and explains when funders need to enact this particular procedure in order to avoid tax penalty.

Edie, John A. *Family Foundations and the Law: What You Need to Know.* 3rd ed. Washington, D.C.: Council on Foundations, 2002.
   Identifies legal issues of concern for members of family foundations and provides user-friendly explanations. Some of the topics explained include rules about charitable deductions, excise taxes, self-dealing, minimum payouts, international grantmaking, administrative issues, and the Form 990-PF.

Hopkins, Bruce R. *Starting and Managing a Nonprofit Organization: A Legal Guide.* 3rd ed. New York, NY: John Wiley & Sons, 2001.
   Readable exploration of the fundamental laws affecting the operation of nonprofit organizations. Examines virtually all aspects of starting and operating a nonprofit group, including reporting revenue, tax exemption, the regulation of fundraising, compensating the nonprofit employee, lobbying, and successful techniques for using for-profit subsidiaries, partnerships, and planned giving.

Hopkins, Bruce R. and Jody Blazek. *The Legal Answer Book for Private Foundations.* Hoboken, NJ: John Wiley & Sons, 2002.
   Provides quick answers in FAQ format for officers, lawyers, and accountants of private foundations. The major topics covered include basic definitions, self-dealing, payout requirements, business holdings, investments, taxable expenditures, unrelated business activities, disclosure rules, and termination, among others.

Kirschten, Barbara L. *Nonprofit Corporation Forms Handbook.* Eagan, MN: West Group, annual.
>   Provides model corporate documents to facilitate the incorporation of nonprofit organizations in various jurisdictions, as well as guidance in applying to the IRS for recognition of exemption from federal income tax.

Mancuso, Anthony. *How to Form a Nonprofit Corporation.* 5th ed. Berkeley, CA: Nolo Press, 2002.
>   A soup-to-nuts guide to forming and operating a tax-exempt corporation under Section 501(c)(3) of the Internal Revenue Code.

Olenick, Arnold J. and Philip R. Olenick. *A Nonprofit Organization Operating Manual: Planning for Survival and Growth.* New York, NY: The Foundation Center, 1991.
>   Leads nonprofits through the maze of tax and legal codes and offers advice on accounting procedures.

Internet resources:

Independent Sector's Public Affairs Program (http://www.independentsector.org/programs/gr/govrelat.html)
>   This site is especially useful for keeping up with legislative and legal issues.

National Center on Philanthropy and the Law—Nonprofit Legal Bibliography Project (http://www.law.nyu.edu/ncpl/library/bibliography.html)
>   A bibliographic database containing citations to materials pertaining to nonprofit law.

Nonprofit Resource Center (http://www.not-for-profit.org)
>   This site's "Nonprofit Laws" area includes links to numerous federal and state regulatory and nonprofit incorporation law Web resources.

Nonprofit Management and Planning

Allison, Michael. *Strategic Planning for Nonprofit Organizations: A Practical Guide and Workbook*. 2nd ed. Hoboken, NJ: John Wiley & Sons, 2004.
　　Divides strategic planning into six steps and contains useful worksheets.

Bernstein, Philip. *Best Practices of Effective Nonprofit Organizations: A Practitioner's Guide*. New York, NY: The Foundation Center, 1997.
　　Identifies and explains the procedures which provide the foundation for social achievement in all nonprofit fields.

Blazek, Jody. *Financial Planning for Nonprofit Organizations*. New York, NY: John Wiley & Sons, 1996.
　　Provides a step-by-step approach to understanding the major areas of financial planning including general administration; the roles and responsibilities of staff, board members, and professional advisors; developing and implementing budgets; asset and resource management; and internal controls to prevent waste and fraud.

Connors, Tracy Daniel. *The Nonprofit Handbook: Management*. 3rd ed. New York, NY: John Wiley & Sons, 2001.
　　This handbook is a comprehensive reference guide to best practices and procedures for nonprofits and consists of contributions from many nonprofit specialists.

DiLima, Sara Nell and Lisa T. Johns, eds. *Nonprofit Organization Management: Forms, Checklists & Guidelines*. 2nd ed. Gaithersburg, MD: Aspen Publishers, 2001.
　　Sample forms, checklists, guidelines, policies, and procedures for various aspects of nonprofit management, including planning, fundraising, human resources, accounting and finance, board relations, and public relations.

La Piana, David. *The Nonprofit Mergers Workbook: The Leader's Guide to Considering, Negotiating, and Executing a Merger.* Saint Paul, MN: Amherst H. Wilder Foundation, 2000. viii, 228 p.

> The initial chapters explain the different forms of mergers available to nonprofits; following this are steps for an internal assessment and for the process of identifying a potential merger partner.

Oertel, Patty. *The Nonprofit Answer Book: An Executive Director's Guide to Frequently Asked Questions.* Los Angeles, CA: Center for Nonprofit Management, 1998.

> Written in FAQ format and in nontechnical language, answers many common questions about nonprofits.

Olenick, Arnold J. and Philip R. Olenick. *A Nonprofit Organization Operating Manual: Planning for Survival and Growth.* New York, NY: The Foundation Center, 1991.

> Addresses the essential financial and legal aspects of managing a nonprofit organization.

Salamon, Lester M., ed. *The State of Nonprofit America.* Washington, D.C.: Brookings Institution Press, 2002.

> Presents a portrait of the nonprofit sector, composed of essays written by specialists covering broad subject areas.

Sandler, Martin W. and Deborah A. Hudson. *Beyond the Bottom Line: How to Do More with Less in Nonprofit and Public Organizations.* New York, NY: Oxford University Press, 1998.

> The authors present the winning strategies of the best-managed nonprofit and government agencies: staying focused on their mission, using mission as a recruiting tool, a unifying force, and setting priorities; using change as an ally to revitalize the organization; creating a climate for innovation by taking risks, tolerating mistakes, and sharing power; careful planning and measuring performance in customer's terms.

Smith, Bucklin & Associates and Wilbur, Robert H., ed. *The Complete Guide to Nonprofit Management.* 2nd ed. New York, NY: John Wiley & Sons, 2000.

> Sections cover mission, governance, fundraising, marketing, educational programs, meetings, public relations, political support, financial

management, information systems, personnel, legal requirements, and selecting and using consultants.

Young, Dennis R., ed. *Effective Economic Decision-Making by Nonprofit Organizations.* New York, NY: Foundation Center, 2004. xvi, 228 p.
   Expert authors explore core operating decisions that face all organizations and provide solutions that are useful to nonprofits of any size. Chapters cover such key decisions as pricing of services, compensation of staff, outsourcing, fundraising expenditures, and investment and disbursement of funds.

Internet resources:

Alliance for Nonprofit Management (http://www.allianceonline.org)
   Members of the Alliance include management support organizations, individual professionals, and a range of national/regional, umbrella, research and academic, publishing, and philanthropic organizations that provide training and consulting to nonprofits.

BoardSource (http://www.boardsource.org)
   Useful information about recruiting and communicating with board members, resolving board conflicts, and developing board job descriptions.

Free Management Library (http://www.managementhelp.org)
   A no-frills collection of free management courses in topics such as board roles and responsibilities, communications skills, finance and taxes, program development, program evaluation, and consultants.

The Nonprofit FAQ (http://www.nonprofits.org/npofaq)
   An online resource of information about and advice for nonprofits, taken from discussions on e-mail lists and other sources.

Nonprofit Resource Center (http://www.not-for-profit.org)
   Designed for managers, board members, and volunteers, this is a one-stop directory for Internet resources of interest to nonprofit

organizations, covering such topics as fundraising, finance and accounting, and management.

The Fundraising Process

Brown, Larissa Golden and Martin John Brown. *Demystifying Grant Seeking: What You Really Need to Do to Get Grants.* San Francisco, CA: Jossey-Bass Publishers, 2001.
    Confronts some common ideas about the fundraising process and offers the building blocks of a systematic grants effort.

Burnett, Ken. *Relationship Fundraising: A Donor-Based Approach to the Business of Raising Money.* San Francisco, CA: Jossey-Bass Publishers, 2002.
    A guidebook that presents a donor-based approach to fundraising. Discusses prospect research, donor attitudes, marketing, donor relations, bequests, common mistakes, and new challenges.

Ciconte, Barbara L. and Jeanne G. Jacob. *Fundraising Basics: A Complete Guide.* 2nd ed. Gaithersburg, MD: Aspen Publishers, 2001.
    Drawing from numerous sources, this resource provides a thorough treatment of the fundraising effort from establishing a philanthropic environment to working with consultants.

Dove, Kent E. *Conducting a Successful Fundraising Program: A Comprehensive Guide and Resource.* San Francisco, CA: Jossey-Bass Publishers, 2001.
    Chapters cover many different types of fundraising, including annual campaigns, major gifts, planned giving, foundation and corporate grants. Additional chapters cover how to choose among the fundraising options, how to motivate volunteers, use of technology in the effort, and accountability.

Greenfield, James M., ed. *The Nonprofit Handbook: Fund Raising.* 3rd ed. New York, NY: John Wiley & Sons, 2001.
    This compilation provides contributions from numerous experts who share information on the entire scope of fundraising, including the "how to" of actual solicitation activities.

New, Anne L. *Raise More Money for Your Nonprofit Organization: A Guide to Evaluating and Improving Your Fundraising.* New York, NY: The Foundation Center, 1991.
   A workbook of questionnaires to help fundraising officials and nonprofit executives evaluate their organization's present state of fundraising and show them what directions to take to improve it.

New, Cheryl Carter and James Aaron Quick. *Grantseeker's Toolkit: A Comprehensive Guide to Finding Funding.* New York, NY: John Wiley & Sons, 1998.
   A grantseeking handbook to help readers achieve success in the grantseeking process. Begins with the design of a project to solve a problem, focuses on the research process for locating potential funders interested in the project, and finishes with the proposal writing process.

Robinson, Andy. *Grassroots Grants: An Activist's Guide to Grantseeking.* 2nd ed. San Francisco, CA: Jossey-Bass Publishers, 2004.
   Provides step-by-step guidance on obtaining funds for grassroots organizations and contains several sample proposals.

Rosso, Henry A. and Eugene R. Tempel, ed. *Hank Rosso's Achieving Excellence in Fund Raising.* 2nd ed. San Francisco, CA: Jossey-Bass Publishers, 2003.
   Provides comprehensive coverage of successful and ethical fundraising principles, concepts, and techniques.

Seltzer, Michael. *Securing Your Organization's Future: A Complete Guide to Fundraising Strategies.* Rev. ed. New York, NY: Foundation Center, 2001.
   Presents a step-by-step approach to creating and sustaining a network of funding sources.

Weinstein, Stanley. *The Complete Guide to Fundraising Management.* 2nd ed. New York, NY: John Wiley & Sons, 2002.
   A comprehensive treatment of fundraising principles and practices, including information about creating case statements, record keeping, prospect research, cultivating donors, major gifts, grants, direct mail, telemarketing, special events, planned giving, and capital campaigns.

Zukowski, Linda M. *Fistfuls of Dollars: Fact and Fantasy about Corporate Charitable Giving.* Redondo Beach, CA: EarthWrites Publishing, 1998.
Covers the basics of corporate giving solicitation as well as the elements of proposals and budgets. Also discusses how to respond to a funding decision.

Internet resources:

Association of Fundraising Professionals (http://www.afpnet.org)
This membership organization offers educational programs and support for career development.

Foundation Center's Orientation to Grantseeking (http://www.fdncenter.org/learn/orient/intro1.html)
A basic primer on the funding research process for both nonprofits and individuals seeking grants.

The Grantsmanship Center (http://www.tgci.com)
A clearinghouse of fundraising information providing training in grantsmanship and proposal writing for nonprofit organizations and government agencies.

Michigan State University Grants and Related Resources (http://www.lib.msu.edu/harris23/grants/grants.htm)
Jon Harrison of the University of Michigan Library System has created a useful site for grantseekers that is well organized and cleanly designed.

Fundraising—Special Topics

ANNUAL GIVING

Dove, Kent E., Jeffrey A. Lindauer, and Carolyn P. Madvig. *Conducting a Successful Annual Giving Program: A Comprehensive Guide and Resource*. San Francisco, CA: Jossey-Bass Publishers, 2001.

A comprehensive textbook covering the primary components and considerations of planning, conducting, and evaluating annual giving campaigns.

Graham, Christine. *Keep the Money Coming: A Step-by-Step Strategic Guide to Annual Fundraising*. Rev. ed. Sarasota, FL: Pineapple Press, 2001.

Basic information on planning an annual fund campaign, with sections on utilizing various fundraising techniques including direct mail, membership, and events.

Greenfield, James M. *Fundraising Fundamentals: A Guide to Annual Giving for Professionals and Volunteers*. New York, NY: John Wiley & Sons, 2002.

A companion volume to *Starting and Managing a Nonprofit Organization: A Legal Guide* (John Wiley & Sons, 2001) that explains various fundraising methods and describes how to manage a comprehensive annual giving program.

CAPITAL CAMPAIGNS AND ENDOWMENTS

Kihlstedt, Andrea and Catherine Schwartz. *Capital Campaigns: Strategies That Work*. 2nd ed. Gaithersburg, MD: Aspen Publishers, 2002.

Written for small to mid-sized nonprofit organizations that are considering a capital campaign. Covers the entire process from planning the campaign to finishing, evaluating, and reporting on the campaign.

Moerschbaecher, Lynda S. *Building an Endowment Right From the Start*. Chicago, IL: Precept Press, 2001.

This resource for fundraisers, executives, accountants, and board members, explains how to create an endowment for a nonprofit.

Differentiates between the different types of gifts that can be used to enhance an endowment.

Schumacher, Edward C. *Building Your Endowment*. San Francisco, CA: Jossey-Bass Publishers, 2003.
A guide written in workbook format that explains planning and implementing endowment fundraising programs. Topics covered include advisory committees, feasibility studies, staff support, budgeting, endowment types, cultivating donors, and stewardship.

Weinstein, Stanley. *Capital Campaigns from the Ground Up: How Nonprofits Can Have the Buildings of Their Dreams*. Hoboken, NJ: John Wiley & Sons, 2004.
Covers all the major elements of a fundraising campaign to construct or renovate buildings. Also devotes chapters to the special situations of churches and historic preservation projects.

DIRECT MAIL/TELEMARKETING

Lautman, Kay Partney. *Direct Marketing for Nonprofits: Essential Techniques for the New Era*. Gaithersburg, MD: Aspen Publishers, 2001.
A workbook that includes advice on planning, choosing list brokers, creating the appeal, testing, premiums, monthly and special donor programs, file maintenance, telemarketing, and future trends.

Lister, Gwyneth J. *Building Your Direct Mail Program*. San Francisco, CA: Jossey-Bass Publishers, 2001.
A workbook that demonstrates the major steps in direct mail campaigns beginning with development of the case statement, assembling the mailing, testing the outcome, and evaluating costs.

Warwick, Mal. *How to Write Successful Fundraising Letters*. San Francisco, CA: Jossey-Bass Publishers, 2001.
A practical handbook that covers the written content of all types of direct mail appeals and provides numerous examples and tips.

ONLINE FUNDRAISING

Schladweiler, Kief, ed. *The Foundation Center's Guide to Grantseeking on the Web.*
2003 ed. New York, NY: Foundation Center, 2003.
> A comprehensive guidebook on utilizing the Web to locate information
> on foundation, corporate, individual donor, and government funding.
> Also includes an extensive listing of nonprofit sites of interest.

Warwick, Mal, Ted Hart, and Nick Allen, eds. *Fundraising on the Internet: The
ePhilanthropyFoundation.org's Guide to Success Online.* 2nd ed. San Francisco, CA:
Jossey-Bass Publishers, 2002.
> The coverage of this compendium by various specialists includes how to
> recruit donors online, managing Web site content, use of charity portals,
> and electronic prospect research, among many other topics.

Internet resources:

e-Philanthropy (http://www.actknowledgeworks.net/ephil/index_html)
> The site allows you to access the report "e-Philanthropy v.2.001," which
> documents the phenomenon of interactive online services for
> philanthropy and voluntarism.

Internet Nonprofit Center (http://www.nonprofits.org/npofaq/misc/
990804olfr.html)
> An excellent listing of companies involved in "online fundraising" and "e-
> philanthropy."

PLANNED GIFTS

Dove, Kent E., Alan M. Spears, and Thomas W. Herbert. *Conducting a Successful
Major Gifts and Planned Giving Program: A Comprehensive Guide and Resource.* San
Francisco, CA: Jossey-Bass Publishers, 2002.
> Explains how to identify prospects for major gifts and how this level of
> philanthropy relates to planned giving.

Jordan, Ronald R. and Katelyn L. Quynn. *Planned Giving: Management, Marketing, and Law.* 3rd ed. Hoboken, NJ: John Wiley & Sons, 2004.

Divided into ten parts: getting started; managing a planned giving program; managing donors and prospects; marketing; types of planned gifts; assets; related disciplines; policies and procedures; specific types of institutions; and planned giving in context.

Internet resource:

National Committee on Planned Giving (http://www.ncpg.org)

A professional association for people whose work involves developing, marketing, and administering charitable planned gifts.

PROSPECT RESEARCH

Bergan, Helen. *Where the Money Is: Advancement Research for Nonprofit Organizations.* Arlington, VA: BioGuide Press, 2001.

A book of techniques for using the Internet to find information on people, companies, and foundations. Names and describes hundreds of Web sites that are useful for fundraisers and advancement personnel.

Hogan, Cecilia. *Prospect Research: A Primer for Growing Nonprofits.* Sudbury, MA: Jones and Bartlett Publishers, 2004.

Explains the terminology, tools, and procedures for prospect research of individuals, corporations, foundations, and government agencies.

Solla, Laura A. *The Guide to Prospect Research & Prospect Management.* 2003–2004 ed. Freeport, PA: Laura A. Solla, 2003.

Defines prospect research and explains how it fits in with an overall fundraising plan.

Internet resources:

Association of Professional Researchers for Advancement (http://www.aprahome.org)
  A professional association for prospect researchers. Its Web site contains links to private and government resources.

Internet Prospector (http://www.internet-prospector.org)
  This nonprofit service to the prospect research community is produced by volunteers nationwide who "mine" the Internet for prospect research nuggets for nonprofit fundraisers.

SPECIAL EVENTS

Armstrong, James S. *Planning Special Events.* San Francisco, CA: Jossey-Bass Publishers, 2001.
  Practical guide for conducting special events and incorporating them into a fundraising program. Explains how to determine the needs of the organization, select the type of event, choose the best location, create a budget, market the event, take advantage of follow-up activities, and measure and analyze the results of the project.

Wendroff, Alan L. *Special Events: Proven Strategies for Nonprofit Fund Raising.* 2nd ed. Hoboken, NJ: John Wiley & Sons, 2004.
  Provides a strategy for conducting special events using the Master Event Timetable as a guide.

Other Sources of Nonprofit Support

GOVERNMENT FUNDING

Dumouchel, J. Robert. *Government Assistance Almanac.* Detroit, MI: Omnigraphics, Inc., annual.
  Outlines the more than 1,500 federal domestic programs currently available. Provides information about the type(s) of assistance offered and complete contact details.

Garvin, Peggy, ed. *Government Information on the Internet*. Lanham, MD: Bernan Press, annual.
 Covers nearly 5,000 government (federal, state, and local) Internet resources. Also includes some primary sites in other countries.

Internet resources:

FirstGov for Nonprofits (http://www.firstgov.gov/Business/Nonprofit.shtml)
 A starting point for information about services provided to nonprofits by federal agencies.

Grants.gov (http://www.grants.gov)
 The federal government's portal for grant opportunities. The site can be searched by subject and in many instances applications can be filled out and submitted online.

National Assembly of State Arts Agencies (http://www.nasaa-arts.org)
 Sponsored by the National Endowment for the Arts, this site is a clearinghouse of information for arts organizations on the Web.

MEMBERSHIPS

Ellis, Susan J. *The Volunteer Recruitment and Membership Development Book*. 3rd ed. Philadelphia, PA: Energize, 2002.
 Provides one chapter about building memberships based on principles of successful volunteer recruitment.

Ethier, Donald and David Karlson. *Association Membership Basics: A Workbook for Membership Directors and Members*. Menlo Park, CA: Crisp Publications Inc., 1997.
 Provides "how to" information on recruiting members, the membership cycle, establishing dues, special handling for new members, forecasting revenue, building value-added services, and other challenges for membership directors.

Robinson, Ellis M. M. *The Nonprofit Membership Toolkit.* San Francisco, CA: Jossey-Bass Publishers, 2003.

> This publication is directed primarily at the smaller nonprofit and is a comprehensive workbook and guide to establishing or enhancing the membership base. Includes numerous worksheets, sample documents, calendars, and other practical items for the development office.

NONPROFIT ENTREPRENEURSHIP

Dees, J. Gregory, Jed Emerson, and Peter Economy. *Enterprising Nonprofits: A Toolkit for Social Entrepreneurs.* New York, NY: John Wiley & Sons, 2001.

> Offers a starting point for understanding and applying the basic concepts of social entrepreneurship.

Larson, Rolfe. *Venture Forth! The Essential Guide to Starting a Moneymaking Business in Your Nonprofit Organization.* Saint Paul, MN: Amherst H. Wilder Foundation, 2002.

> A guide for developing nonprofit business ventures that align with an organization's mission and financial goals.

Robinson, Andy. *Selling Social Change (Without Selling Out): Earned Income Strategies for Nonprofits.* San Francisco, CA: Jossey-Bass Publishers, 2002.

> Discusses the growing importance of social entrepreneurship in the nonprofit sector and identifies specific steps to help an organization generate more money from its programs.

Proposal Development

Anderson, Cynthia. *Write Grants, Get Money.* Worthington, OH: Linworth Publishing, 2001.

> A proposal writing guidebook for school media specialists and other K-12 librarians to improve library programs and facilities.

Carlson, Mim. *Winning Grants Step by Step: The Complete Workbook for Planning, Developing and Writing Successful Proposals.* 2nd ed. San Francisco, CA: Jossey-Bass Publishers, 2002.
> Contains instructions and exercises designed to help with proposal planning and writing skills to meet the requirements of both government agencies and private funders.

Clarke, Cheryl A. *Storytelling for Grantseekers: The Guide to Creative Nonprofit Fundraising.* San Francisco, CA: Jossey-Bass Publishers, 2001.
> Puts forward the notion that proposals share much with great stories: characters, setting, and plot. Shows proposal writers how to craft documents that include elements of drama.

Collins, Sarah, ed. *The Foundation Center's Guide to Winning Proposals.* New York, NY: Foundation Center, 2003.
> Reprints 20 proposals and four letters of inquiry in their original form that succeeded in securing foundation support. Each proposal is accompanied by commentary by the funder who awarded the grant and proposal writing advice.

Geever, Jane C. *The Foundation Center's Guide to Proposal Writing.* 4th ed. New York, NY: The Foundation Center, 2004.
> Guides the grantwriter from pre-proposal planning to post-grant follow-up. Incorporates excerpts from actual grant proposals and interviews with foundation and corporate grantmakers about what they look for in a proposal.

Geever, Jane C., Liliana Castro Trujillo (trans.), and Marco A. Mojica (trans.) *Guía para escribir propuestas.* 3rd ed. New York, NY: Foundation Center, 2003.
> Spanish translation of the third edition of *The Foundation Center's Guide to Proposal Writing.* Includes new appendix of technical assistance providers that assist Hispanic nonprofits.

Hall, Mary Stewart. *Getting Funded: A Complete Guide to Proposal Writing*. 4th ed. Portland, OR: Continuing Education Publications, 2003.
> This guidebook to proposal writing is organized along a logical pattern of planning, beginning with a discussion of ideas for projects and ending with considerations about submissions, negotiation, and project renewal.

Karsh, Ellen and Arlen Sue Fox. *The Only Grant-Writing Book You'll Ever Need*. New York, NY: Carroll & Graf, 2003.
> Organized into a series of lessons, this book provides guidance to both nonprofits and individuals who are preparing proposals for public and private funders.

Knowles, Cynthia. *The First-Time Grantwriter's Guide to Success*. Thousand Oaks, CA: Corwin Press Inc., 2002.
> A toolkit for applying for funding from government and private sources. Covers the elements of the proposal package, writing style, budget development, and other aspects of completing the application.

Miner, Lynn E. and Jeremy T. Miner. *Proposal Planning and Writing*. 3rd ed. Westport, CT: Greenwood Press, 2003.
> Covers the proposal development process focusing primarily on protocols for federal government grants, but also covering the standard elements of proposals to private foundations and corporate funding sources.

Quick, James Aaron and Cheryl Carter New. *Grant Seeker's Budget Toolkit*. New York, NY: John Wiley & Sons, 2001.
> Explains the calculation of direct costs with chapters specifically describing personnel and travel costs.

Internet resources:

The Foundation Center's Proposal Writing Short Course (http://www.fdncenter.org/learn/shortcourse/prop1.html)
> Basic information about proposal writing, excerpted from *The Foundation Center's Guide to Proposal Writing*.

The Foundation Center's FAQs on Proposal Writing (http://www.fdncenter.org/learn/faqs/section_3d.html)
> Covers proposal writing, letters of inquiry, and information on examples of "already-written" proposals and proposal templates.

Grantproposal.com (http://www.grantproposal.com)
> Provides free resources for both advanced grantwriting consultants and inexperienced nonprofit staff.

Specialized Funding Directories

Annual Register of Grant Support: A Directory of Funding Sources. Medford, NJ: Information Today, Inc., annual.

Baynes, Louise, ed. *The Grants Register.* New York, NY: Palgrave Publishers Ltd., annual.

The Catholic Funding Guide: A Directory of Resources for Catholic Activities. 3rd ed. Washington, D.C.: Foundations and Donors Interested in Catholic Activities, Inc., 2003.

Eckstein, Richard M., ed. *Directory of Building and Equipment Grants.* 6th ed. Loxahatchee, FL: Research Grant Guides, 2001.

Eckstein, Richard M., ed. *Directory of Grants for Organizations Serving People with Disabilities.* 11th ed. Loxahatchee, FL: Research Grant Guides, 2000.

Eckstein, Richard M., ed. *Directory of Operating Grants.* 7th ed. Loxahatchee, FL: Research Grant Guides, 2003.

Environmental Grantmaking Foundations. 10th ed. Rochester, NY: Resources for Global Sustainability, Inc., 2003.

Ferguson, Jacqueline. *Grants for Schools: How to Find and Win Funds for K–12 Programs.* 4th ed. Alexandria, VA: Capitol Publications, 2000.

Ferguson, Jacqueline. *Grants for Special Education and Rehabilitation: How to Find and Win Funds for Research, Training and Services.* 4th ed. Alexandria, VA: Capitol Publications, 2000.

Foundation Grants to Individuals. New York, NY: The Foundation Center, biennial.

Funders of Lesbian, Gay, Bisexual and Transgender Programs: A Directory for Grantseekers. 5th ed. New York, NY: Funders for Lesbian and Gay Issues, 2002.

Funding Sources for Community and Economic Development: A Guide to Current Sources for Local Programs and Projects. 9th ed. Phoenix, AZ: Oryx Press, 2003.

Funding Sources for K-12 Schools and Adult Basic Education. 2nd ed. Phoenix, AZ: Oryx Press, 2001.

Guide to Funding for International and Foreign Programs. 7th ed. New York, NY: The Foundation Center, 2002.

Kerber, Beth-Ann. *The Health Funds Grants Resources Yearbook.* 10th ed. Manasquan, NJ: Health Resources Publishing, 2004.

Morris, James McGrath and Laura Adler. *Grant Seekers Guide: Foundations that Support Social & Economic Justice.* 6th ed. Wakefield, RI: Moyer Bell, 2003.

National Guide to Funding for Libraries and Information Services. 7th ed. New York, NY: The Foundation Center, 2003.

National Guide to Funding for the Environment and Animal Welfare. 7th ed. New York, NY: The Foundation Center, 2004.

National Guide to Funding in AIDS. 3rd ed. New York, NY: The Foundation Center, 2003.

National Guide to Funding in Arts and Culture. 8th ed. New York, NY: The Foundation Center, 2004.

National Guide to Funding in Health. 8th ed. New York, NY: The Foundation Center, 2003.

National Guide to Funding in Religion. 7th ed. New York, NY: The Foundation Center, 2003.

Paul, Eileen (ed.) *Religious Funding Resource Guide.* 16th ed. Washington, D.C.: ResourceWomen. 2000.

Webster, Valerie J. (ed.) *Awards, Honors, and Prizes.* Farmington Hills, MI: Gale Group, annual.

Periodicals on Foundations and Fundraising—A Selected Listing

Advancing Philanthropy. Association of Fundraising Professionals, 1101 King Street, Suite 700, Alexandria, VA 22314. Quarterly. (http://www.afpnet.org)
    Covers trends and issues impacting philanthropy and fundraising, new ideas and success stories, interviews with nonprofit leaders, and book reviews.

Chronicle of Philanthropy. 1255 23rd Street, NW, Washington, D.C. 20037. Biweekly. (http://www.philanthropy.com)
    Reports on issues and trends in the nonprofit sector, covering corporate and individual giving, foundation profiles, updates on fundraising campaigns, taxation, regulation, and management.

Corporate Philanthropy Report. Aspen Publishers, Inc., 7201 McKinney Circle, Frederick, MD 21704. Monthly. (http://www.aspenpublishers.com)
    Articles on issues and trends, reviews of current giving by companies and industry, and news items.

CURRENTS. Council for the Advancement and Support of Education, 1307 New York Avenue, Suite 1000, Washington, D.C. 20005-1973. Monthly. (http://www.case.org/CURRENTS)
    Articles on management, fundraising, and development for educational institutions. Book reviews and conference listings are also included.

Foundation News & Commentary. Council on Foundations, 1828 L Street, N.W. Washington, D.C. 20036. Bimonthly. (http://www.foundationnews.org)
   Articles on grantmaking activities, foundation leaders and people in the news, and trends in the field.

Grantsmanship Center Magazine. The Grantsmanship Center, P.O. Box 17220, Los Angeles, CA 90017. Quarterly. (http://www.tgci.com/magazine/archives.asp)
   Articles, summaries of publications, and listings of Grantsmanship Center training programs and seminars.

Grassroots Fundraising Journal. Grassroots Fundraising, 3781 Broadway, Oakland, CA 94611. Bimonthly. (http://www.grassrootsfundraising.org)
   Contains articles about basic fundraising techniques, alternative sources of funding, book reviews, and bibliographies, all designed especially for the smaller nonprofit.

New Directions for Philanthropic Fundraising. Jossey-Bass / John Wiley. 111 River Street, Hoboken, NJ 07030-5774. Quarterly. (http://www.josseybass.com)
   Quarterly journal addressing how the concepts of philanthropy pertain to fundraising practice.

The Nonprofit Quarterly. Third Sector New England, 18 Tremont Street, Suite 700, Boston, MA 02108. Quarterly. (http://www.nonprofitquarterly.org)
   Each issue focuses on a theme of critical importance to the nonprofit sector.

NonProfit Times. 120 Littleton Rd., Suite 120, Parsippany, NY 07054-1803. Monthly. (http://www.nptimes.com)
   News articles focusing on trends, legislation, fundraising, and management of nonprofits.

Stanford Social Innovation Review. 518 Memorial Way, Stanford University, Stanford, CA 94305-5015. Quarterly. (http://www.ssireview.com)
   Articles about nonprofit management, philanthropy, and corporate citizenship.

ONLINE JOURNALS:

Charity Channel (http://www.charitychannel.com)
Features reviews of nonprofit periodicals, books, and software written by a volunteer community of nonprofit sector professionals; free discussion forums with thousands of participants; and a searchable career database.

Internet Prospector (http://www.internet-prospector.org)
A newsletter focusing on information for prospect researchers.

Philanthropy Journal Online (http://www.philanthropyjournal.org)
Up-to-date news for the nonprofit sector. Includes job listings.

Philanthropy News Digest (http://www.fdncenter.org/pnd)
The Foundation Center's summary of news about philanthropy taken from the popular print and online press.

Appendix B

State Charities Registration Offices

ALABAMA

Rhonda Barber
Office of the Attorney General
11 South Union Street, 3rd Floor
Montgomery, AL 36130
(334) 242-7335
e-mail: rbarber@ago.state.al.us
http://www.ago.state.al.us/
   consumer_charities.cfm

ALASKA

Shelly J. McCormick, Law Office Assistant
State of Alaska
Fair Business Practices Section
Department of Law
Attorney General's Office
1031 West 4th Avenue, Suite 200
Anchorage, AK 99501
(907) 269-5100
e-mail: Shelly_mcCormick@law.state.ak.us
http://www.law.state.ak.us/department/
   civil/consumer/
   cp_charities.html#c_reqs

ARIZONA

Kerrie Pesserillo
Office of the Secretary of State
Attn.: Charities
1700 West Washington Street, 7th Floor
Phoenix, AZ 85007
(602) 542-6187
e-mail: charities@sos.state.az.us
http://www.sosaz.com/business_services/
    Charities.htm

ARKANSAS

Marie Peters
Office of the Attorney General
Consumer Protection Division
323 Center Street, Suite 200
Little Rock, AR 72201-2610
(501) 682-6150
e-mail: marie.peters@ag.state.ar.us
http://www.ag.state.ar.us/consumer/
    charity.htm

CALIFORNIA

Gena Ensey
Registration Unit
Registry of Charitable Trusts
P.O. Box 903447
Sacramento, CA 94203-4470
(916) 323-0785
e-mail: gena.ensey@doj.ca.gov
http://caag.state.ca.us/charities/forms.htm

COLORADO

Russell K. Subiono, Charities Program
    Assistant
Charitable Solicitations Section
Colorado Secretary of State
1560 Broadway, Suite 200
Denver, CO 80202
(303) 894-2200 ext. 6408
Fax: (303) 869-4871
e-mail: Russell.Subiono@sos.state.co.us
http://www.sos.state.co.us

CONNECTICUT

Public Charities Unit
c/o Office of the Attorney General
55 Elm Street
P.O. Box 120
Hartford, CT 06141-0120
(860) 808-5030
Fax: (860) 808-5347
http://www.cslib.org/attygenl/mainlinks/
    tabindex8.htm

DELAWARE

*No registration required for nonprofits
    in Delaware.*
Civil Division - Charities Group
Office of the Attorney General
Carvel State Building
820 North French Street
Wilmington, DE 19801
(302) 577-8400
http://www.state.de.us/attgen

DISTRICT OF COLUMBIA

Corporations Division
Department of Consumer and Regulatory
    Affairs
941 North Capitol Street NE
Washington, D.C. 20002
(202) 442-4432
e-mail: patricia.grays@dc.gov
http://www.dcra.dc.gov

FLORIDA

Emily Gaskin
Florida Department of Agriculture &
    Consumer Services Division
2005 Apalachee Parkway
Tallahassee, FL 32399-6500
(850) 410-3721
Fax: (850) 410-3804
e-mail: gaskin@doacs.state.fl.us
http://doacs.state.fl.us/onestop/cs/
    solicit.html

GEORGIA

Bre Parker
Office of the Secretary of State
Division of Securities and Business
    Regulations
2 Martin Luther King, Jr. Drive,
    SE, Suite 802, West Tower
Atlanta, GA 30334
(404) 656-4911
bparker@sos.state.ga.us
http://www.sos.state.ga.us

HAWAII

*No registration required for nonprofits
    in Hawaii.*
Department of Commerce & Consumer
    Affairs
Office of the Attorney General
830 Punchbowl Street, Room 219
Honolulu, HI 96813
(808) 586-2727
e-mail: ocp@dcca.hawaii.gov
http://www.hawaii.gov/dcca/ocp

IDAHO

*No registration required for nonprofits
    in Idaho.*
Office of the Attorney General
Consumer Protection Unit
P.O. Box 83720
Boise, ID 83720
(208) 334-2400
Fax: (208) 334-2530
http://www2.state.id.us/ag

ILLINOIS

Carolyn Beck
Office of the Attorney General
Charitable Trust Bureau
100 West Randolph Street, 3rd Floor
Chicago, IL 60601
(312) 814-2595
e-mail: cbeck@atg.state.il.us
http://www.ag.state.il.us/charities

INDIANA

No registration required for nonprofits in Indiana.
Roger Smith, Deputy Attorney General
Charitable Fundraising
Office of the Indiana Attorney General
Government Center South, 5th Floor
302 West Washington Street
Indianapolis, IN 46204
(317) 232-6201
Fax: (317) 232-7979
rsmith@atg.state.in.us
http://www.in.gov/attorneygeneral/
consumer/charityfundraisers.html

IOWA

No registration required for nonprofits in Iowa.
Department of Justice
Consumer Protection Division
Hoover Building, 2nd Floor
1300 East Walnut
Des Moines, IA 50319
(515) 281-5926
e-mail: webteam@ag.state.ia.us
http://www.state.ia.us/government/ag/
consumer.html

KANSAS

Mary Beth Acree
Office of the Secretary of State
Corporations Division
120 SW 10th Street, 1st Floor
Topeka, KS 66612
(785) 296-4565
e-mail: corp@kssos.org
http://www.kssos.org

KENTUCKY

Bonnie Foley
Office of the Attorney General
Consumer Protection Division
1024 Capital Center Dr., Suite 200
Frankfort, KY 40601
(502) 696-5389
http://www.law.state.ky.us/cp/charity.htm

LOUISIANA

Fonja Anderson
Office of the Attorney General
Consumer Protection Section
P.O. Box 94005
Baton Rouge, LA 70804-9005
(225) 326-6465
e-mail: andersons@ag.state.la.us
http://www.ag.state.la.us

MAINE

Marlene M. McFadden
Department of Professional & Financial
Regulation
Office of Licensing & Registration
35 State House Station
Augusta, ME 04333
(207) 624-8624
Fax: (207) 624-8637
e-mail: marlene.m.mcfadden@maine.gov
http://www.state.me.us/pfr/pfrhome.htm

MARYLAND

Kim Smith
Office of the Secretary of State
Charitable Organizations Division
State House
Annapolis, MD 21401
(410) 974-5534
e-mail: KSmith@sos.state.md.us
http://www.sos.state.md.us/sos/charity/
    html/cod.html

MASSACHUSETTS

Division of Public Charities
Office of the Attorney General
One Ashburton Place, Room 1413
Boston, MA 12108
(617) 727-2200 ext. 2101
http://www.ago.state.ma.us

MICHIGAN

Marion Y. Gorton
Charitable Trust Administrator
Charitable Trust Section
Protection Division of the Department of
    the Attorney General
P.O. Box 30214
Lansing, MI 48909
(517) 373-1152
Fax: (517) 241-7074
e-mail: Gorton@michigan.gov
http://www.michigan.gov/ag

MINNESOTA

Cindy Nelson
Charities Unit
NCL Tower, #1200
445 Minnesota Street
St. Paul, MN 55101-2131
(651) 296-6172
http://www.ag.state.mn.us

MISSISSIPPI

Kathy French
Office of the Secretary of State
Regulation & Enforcement Division
P.O. Box 136
Jackson, MS 39205
(601) 359-1350
e-mail: kfrench@sos.state.ms.us
http://www.sos.state.ms.us/busserv/
    charities/charities.html

MISSOURI

Kimberly Haddix, Registration Specialist
Investigator
Missouri Attorney General's Office
Consumer Protection Division
P.O. Box 899
Jefferson City, MO 65102-0899
(573) 751-1197
Fax: (573) 751-7948
e-mail: Kim.Haddix@ago.mo.gov
http://www.ago.state.mo.us

MONTANA

No registration required for nonprofits in Montana.
Consumer Protection Office
1219 8th Avenue
P.O. Box 200501
Helena, MT 59620-0501
(406) 444-4500
http://www.doj.state.mt.us/ago

NEBRASKA

No registration required for nonprofits in Nebraska.
Office of the Secretary of State
P.O. Box 94608
Lincoln, NE 68509-4608
(402) 471-2554
http://www.sos.state.ne.us/htm/
   Charitablesol.htm

NEVADA

Nevada Secretary of State
Securities Division
Corporations
206 North Carson Street
Carson City, NV 89701-4299
e-mail: sosmail@govmail.state.nv.us
http://www.secretaryofstate.biz

NEW HAMPSHIRE

Christine Gauntt
Department of Charitable Trusts
New Hampshire Department of Justice
33 Capitol Street
Concord, NH 03301
(603) 271-3591
e-mail: Christine.Gauntt@doj.nh.gov
http://www.doj.nh.gov/charitable

NEW JERSEY

New Jersey Department of Law and
   Public Safety
Division of Consumer Affairs
Office of Consumer Protection
Charitable Registration and Investigation
   Section
P.O. Box 45021
Newark, NJ 07101
(973) 504-6215
e-mail: Affairs@lps.state.nj.us
http://www.state.nj.us/lps/ca

NEW MEXICO

Special Consumer Projects
Attorney General of New Mexico
Leah Quesada, Assistant to the Registrar of
   Charitable Organizations or
Christine Turner, Registrar of Charitable
   Organizations
111 Lomas Boulevard, NW, Suite 300
Albuquerque, NM 87102
(505) 222-9090
e-mail: Charity.Registrar@ago.state.nm.us
http://www.ago.state.nm.us/divs/spcons/
   charities/spcons_charities.htm

NEW YORK

Department of Law
Charities Bureau-Registration Section
Office of the Attorney General
120 Broadway
New York, NY 10271
(212) 416-8401
http://www.oag.state.ny.us/charities/
   charities.html

NORTH CAROLINA

Lionel J. Randolph, CSL Supervisor
Department of the Secretary of State
Charitable Solicitation Licensing Section
P.O. Box 29622
Raleigh, NC 27626-0622
(919) 807-2211
e-mail: csl@sosnc.com
http://www.secretary.state.nc.us/csl

NORTH DAKOTA

Business Division
Secretary of State
600 East Boulevard Avenue, Department
 108
Bismarck, ND 58505-0500
(701) 328-3665
Fax: (701) 328-2992
e-mail: sosbir@state.nd.us
http://www.state.nd.us/sec

OHIO

Ohio Attorney General Jim Petro
Charitable Law Section
150 East Gay Street, 23rd Floor
Columbus, OH 43215-3130
(614) 466-3180
e-mail: MFarrin@ag.state.oh.us
http://www.ag.state.oh.us

OKLAHOMA

Charlene Dickerson
Secretary of State's Office
Business Filing Division/Charitable
 Organizations
2300 North Lincoln Boulevard, Suite 101
Oklahoma City, OK 73105-4897
(405) 521-3912
e-mail: charlene.dickerson@sos.state.ok.us
http://www.sos.state.ok.us

OREGON

Rhonda Powell
Charitable Activities Section
Oregon Department of Justice
1515 SW Fifth Avenue, Suite 410
Portland, OR 97201
(503) 229-5725
e-mail: rhonda.powell@state.or.us
http://www.doj.state.or.us/ChariGroup/
 Howtobe.htm

PENNSYLVANIA

Bureau of Charitable Organizations
207 North Office Building
Harrisburg, PA 17120
(717) 783-1720 or (800) 732-0999 (PA)
Fax: (717) 783-6014
e-mail: ST-CHARITY@state.pa.us
http://www.dos.state.pa.us/char

RHODE ISLAND

Alicia Milder
Department of Business Regulation
Securities Division
233 Richmond Street, Suite 232
Providence, RI 02903-4232
(401) 222-3048
http://www.dbr.state.ri.us

SOUTH CAROLINA

Carolyn Hatcher
Secretary of State's Office
Public Charity Division
P.O. Box 11350
Columbia, SC 29211
(803) 734-1796
e-mail: cjhatcher@infoave.net
http://www.scsos.com

SOUTH DAKOTA

No registration required for nonprofits in South Dakota, unless registered as a corporation.
Office of the Attorney General
Division of Consumer Protection
500 East Capitol
Pierre, SD 57501
(605) 773-4400 or (800) 300-1986 (SD)
e-mail: consumerhelp@state.ad.us
http://www.state.sd.us/attorney/office/
divisions/consumer
To register as a corporation:
Secretary of State
500 East Capitol
Pierre, SD 57501
http://www.state.sd.us/sos/
CORPADMN.HTM

TENNESSEE

Graham Sugg, Assistant Director
Division of Charitable Solicitations
312 Eighth Avenue North
8th Floor, William R. Snodgrass Tower
Nashville, TN 37243
(615) 741-2555
e-mail: graham.sugg@state.tn.us
http://www.state.tn.us/sos/charity.htm

TEXAS

Under Texas law, most charities or non-profit organizations are not required to register with the state. Exceptions exist, however, for organizations that solicit for law enforcement, public safety, or veterans' causes.
Secretary of State
Corporations Section
P.O. Box 13697
Austin, TX 78711-3697
(512) 463-5555
Fax: (512) 463-5709
e-mail: corpinfo@sos.state.tx.us
http://www.sos.state.tx.us/corp/
forms.shtml

UTAH

Shauna DeWolf
Division of Consumer Protection
Heber M. Wells Building
160 East 300 South, 2nd Floor
SM 146704
Salt Lake City, UT 84114
(801) 530-6601
Fax: (801) 530-6001
e-mail: commerce@utah.gov
http://commerce.utah.gov/dcp/registration

VERMONT

Division of Corporations and UCCs
Secretary of State
81 River Street
Drawer 09
Heritage Building
Montpelier, VT 05609-1101
(802) 828-2386
Fax: (802) 828-2853
e-mail: Webmaster@sec.state.vt.us
http://www.sec.state.vt.us

VIRGINIA

Department of Agriculture and Consumer
    Services
Office of Consumer Affairs
Charitable Solicitations
P.O. Box 526
Richmond, VA 23218
(804) 786-1343
http://www.vdacs.state.va.us

WASHINGTON

Office of the Secretary of State
Charities Program
P.O. Box 40234
801 Capitol Way South
Olympia, WA 98504-0234
(360) 753-0863, menu option 5
e-mail: charities@secstate.wa.gov
http://www.secstate.wa.gov/charities

WEST VIRGINIA

Jennifer Twyman
Charities Division
Office of the Secretary of State
State Capitol Building, 1, Suite 157-K
1900 Kanawha Boulevard, East
Charleston, WV 25305-0770
(304) 558-6000
Fax: (304) 558-5758
e-mail: jtwyman@wvsos.com
http://www.wvsos.com

WISCONSIN

Attn.: Mick Daly
Department of Regulation & Licensing
Bureau of Real Estate & Direct Licensing
P.O. Box 8935
Madison, WI 53708-8935
(608) 266-2112
e-mail: dorl@drl.state.wi.us
http://drl.wi.gov

WYOMING

*No registration required for nonprofits in
    Wyoming.*
Jeanne Sawyer
Corporations/UCC
Office of the Secretary of State
State Capitol Building
Cheyenne, WY 82002
(307) 777-5334
Fax: (307) 777-5339
e-mail: jsawyer@state.wy.us
http://soswy.state.wy.us

Appendix C

The Foundation Center's Grants Classification System and The National Taxonomy of Exempt Entities (NTEE)

The Foundation Center began to record and categorize grants in 1961. It established a computerized grants reports system in 1972. From 1979 to 1988, the Center relied on a "facet" classification system, employing a fixed vocabulary of four-letter codes that permitted categorization of each grant by subject, type of recipient, population group, type of support, and scope of grant activity.

In 1989, following explosive growth in the number of grants indexed annually, the Center introduced a new classification system with links to the National Taxonomy of Exempt Entities (NTEE), a comprehensive coding scheme developed by the National Center for Charitable Statistics. This scheme established a unified national standard for classifying nonprofit organizations while permitting a multidimensional structure for analyzing grants. The new system also provided a more concise and consistent hierarchical method with which to classify and index grants.

The Center's Grants Classification System uses two- or three-character alphanumeric codes to track institutional fields and entities, governance or auspices, population groups, geographic focus, and types of support awarded. The universe of institutional fields is organized into 26 "major field" areas (A to Z), following the ten basic divisions established by the NTEE:

I.	Arts, Culture, Humanities	A
II.	Education	B
III.	Environment/Animals	C, D
IV.	Health	E, F, G, H
V.	Human Services	I, J, K, L, M, N, O, P
VI.	International/Foreign Affairs	Q
VII.	Public Affairs/Society Benefit	R, S, T, U, V, W
VIII.	Religion	X
IX.	Mutual/Membership Benefit	Y
X.	Nonclassifiable Entities	Z

The first letter of each code denotes the field, such as "A" for Arts and "B" for Education. Within each alpha subject area, numbers 20 to 99 identify services, disciplines, or types of institutions unique to that field, organized in a hierarchical structure. These subcategories cover most activities in the nonprofit field. As a result, hundreds of specific terms can be researched with consistent results and grant dollars can be tallied to determine distribution patterns.

While based on NTEE, the Center's system added indexing elements not part of the original taxonomy, including the ability to track awards to government-sponsored organizations such as public schools, state universities, and municipal or federal agencies; a secondary set of codes to classify 42 specific types of grant support; and a third set of codes to track 41 different grant beneficiary populations. More evolutionary than revolutionary, the new system does introduce two new fields not previously tracked by the Foundation Center: Auspices (NTEE's governance codes are used) and Country of Activity (not part of NTEE). This last field is used to track the foreign locations of grant activities, for example, an award to the New York office of UNESCO for relief services in Ethiopia.

For a complete explanation of the Foundation Center's Grants Classification System, see *The Foundation Center's Grants Classification System Indexing Manual with Thesaurus*, available in all Center libraries and in many Cooperating Collections. The

Manual can also be purchased from the Center at its libraries, via telephone (1-800-424-9836), or on the Center's Web site (http://www.fdncenter.org).

For more information on "How the Foundation Center Indexes Grants," see http://www.fdncenter.org/research/grants_class/how.html. The complete list of all the NTEE terms and definitions can be found at the Center's Web site at http://www.fdncenter.org/research/grants_class. The complete lists of the population beneficiary codes, the type of support codes, and the recipient auspice codes can also be found at the Center's Web site.

Appendix D

Types of Support Definitions

A grantmaker may limit its giving to certain types of support. The types of support indexes in Foundation Center print and electronic publications are used to locate grants that are in the form of a specific type of funding. The following is a list of terms in these indexes with their definitions.

Please note: *The Foundation Directory Online* and *FC Search: The Foundation Center's Database on CD-ROM* have separate lists of types of support terms for their Grantmaker and Grants files. These are similar but not identical to each other. Unless otherwise noted, the following terms are used in both the Grantmaker and Grants files of these electronic databases.

Annual campaigns: Any organized effort by a nonprofit to secure gifts on an annual basis; also called annual appeals.

Awards/prizes/competitions: Grants for artists' awards, prizes, competitions, housing, living space, and workspace. Grants file only.

Building/renovation: Grants for constructing, renovating, remodeling, or rehabilitating property. Includes general or unspecified capital support awards.

Capital campaigns: Campaigns to raise funds for a variety of long-term purposes such as building construction or acquisition, endowments, land acquisition, etc.

Cause-related marketing: The practice of linking gifts to charity with marketing promotions. This may involve donating products that will then be auctioned or given away in a drawing with the proceeds benefiting a charity. The advertising campaign for the product will be combined with the promotion for the charity. In other cases it will be advertised that when a customer buys the product a certain amount of the proceeds will be donated to charity. Grantmaker file only.

Collections acquisition: Grants to libraries or museums to acquire permanent materials as part of a collection, usually books or art. Grants file only.

Collections management/preservation: Grants for maintenance, preservation, and conservation of materials. Grants file only.

Commissioning new works: Grants to support the creation of new artistic works. Grants file only.

Computer systems/equipment: Grants to purchase or develop automated systems. Grants file only.

Conferences/seminars: Includes workshops.

Consulting services: Professional staff support provided by the foundation to a nonprofit to consult on a project of mutual interest or to evaluate services (not a cash grant). Grantmaker file only.

Continuing support: Grants renewed on a regular basis.

Curriculum development: Awards to schools, colleges, universities, and educational support organizations to develop general or discipline-specific curricula.

Debt reduction: Grant to reduce the recipient organization's indebtedness; also referred to as deficit financing. Frequently refers to mortgage payments.

Donated equipment: Surplus furniture, office machines, paper, appliances, laboratory apparatus, or other items that may be given to charities, schools, or hospitals. Grantmaker file only.

Donated land: Land or developed property. Institutions of higher education often receive gifts of real estate; land has also been given to community groups for housing development or for parks or recreational facilities. Grantmaker file only.

Donated products: Companies giving away what they make or produce. Product donations can include periodic clothing donations to a shelter for the homeless or regular donations of pharmaceuticals to a health clinic resulting in a reliable supply. Grantmaker file only.

Electronic media/online services: Grants for support of projects on the Internet and World Wide Web, including online publications and databases, development of Web sites, electronic networking and messaging services, CD-ROM products, and interactive educational programs. Grants file only.

Emergency funds: One-time grants to cover immediate short-term funding needs of a recipient organization on an emergency basis.

Employee matching gifts: Usually made by corporate foundations to match gifts made by corporate employees. Grantmaker file only.

Employee volunteer services: Effort through which a company promotes involvement with nonprofits on the part of employees. Grantmaker file only.

Employee-related scholarships: Scholarship programs funded by a company-sponsored foundation usually for children of employees; programs are frequently administered by the National Merit Scholarship Corporation which is responsible for selection of scholars. Grantmaker file only.

Endowments: Bequests or gifts intended to be kept permanently and invested to provide income for continued support of an organization.

Equipment: Grants to purchase equipment, furnishings, or other materials.

Exchange programs: Usually refers to funds for educational exchange programs for foreign students. Grantmaker file only.

Exhibitions: Awards to institutions such as museums, libraries or historical societies specifically to mount an exhibit or to support the installation of a touring exhibit. Grants file only.

Faculty/staff development: Grants to institutions or organizations to train or further educate staff or faculty members. Grants file only.

Fellowships: Indicates funds awarded to educational institutions or organizations to support fellowship programs. A few foundations award fellowships directly to individuals.

Film/video/radio production: Grants to fund a specific film, video, or radio production. Grants file only.

General/operating support: Grants for the day-to-day operating costs of an existing program or organization or to further the general purpose or work of an organization; also called "unrestricted grants."

Grants to individuals: These awards are given directly to individuals, not through other nonprofit organizations. Many grantmakers have a specific limitation stating no grants to individuals. In order to make grants to individuals, a foundation must have a program that has received formal IRS approval. Grantmaker file only.

In-kind gifts: Contributions of equipment, supplies, or other property as distinct from monetary grant. Grantmaker file only.

Income development: Grants for fundraising, marketing, and to expand audience base.

Internship funds (institutional support): Funds awarded to an institution or organization to support an internship program, rather than a grant to an individual.

Land acquisition: Grants to purchase real estate property.

Loaned talent: Usually involves employee-loaned professionals and executive staff who are helping a non-profit in an area involving their particular skills. Grantmaker file only.

Management development: Grants for salaries, staff support, staff training, strategic and long-range planning, budgeting and accounting.

Matching/challenge support: Grants made to match funds provided by another donor and grants paid only if the donee is able to raise additional funds from another source.

Performance/productions: Grants to cover costs specifically associated with mounting performing arts productions. Grants file only.

Professorships: Grants to educational institutions to endow a professorship or chair.

Program development: Grants to support specific projects or programs as opposed to general purpose grants.

Program evaluation: Grants to evaluate a specific project or program; includes awards both to agencies to pay for evaluation costs and to research institutes and other program evaluators.

Program-related investments/loans: Loans or other investments (as distinguished from grants) to organizations to finance projects related to the foundation's stated charitable purpose and interests. Student loans are classified under "Student aid funds." Grantmaker file only.

Public relations services: May include printing and duplicating, audio-visual and graphic arts services, helping to plan special events such as festivals, piggyback advertising (advertisements that mention a company while also promoting a nonprofit), and public service advertising. Grantmaker file only.

Publication: Grants to fund reports or other publications issued by a nonprofit resulting from research or projects of interest to the funder.

Research: Funds to cover the costs of investigations and clinical trials, including demonstration and pilot projects. (Research grants for individuals are usually referred to as fellowships.)

Scholarship funds (institutional support): Grants to educational institutions or organizations to support a scholarship program, mainly for students at the undergraduate level; the donee institution then distributes the funds to individuals through their own programs.

Scholarships—to individuals: These are funds awarded to individuals through programs administered by the grantmaker. Grantmaker file only.

Seed money: Grants to start, establish, or initiate new projects or organizations; may cover salaries and other operating expenses of a new project; also called "start-up funds."

Sponsorships: Endorsements of charities by corporations or corporate contributions to charitable events. Grantmaker file only.

Student aid (institutional support): Assistance in the form of educational grants, loans, or scholarships. Grants file only.

Student loans—to individuals: These are loans distributed directly to individuals through programs administered by the grantmaker. Grantmaker file only.

Technical assistance: Operational or management assistance given to nonprofit organizations, including fundraising assistance, budgeting and financial planning, program planning, legal advice, marketing, and other aids to management.

Use of facilities: May include rent-free office space for temporary periods, dining and meeting facilities, telecommunications services, mailing services, transportation services, or computer services. Grantmaker file only.

Appendix E

Resources of the Foundation Center

The Foundation Center is a national service organization founded and supported by foundations to provide a single authoritative source of information on foundation and corporate giving. The Center's programs are designed to help grantseekers select those funders that may be most interested in their projects from the more than 75,000 active U.S. grantmakers. Among its primary activities toward this end are offering searchable databases online and on CD-ROM as well as publishing print directories covering foundation and corporate philanthropy; disseminating information on grantmaking, grantseeking, and related subjects through its site on the Internet; offering educational courses and workshops; and maintaining a nationwide network of library/learning centers and Cooperating Collections.

Databases and publications of the Foundation Center are the primary working tools of every serious grantseeker. They are also used by grantmakers, scholars, journalists, and legislators—in short, by anyone seeking any type of factual information on philanthropy. All private foundations and a significant number of corporate grantmakers actively engaged in grantmaking, regardless of size or geographic location, are included in one or more of the Center's databases or publications.

For those who wish to access information on grantmakers and their grants electronically, *The Foundation Directory Online Basic* provides information on 10,000 of the nation's largest foundations. *The Foundation Directory Online Plus* contains the top 10,000 foundations plus a searchable database of nearly 400,000 grants. *The Foundation Directory Online Premium* includes 20,000 foundations plus nearly 400,000 grants. *The Foundation Directory Online Platinum* includes more than 75,000 grantmakers plus nearly 400,000 grants.

The Center also issues *FC Search: The Foundation Center's Database on CD-ROM* containing the full universe of more than 75,000 grantmakers and more than 320,000 associated grants.

Foundation Center print publications are of three kinds: directories that describe specific funders, characterizing their program interests and providing fiscal and personnel data; grants indexes that list and classify by subject recent foundation and corporate awards; and guides, monographs, and bibliographies that introduce the reader to funding research, elements of proposal writing, and nonprofit management issues.

In addition, the Center's award-winning Web site features a wide array of free information about the philanthropic community.

The Foundation Center's electronic and print products may be ordered from the Foundation Center, 79 Fifth Avenue, New York, NY 10003-3076, or online at our Web site. For more information about any aspect of the Center's programs or for the name of the Center's library collection nearest you, call 1-800-424-9836, or visit us on the Web at www.fdncenter.org. Please visit our Web site for the most current information available on new products and services of the Foundation Center.

ONLINE DATABASES

THE FOUNDATION DIRECTORY ONLINE SUBSCRIPTION PLANS

The Foundation Directory Online Basic

Search for foundation funding prospects from among the nation's largest 10,000 foundations and search the index of over 64,000 names of trustees, officers, and donors. Perform searches using up to twelve search fields and print results that appear in the browser window.

Monthly subscriptions start at $19.95 per month
Annual subscriptions start at $195 per year

The Foundation Directory Online Plus

Plus service allows users to search the 10,000 largest foundations in the U.S. and the index of over 64,000 names of trustees, officers, and donors—plus nearly 400,000 grants awarded by major foundations.

Monthly subscriptions start at $29.95 per month
Annual subscriptions start at $295 per year

The Foundation Directory Online Premium

Research and identify more foundation funding sources online with *The Foundation Directory Online Premium*. In addition to featuring 20,000 of the nation's large and mid-sized foundations and an index of more than 111,000 names of trustees, officers, and donors—*Premium* service includes a searchable database of nearly 400,000 grants awarded by major U.S. foundations.

Monthly subscriptions start at $59.95 per month
Annual subscriptions start at $595 per year

The Foundation Directory Online Platinum

Search our entire universe of U.S. foundations, corporate giving programs, and grantmaking public charities—75,000+ funders in all—in our most comprehensive online subscription service. In addition to more funders, you'll get access to more in-depth data and an index of more than 340,000 names of trustees, officers, and donors. Only *The Foundation Directory Online Platinum* offers extensive program details for more than 1,500 leading foundations; detailed application guidelines for more than 7,200 foundations; and sponsoring company information for corporate givers. This service also includes a searchable file of nearly 400,000 grants awarded by the largest U.S. foundations.

Monthly subscriptions start at $149.95 per month
Annual subscriptions start at $995 per year

Foundation and grants data are updated every week for the above databases.
Monthly, annual, multi-user, and institution-wide access subscription options are available.
Please visit www.fconline.fdncenter.org to subscribe.

Foundation Grants to Individuals Online

Foundation Grants to Individuals Online features more than 6,000 foundation funding sources for individual grantseekers in education, research, arts and culture, or for special needs. Updated quarterly, users may choose from up to nine different search fields to discover prospective funders. Foundation records include current, authoritative data on the funder, including the name, address, and contact information; fields of interest; types of support; application information; and descriptions of funding opportunities for individual grantseekers.

One-month subscription: $9.95 Three-month subscription: $26.95 Annual subscription: $99.95

DIALOG

The Center's grantmaker and grants databases are also available online through The Dialog Corporation. For further information, contact The Dialog Corporation at 1-800-334-2564.

CD-ROMs

FC SEARCH: The Foundation Center's Database on CD-ROM, Version 8.0

The Foundation Center's comprehensive database of grantmakers and their associated grants can be accessed in this fully searchable CD-ROM format. *FC Search* contains more than 75,000 grantmaker records, including all known active foundations and corporate giving programs in the United States. It also includes more than 320,000 newly reported grants from the largest foundations and the names of more than 350,000 trustees, officers, and donors which can be quickly linked to their foundation affiliations. Users can also link from *FC Search* to the Web sites of 4,000+ grantmakers and 2,200+ corporations.

Grantseekers and other researchers may select multiple criteria and create customized prospect lists that can be printed or saved. Basic or Advanced search modes and special search options enable users to make searches as broad or as specific as required. Up to 21 different criteria may be selected:

- grantmaker name
- grantmaker type
- grantmaker city
- grantmaker state

- geographic focus
- fields of interest
- types of support
- total assets

- total giving
- trustees, officers, and donors
- establishment date
- corporate name
- corporate location
- recipient name
- recipient city

- recipient state
- recipient type
- subject
- grant amount
- year grant authorized
- text search field

FC Search is a sophisticated fundraising research tool, but it is also user-friendly. It has been developed with both the novice and experienced researcher in mind. Assistance is available through Online Help, a *User Manual* that accompanies *FC Search*, as well as through a free User Hotline.

FC Search, Version 8.0, April 2004 (prices include fall 2004 Update disk plus one User Manual).
Standalone (single user) version: $1,195
Local Area Network (2–8 users in one building) version: $1,895*
Additional copies of User Manual: $19.95
New editions of FC Search are released each spring.
*Larger local area network versions, site licenses, and wide area network versions are also
available. For more information, call the Electronic Product Support Line (Mon.–Fri., 9 am–5 pm
EST) 1-800-478-4661.

THE FOUNDATION DIRECTORY 1 & 2 ON CD-ROM, Version 4.0

We've combined the authoritative data found in our two print classics, *The Foundation Directory* and *The Foundation Directory Part 2*, to bring you 20,000 of the nation's largest and mid-sized foundations in this searchable CD-ROM. Search for funding prospects by choosing from 12 search fields:

- grantmaker name
- grantmaker state
- grantmaker city
- fields of interest
- types of support
- trustees, officers, and donors

- geographic focus
- grantmaker type
- total giving
- total assets
- establishment date
- text search

The CD-ROM includes links to close to 1,700 foundation Web sites, a list of sample grants in more than 10,500 foundation records, and a searchable index of more than 111,000 trustees, officers, and donors.

The Foundation Directory 1 & 2 on CD-ROM (includes March 2004 release and Fall 2004 Update disk) / Standalone (single-user) version: $495 / Local Area Network version (2-8 users in one building): $795

THE FOUNDATION GRANTS INDEX ON CD-ROM, Version 4.0

The same data found in our former print publication, *The Foundation Grants Index,* is available for the first time in a fast-speed CD-ROM format. Search our database of close to 125,000 recently awarded grants by the largest 1,000 funders to help you target foundations by the grants they have already awarded. Choose from twelve search fields:

- Recipient Name
- Recipient State
- Recipient City
- Recipient Type
- Grantmaker Name
- Grantmaker State
- Geographic Focus
- Subject
- Types of Support
- Grant Amount
- Year Authorized
- Text Search

The Foundation Grants Index on CD-ROM
December 2004 / Single User / ISBN 1-59542-009-6 /$175
Call 1-800-478-4661 for network versions.

GUIDE TO GREATER WASHINGTON D.C. GRANTMAKERS ON CD-ROM, Version 3.0

Compiled with the assistance of Washington Grantmakers, this CD-ROM covers more than 2,500 grantmakers located in the D.C. region or that have an interest in D.C.-area nonprofits. It also contains close to 3,000 selected grants and a searchable index of 8,000+ trustees, officers, and donors and their grantmaker affiliations.

Users can generate prospect lists using twelve search fields. Grantmaker portraits feature crucial information: address, phone number, contact name, financial data, giving limitations, and names of key officials. For the large foundations—those that give at least $50,000 in grants per year—the volume provides more data, including application procedures and giving interest statements. The CD-ROM connects to a special Web page with resources of value to D.C. grantseekers.

June 2004 / ISBN 1-931923-97-3 / $75

GUIDE TO OHIO GRANTMAKERS ON CD-ROM

Guide to Ohio Grantmakers on CD-ROM is produced in collaboration with the Ohio Grantmakers Forum and the Ohio Association of Nonprofit Organizations. This new CD-ROM features profiles of more than 3,400 foundations in Ohio, plus more than 400 funders outside the state that award grants in Ohio. This comprehensive searchable database provides current information on the foundations, corporate givers and public charities that make grants to Ohio-based nonprofits: contact information, financial data, names of key officials, and in many cases, application procedures, giving interest statements, and a list of recent grants.

November 2003 / ISBN 1-931923-64-7 / $125

SYSTEM CONFIGURATIONS FOR CD-ROM PRODUCTS

- Windows-based PC

- Microsoft Windows™ ME, Windows™ 98, Windows™ 95, Windows™ 2000, Windows™ NT, or Windows™ XP

- Pentium microprocessor 64MB memory

Note: *Internet access and Netscape's Navigator or Communicator or Microsoft's Internet Explorer browser required to access grantmaker Web sites and Foundation Center Web site.*

GENERAL RESEARCH DIRECTORIES

THE FOUNDATION DIRECTORY, 2004 Edition

The Foundation Directory has been widely known and respected in the field for more than 40 years. It includes the latest information on the 10,000 largest U.S. foundations based on total giving. The 2004 Edition includes more than 1,600 foundations that are new to this edition. *Directory* foundations hold more than $380 billion in assets and award over $27 billion in grants annually.

Each *Directory* entry contains information on application procedures, giving limitations, types of support awarded, the publications of each foundation, and foundation staff. In addition, each entry features such vital data as the grantmaker's giving interests, financial data, grant amounts, address, and telephone number. This edition includes more than 51,000 selected grants. The Foundation Center works closely with foundations to ensure the accuracy and timeliness of the information provided.

The *Directory* includes indexes by foundation name; subject areas of interest; names of donors, officers, and trustees; geographic location; international interests; types of support awarded; and grantmakers new to the volume. Also included are analyses of the foundation community by geography, asset and grant size, and the different foundation types.

Also available on CD-ROM and Online. / March 2004 / ISBN 1-931923-87-6 / $215
Published annually

THE FOUNDATION DIRECTORY PART 2, 2004 Edition

The Foundation Directory Part 2 brings you the same thorough coverage for the next largest set of 10,000 foundations. It includes *Directory*-level information on mid-sized foundations, an important group of grantmakers responsible for millions of dollars in funding annually. Essential data on foundations is included along with more than 45,000 recently awarded foundation grants, providing an excellent overview of the foundations' giving interests. Quick access to foundation entries is facilitated by seven indexes, including foundation name; subject areas of interest; names of donors, officers, and trustees; geographic location; international interests; types of support awarded; and grantmakers new to the volume.

March 2004 / ISBN 1-931923-88-4 / $185 Published annually

THE FOUNDATION DIRECTORY SUPPLEMENT

The Foundation Directory Supplement provides new information on *Foundation Directory* and *Foundation Directory Part 2* grantmakers six months after those volumes are published. The *Supplement* ensures that users of the *Directory* and *Directory Part 2* always have the latest addresses, contact names, policy statements, application guidelines, and financial data for the foundations they're approaching for funding.

September 2004 / ISBN 1-931923-89-2 / $125 Published annually

GUIDE TO U.S. FOUNDATIONS, THEIR TRUSTEES, OFFICERS, AND DONORS

This fundraising reference tool provides fundraisers with current, accurate information on more than 67,000 private and community foundations in the U.S. The three-volume set also includes a master list of the names of the people who establish, oversee, and manage those institutions so that fundraisers can discover the philanthropic connections of current donors, board members, volunteers, and prominent families in their geographic area. Each entry includes asset and giving amounts as well as geographic limitations, allowing fundraisers to quickly determine whether or not to pursue a particular grant source.

The *Guide to U.S. Foundations* is the only source of published data on thousands of local foundations. (It includes more than 46,000 grantmakers not covered in other print publications.) Each entry also tells you whether you can find more extensive information on the grantmaker in another Foundation Center reference work.

April 2004/ 1-931923-91-4 / $325 Published annually

THE FOUNDATION 1000

The Foundation 1000 provides access to extensive and accurate information on the 1,000 largest foundations in the country. *Foundation 1000* grantmakers hold over $290 billion in assets and awarded close to 250,000 grants worth nearly $17 billion to nonprofit organizations nationwide in the most current year of record.

The Foundation 1000 provides thorough analyses of the 1,000 largest foundations and their extensive grant programs, including all the data fundraisers need when applying for grants from these top-level grantmakers. Each multi-page profile features a full foundation portrait, a detailed breakdown of the foundation's grant programs, and extensive lists of recently awarded grants.

Five indexes target potential funders in a variety of ways: by subject field, type of support, geographic location, international giving, and the names of foundation officers, donors, and trustees.

October 2004 / ISBN 1-59542-007-X / $295 Published annually

NATIONAL DIRECTORY OF CORPORATE GIVING, 10th Edition

The *National Directory of Corporate Giving* offers authoritative information on more than 3,900 company-sponsored foundations and direct corporate giving programs.

It features detailed portraits of more than 2,500 company-sponsored foundations plus more than 1,400 direct corporate giving programs. Fundraisers will find essential information on these corporate grantmakers, including application information, key personnel, types of support generally awarded, giving limitations, financial data, and purpose and activities statements. Also included in the 10th Edition are more than 6,500 selected grants, providing the best indication of a grantmaker's funding priorities by identifying nonprofits it has already funded. The volume also provides data on the companies that sponsor foundations and direct-giving programs. Each entry gives the company's name and address, a listing of its types of business, its financial data (complete with Forbes and Fortune ratings), a listing of its subsidiaries, divisions, plants, and offices, and a charitable-giving statement.

The *National Directory of Corporate Giving* also features an extensive bibliography to guide you to further research on corporate funding. Seven essential indexes target funding prospects by geographic region; international giving; types of support; subject area; officers, donors, and trustees; types of business; and the names of the corporation, its foundation, and its direct-giving program.

August 2004/ ISBN 1-59542-004-5 / $195 Published annually

DIRECTORY OF MISSOURI GRANTMAKERS, 5th Edition

The *Directory of Missouri Grantmakers* provides a comprehensive guide to grantmakers in the state or that have an interest in Missouri nonprofits—more than 2,300 foundations, corporate giving programs, and public charities—from the largest grantmakers to local family foundations. The volume will facilitate your grantseeking with entries that list giving amounts, fields of interest, purpose statements, selected grants, and more. Indexes help you target the most appropriate funders by subject interest, types of support, and names of key personnel.

June 2003 / ISBN 1-931923-46-9 / $75 Published biennially

FOUNDATION GRANTS TO INDIVIDUALS, 13th Edition

The only publication devoted entirely to foundation grant opportunities for qualified individual applicants, the 13th Edition of this volume features more than 5,500 entries, all of which profile foundation grants to individuals. Entries include foundation addresses and telephone numbers, financial data, giving limitations, and application guidelines. This volume will save individual grantseekers countless hours of research. Indexes include:

- Geographic Focus
- Company Name
- Specific Schools

- Types of Support
- Subject
- Foundation Name

June 2003 / ISBN 1-931923-45-0 / $65 Published biennially

SUBJECT DIRECTORIES

The Foundation Center's National Guide to Funding series is designed to facilitate grantseeking within specific fields of nonprofit activity. Each of the directories described below identifies a set of grantmakers that have already stated or demonstrated an interest in a particular field. Entries provide access to foundation addresses, financial data, giving priorities, application procedures, contact names, and key officials. Many entries also feature recently awarded grants, the best indication of a grantmaker's funding priorities. A variety of indexes help fundraisers target potential grant sources by subject area, geographic preferences, types of support, and the names of donors, officers, and trustees.

Subject guides are published biennially.

GUIDE TO FUNDING FOR INTERNATIONAL AND FOREIGN PROGRAMS, 7th Edition

The *Guide to Funding for International and Foreign Programs* covers more than 1,500 grantmakers interested in funding projects with an international focus, both within the U.S. and abroad. Program areas covered include international relief, disaster assistance, human rights, civil liberties, community development, education, and more. The volume also includes descriptions of more than 9,500 recently awarded grants.

May 2004 / ISBN 1-931923-95-7 / $125

NATIONAL GUIDE TO FUNDING IN AIDS, 3rd Edition

This volume covers more than 560 foundations, corporate giving programs, and public charities that support AIDS- and HIV-related nonprofit organizations involved in direct relief, medical research, legal aid, preventative education, and other programs for persons with AIDS and AIDS-related diseases. More than 500 recently awarded grants show the types of projects funded by grantmakers.

June 2003/ ISBN 1-931923-44-2 / $115

NATIONAL GUIDE TO FUNDING IN ARTS AND CULTURE, 8th Edition

This volume covers more than 9,600 grantmakers with an interest in funding dance companies, museums, theaters, and other types of arts and culture projects and institutions. The volume also includes more than 19,700 descriptions of recently awarded grants.

May 2004 / ISBN 1-931923-94-9 / $155

NATIONAL GUIDE TO FUNDING FOR THE ENVIRONMENT AND ANIMAL WELFARE, 7th Edition

This guide covers over more than 3,500 grantmakers that fund nonprofits involved in international conservation, ecological research, waste reduction, animal welfare, and more. The volume includes descriptions of more than 7,200 recently awarded grants.

June 2004 / ISBN 1-931923-93-0 / $125

NATIONAL GUIDE TO FUNDING IN HEALTH, 8th Edition

The *National Guide to Funding in Health* contains essential facts on nearly 10,700 grantmakers interested in funding hospitals, universities, research institutes, community-based agencies, national health associations, and a broad range of other health-related programs and services. The volume also includes descriptions of more than 16,000 recently awarded grants.

May 2003 / ISBN 1-931923-42-6 / $155

NATIONAL GUIDE TO FUNDING FOR LIBRARIES AND INFORMATION SERVICES, 7th Edition

This volume provides data on more than 800 grantmakers that support a wide range of organizations and initiatives, from the smallest public libraries to major research institutions, academic/research libraries, art, law, and medical libraries, and other specialized information centers. The volume also includes descriptions of more than 600 recently awarded grants.

May 2003 / ISBN 1-931923-43-4 / $115

NATIONAL GUIDE TO FUNDING IN RELIGION, 7th Edition

With this volume, fundraisers who work for nonprofits affiliated with religious organizations have access to information on nearly 8,400 grantmakers that have a demonstrated or stated interest in funding churches, missionary societies, religious welfare and education programs, and many other types of projects and institutions. The volume also includes descriptions of more than 10,000 recently awarded grants.

May 2003/ ISBN 1-931923-41-8 / $155

GRANT DIRECTORIES

GRANT GUIDES

Designed for fundraisers who work within defined fields of nonprofit development, this series of guides lists actual foundation grants of $10,000 or more in 12 key areas of grantmaking.

Each title in the series affords immediate access to the names, addresses, and giving limitations of the foundations listed. The grant descriptions provide fundraisers with the grant recipient's name and location; the amount of the grant; the date the grant was authorized; and a description of the grant's intended use.

In addition, each *Grant Guide* includes three indexes: by the type of organization generally funded by the grantmaker, the subject focus of the foundation's grants, and the geographic area in which the foundation has already funded projects.

Each *Grant Guide* also includes a concise overview of the foundation spending patterns within the specified field. The introduction uses a series of statistical tables to document such important findings as (1) the 25 top funders in the given area of interest (by total dollar amount of grants); (2) the 15 largest grants reported; (3) the total dollar amount and number of grants awarded for specific types of support, recipient organization type, and population group; and (4) the total grant dollars received in each U.S. state and many foreign countries.

Series published annually in December / 2004–2005 Editions / $75 each

GUIDEBOOKS, MANUALS, AND REPORTS

ARTS FUNDING IV: An Update on Foundation Trends

Prepared in cooperation with Grantmakers in the Arts, this report provides a framework for understanding trends in foundation funding for arts and culture through 2001. Based on a sample of 800+ foundations, it compares growth in arts funding with other sources of public and private support, examines changes in giving for specific arts disciplines, analyzes giving patterns by region, and explores shifts in the types of support funders award.

July 2003 / ISBN 1-931923-48-5 / $19.95

FAMILY FOUNDATIONS: A Profile of Funders and Trends

Prepared in cooperation with the National Center for Family Philanthropy, *Family Foundations* is an essential resource for anyone interested in understanding the fastest growing segment of foundation philanthropy. The report provides a comprehensive measurement of the size and scope of the U.S. family foundation community. Through the use of objective and subjective criteria, the report identifies the number of family foundations and their distribution by region and state, size, geographic focus, and decade of establishment; and includes analyses of staffing and public reporting by these funders. *Family Foundations* also examines trends in giving by a sample of larger family foundations between 1993 and 1998 and compares these patterns with independent foundations overall.

August 2000 / ISBN 0-87954-917-3 / $19.95

INTERNATIONAL GRANTMAKING III: An Update on U.S. Foundation Trends

Prepared in cooperation with the Council on Foundations as an update to the 2000 *International Grantmaking II* study, this report examines perspectives on the post-9/11 funding climate and the current outlook for the field based on a 2004 survey of more than 65 leading U.S. international grantmakers. It also documents trends in international giving based on the grants of more than 600 larger U.S. foundations. In particular, the study analyzes shifts in giving priorities, countries/regions targeted for support, and the impact of large new funders.

November 2004 / ISBN 1-59542-008-8 / $40

THE FOUNDATION CENTER'S GRANTS CLASSIFICATION SYSTEM INDEXING MANUAL WITH THESAURUS, Revised Edition

A complete "how-to" guide, the *Grants Classification Manual* is an excellent resource for any organization that wants to classify foundation grants or their recipients. The *Manual* includes a complete set of classification codes to facilitate precise tracking of grants and recipients by subject, recipient type, and population categories. It also features a revised thesaurus to help identify the "official" terms and codes that represent thousands of subject areas and recipient types in the Center's system of grants classification.

May 1995 / ISBN 0-87954-644-1 / $95

FOUNDATIONS TODAY SERIES, 2004 Edition

The *Foundations Today* series provides the latest information on foundation growth and trends in foundation giving.

Foundation Giving Trends: Update on Funding Priorities—Examines 2003 grantmaking patterns of a sample of more than 1,000 larger U.S. foundations and compares current giving priorities with trends since 1980.
February 2004/ISBN 1-931923-71-X/$45

Foundation Growth and Giving Estimates: 2003 Preview—Provides a first look at estimates of foundation giving for 2003 and final statistics on actual giving and assets for 2002. Presents new top 100 foundation lists.
April 2004/ISBN 1-931923-72-8/$20

Foundation Yearbook: Facts and Figures on Private and Community Foundations—Documents the growth in number, giving, and assets of all active U.S. foundations from 1975 through 2002.
June 2004/ISBN 1-931923-96-5/$45

Three Book Set / ISBN 1-931923-96-5 / $95

THE FOUNDATION CENTER'S GUIDE TO GRANTSEEKING ON THE WEB, 2003 Edition

Packed with a wealth of information, the *Guide to Grantseeking on the Web* provides both novice and experienced Web users with a gateway to the numerous online resources available to grantseekers. Foundation Center staff experts have team-authored this guide, contributing their extensive knowledge of Web content as well as their tips and strategies on how to evaluate and use Web-based funding materials. Presented in a concise, "how-to" style, the *Guide* will introduce you to the Web and structure your funding research with a toolkit of resources. These resources include foundation and corporate Web sites, searchable databases for grantseeking, government funding sources, online journals, and interactive services on the Web for grantseekers.

September 2003 / Book / ISBN 1-931923-67-1 / $29.95
CD-ROM / ISBN 1-931923-73-6 / $29.95
Book and CD-ROM / $49.95

THE FOUNDATION CENTER'S GUIDE TO PROPOSAL WRITING, 4th Edition

The *Guide* is a comprehensive manual on the strategic thinking and mechanics of proposal writing. It covers each step of the process, from pre-proposal planning to the writing itself to the essential post-grant follow-up. The book features many extracts from actual grant proposals and also includes candid advice from grantmakers on the "do's and don't's" of proposal writing. Written by a professional fundraiser who has been creating successful proposals for more than 25 years, *The Foundation Center's Guide to Proposal Writing* offers the kind of valuable tips and in-depth, practical instruction that no other source provides.

March 2004 / ISBN 1-931923-92-2 / $34.95

GUÍA PARA ESCRIBIR PROPUESTAS

The Spanish language edition of the 3rd edition of the *Foundation Center's Guide to Proposal Writing* includes a special appendix listing consultants and technical assistance providers who can help Spanish speakers craft proposals in English, or give advice on fundraising.

March 2003 / ISBN 1-931923-16-7 / $34.95

THE FOUNDATION CENTER'S GUIDE TO WINNING PROPOSALS

The *Guide to Winning Proposals* features twenty grant proposals that have been funded by some of today's most influential grantmakers. Each proposal—reprinted in its entirety—includes a critique by the program officer, executive director, or other funding decision-maker who granted the request. The accompanying commentary points to the strengths and weaknesses of each proposal and provides insights into what makes some proposals more successful than others.

To represent the diversity of nonprofits throughout the country, proposals have been selected from large and small, local and national organizations, and for many different purposes, including basic budgetary support, special projects, construction, staff positions, and more. The *Guide to Winning Proposals* also includes actual letters of inquiry, budgets, cover letters, and supplementary documents needed to develop a complete proposal.

October 2003 / ISBN 1-931923-66-3 / $34.95

NEW YORK METROPOLITAN AREA FOUNDATIONS: A Profile of the Grantmaking Community

Prepared in cooperation with the New York Regional Association of Grantmakers, this study examines the size, scope, and giving patterns of foundations based in the eight-county New York metropolitan area. It documents the New York area's share of all U.S. foundations; details the growth of area foundations through 2000; profiles area foundations by type, size, and geographic focus; compares broad giving trends of New York area and all U.S. foundations between 1992 and 2000; and examines giving by non-New York area grantmakers to recipients in the New York area.

December 2002 / ISBN 1-931923-52-3/ $24.95

THE PRI DIRECTORY: Charitable Loans and Other Program-Related Investments by Foundations, 2nd Edition

Certain foundations have developed an alternative financing approach—known as program-related investing—for supplying capital to the nonprofit sector. PRIs have been used to support community revitalization, low-income housing, microenterprise development, historic preservation, human services, and more. This directory lists leading PRI providers and includes tips on how to seek out and manage PRIs. Foundation listings include funder name and state; recipient name, city, and state (or country); and a description of the project funded. There are several helpful indexes by foundation/recipient location, subject/type of support, and recipient name, as well as an index to donors, officers, and trustees.

September 2003/ ISBN 1-931923-49-3 / $75

SOUTHEASTERN FOUNDATIONS II: A Profile of the Region's Grantmaking Community

Produced in cooperation with the Southeastern Council of Foundations, *Southeastern Foundations II* provides a detailed examination of foundation philanthropy in the 12-state Southeast region. The report includes an overview of the Southeast's share of all U.S. foundations, measures the growth of Southeastern foundations since 1992, profiles Southeastern funders by type, size, and geographic focus, compares broad giving trends of Southeastern and all U.S. foundations in 1992 and 1997, and details giving by non-Southeastern grantmakers to recipients in the region.

November 1999 / ISBN 0-87954-775-8 / $19.95

OTHER PUBLICATIONS

AMERICA'S NONPROFIT SECTOR: A Primer, 2nd Edition
by Lester M. Salamon

In this revised edition of his classic book, Lester M. Salamon clarifies the basic structure and role of the nonprofit sector in the U.S. He places the nonprofit sector into context in relation to the government and business sectors. He also shows how the position of the nonprofit sector has changed over time, both generally and in the major fields in which the sector is active. Illustrated with numerous charts and tables, Salamon's book is an easy-to-understand primer for government officials, journalists, and students—in short, for anyone who wants to comprehend the makeup of America's nonprofit sector.

February 1999 / ISBN 0-87954-801-0 / $14.95

BEST PRACTICES OF EFFECTIVE NONPROFIT ORGANIZATIONS: A Practitioner's Guide
by Philip Bernstein

This volume provides guidance for nonprofit professionals eager to advance their organizations' goals. Philip Bernstein has drawn on his own extensive experience as a nonprofit executive, consultant, and volunteer to produce this review of "best practices" adopted by successful nonprofit organizations. Topics include defining purposes and goals, creating comprehensive financing plans, evaluating services, and effective communication.

February 1997 / ISBN 0-87954-755-3 / $29.95

THE BOARD MEMBER'S BOOK: Making a Difference in Voluntary Organizations, 3rd Edition
by Brian O'Connell

The revised and expanded edition of this popular title by former Independent Sector President, Brian O'Connell, is a guide to the issues, challenges, and possibilities that emerge from the interchange between a nonprofit organization and its board. O'Connell offers practical advice on how to be a more effective board member as well as on how board members can help their organizations make a difference.

March 2003 / ISBN 1-931923-17-5 / $29.95

INVESTING IN CAPACITY BUILDING: A Guide to High-impact Approaches
by Barbara Blumenthal

This publication by Barbara Blumenthal offers guidance to grantmakers and consultants in designing better approaches to helping nonprofits, while showing nonprofit managers how to obtain more effective assistance. Based on interviews with more than 100 grantmakers, intermediaries, and consultants; 30 evaluations of capacity building programs; and a review of research on capacity building; *Investing in Capacity Building* identifies the most successful strategies for helping nonprofits improve organizational performance.

September 2003 / ISBN 1-931923-65-5 / $34.95

CAREERS FOR DREAMERS AND DOERS: A Guide to Management Careers in the Nonprofit Sector
by Lilly Cohen and Dennis R. Young

A timeless guide to management positions in the nonprofit world, *Careers for Dreamers and Doers* offers practical advice for starting a job search and suggests strategies used by successful managers throughout the voluntary sector.

November 1989 / ISBN 0-87954-294-2 / $29.95

ECONOMICS FOR NONPROFIT MANAGERS
by Dennis R. Young and Richard Steinberg

In *Economics for Nonprofit Managers*, Young and Steinberg treat micro-economic analysis as an indispensable skill for nonprofit managers. They introduce and explain concepts such as opportunity cost, analysis at the margin, market equilibrium, market failure, and cost-benefit analysis. This volume also focuses on issues of particular concern to nonprofits, such as the economics of fundraising and volunteer recruiting, the regulatory environment, the impact of competition on nonprofit performance, interactions among sources of revenue, and more.

July 1995 / ISBN 0-87954-610-7 / $34.95

EFFECTIVE ECONOMIC DECISION-MAKING BY NONPROFIT ORGANIZATIONS
by Dennis R. Young

Editor Dennis R. Young offers useful, practical guidelines to support today's nonprofit managers in their efforts to maximize the effectiveness with which their organizations employ their valuable resources. A group of expert authors explores core operating decisions that face all organizations and provides solutions that are unique to nonprofits of any size. Chapters cover such decision-making areas as pricing of services, compensation of staff, outsourcing, fundraising expenditures, and investment and disbursement of funds. Published by the National Center on Nonprofit Enterprise and the Foundation Center.

December 2003 / ISBN 1-931923-69-8 / $34.95

FOUNDATION FUNDAMENTALS, 7th Edition

Foundation Fundamentals, often used as a basic primer in academic programs on the nonprofit sector, has been thoroughly updated to introduce beginners to the world of foundations. While prior editions of this guide focused on effective use of print resources, this new edition places particular emphasis on harnessing electronic databases and the Web to uncover information on grantmakers and their grants. Research strategies are explored that utilize subject, geographic and types of support approaches to finding funders. In addition, the guide features chapters on planning a funding research strategy, corporate giving, and presenting ideas to funders. A variety of worksheets and illustrations are provided throughout the text. The expanded and updated bibliography includes the latest publications as well as descriptions of the most relevant Web sites.

September 2004 / ISBN 1-59542-006-1 / $24.95

THE NONPROFIT ENTREPRENEUR: Creating Ventures to Earn Income
Edited by Edward Skloot

In a well-organized topic-by-topic approach to nonprofit venturing, consultant and entrepreneur Edward Skloot demonstrates how nonprofits can launch successful earned-income enterprises without compromising their missions. Skloot has compiled a collection of writings by the nation's top practitioners and advisors in nonprofit enterprise. Topics covered include legal issues, marketing techniques, business planning, avoiding the pitfalls of venturing for smaller organizations, and a special section on museums and their retail operations.

September 1988 / ISBN 0-87954-239-X / $19.95

A NONPROFIT ORGANIZATION OPERATING MANUAL: Planning for Survival and Growth
by Arnold J. Olenick and Philip R. Olenick

This straightforward, all-inclusive desk manual for nonprofit executives covers all aspects of starting and managing a nonprofit. The authors discuss legal problems, obtaining tax exemption, organizational planning and development, and board relations; operational, proposal, cash, and capital budgeting; marketing, grant proposals, fundraising, and for-profit ventures; computerization; and tax planning and compliance.

July 1991 / ISBN 0-87954-293-4 / $29.95

PEOPLE POWER: SERVICE, ADVOCACY, EMPOWERMENT
by Brian O'Connell

People Power, a selection of O'Connell's most powerful writings, provides thought-provoking commentary on the nonprofit world. The 25+ essays included in this volume range from keen analyses of the role of voluntarism in American life, to sound advice for nonprofit managers, to suggestions for developing and strengthening the nonprofit sector of the future.

October 1994 / ISBN 0-87954-563-1 / $24.95

PHILANTHROPY'S CHALLENGE: Building Nonprofit Capacity Through Venture Grantmaking
by Paul B. Firstenberg

In this book, Paul Firstenberg challenges grantors to proactively assist grantee management as the way to maximize the social impact of nonprofit programs, while showing grantseekers how the growing grantor emphasis on organizational capacity building will impact their efforts to win support. The author draws on his years of experience working in both nonprofit and for-profit organizations to explore the roles of grantor and grantee within various models of venture grantmaking. A full chapter is devoted to governance issues and responsibilities.

January 2003
Softbound: ISBN 1-931923-15-9 / $29.95 / Hardbound: ISBN 1-931923-53-1 / $39.95

PROMOTING ISSUES AND IDEAS: A Guide to Public Relations for Nonprofit Organizations,
Revised Edition
by M Booth & Associates

M Booth & Associates are specialists in promoting the issues and ideas of nonprofit groups. Their book presents proven strategies that will attract the interest of the people you wish to influence and inform. Included are the "nuts-and-bolts" of advertising, publicity, speech-making, lobbying, and special events; how to write and produce informational literature that leaps off the page; public relations on a shoe-string budget; how to plan and evaluate PR efforts; the use of rapidly evolving communication technologies; and a new chapter on crisis management.

December 1995 / ISBN 0-87954-594-1 / $29.95

RAISE MORE MONEY FOR YOUR NONPROFIT ORGANIZATION:
A Guide to Evaluating and Improving Your Fundraising
by Anne L. New

In *Raise More Money*, Anne New sets guidelines for a fundraising program that will benefit the incipient as well as the established nonprofit organization. The author divides her text into three sections: "The Basics," which delineates the necessary steps a nonprofit must take before launching a development campaign; "Fundraising Methods," which encourages organizational self-analysis and points the way to an effective program involving many sources of funding; and "Fundraising Resources," a 20-page bibliography that highlights useful research and funding directories.

January 1991 / ISBN 0-87954-388-4 / $14.95

SECURING YOUR ORGANIZATION'S FUTURE: A Complete Guide to Fundraising Strategies, Revised Edition
by Michael Seltzer

In this completely updated edition, Michael Seltzer acts as your personal fundraising consultant. Beginners get bottom-line facts and easy-to-follow worksheets; veteran fundraisers receive a complete review of the basics plus new money-making ideas. Seltzer supplements his text with an extensive bibliography of selected readings and resource organizations. Highly recommended for use as a text in nonprofit management programs at colleges and universities.

February 2001 / ISBN 0-87954-900-9 / $34.95

SUCCEEDING WITH CONSULTANTS: Self-Assessment for the Changing Nonprofit
by Barbara Kibbe and Fred Setterberg

This inspirational book, written by Barbara Kibbe and Fred Setterberg and supported by the David and Lucile Packard Foundation, guides nonprofits through the process of selecting and utilizing consultants to strengthen their organizations' operations. The book emphasizes self assessment tools and covers six different areas in which a nonprofit organization might benefit from a consultant's advice: governance, planning, fund development, financial management, public relations and marketing, and quality assurance.

April 1992 / ISBN 0-87954-450-3 / $19.95

THE 21ST CENTURY NONPROFIT
by Paul B. Firstenberg

In *The 21st Century Nonprofit*, Paul B. Firstenberg provides nonprofit managers with the know-how to make their organizations effective agents of change. *The 21st Century Nonprofit* encourages managers to adopt strategies developed by the for-profit sector in recent years. These strategies will help them to expand their revenue base by diversifying grant sources, exploit the possibilities of for-profit enterprises, and develop human resources by learning how to attract and retain talented people. The book also explores the nature of leadership through short profiles of three nonprofit CEOs.

July 1996 / ISBN 0-87954-672-7 / $34.95

MEMBERSHIP PROGRAM

ASSOCIATES PROGRAM

The Associates Program puts essential facts and figures at your fingertips through an e-mail and toll-free telephone reference service, helping you to:

- Identify potential sources of foundation and corporate funding for your organization; and

- Gather important information to use in targeting and presenting your proposals effectively.

An annual $995 membership in the Associates Program gives you vital information on a timely basis, saving you hundreds of hours of research time. As a member, you may place an unlimited number of requests for assistance. Our staff will refer to any resource available to us in any of our five library/learning centers. Unlike non-members who must visit one of our locations and conduct their own research, you may ask our staff to do it for you.

Members also receive a special monthly e-newsletter and have access to an exclusive extranet site, which includes information about the newest foundations, changes at more established foundations, special discounts and invitations to members-only briefings, and more.

Since the mid-1970s, thousands of professional fundraisers have discovered the Associates Program to be a highly reliable and extremely cost-effective service. In times when budgets are tight, nonprofit staffers wearing many hats at once find it especially useful. For more information, call (800) 634-2953 or visit online at http://www.fdncenter.org/marketplace and learn how we can serve your specific needs.

FOUNDATION CENTER'S WEB SITE
www.fdncenter.org

Helping grantseekers succeed, helping grantmakers make a difference.

The Foundation Center's Web site (http://www.fdncenter.org) is the premier online source of fundraising information. Updated and expanded on a daily basis, the Center's site provides grantseekers, grantmakers, researchers, journalists, and the general public with easy access to a range of valuable resources, among them:

- Personalization at the Center's Web site allows registered users to receive content tailored to their fundraising and research interests at key areas of the site, including the home page, *Philanthropy News Digest,* FC Stats, and the Marketplace.

- A Grantmaker Web Sites area provides annotated links to more than 2,600 grantmaker sites that can be searched by subject or geographic key words.

- Foundation Finder, our free foundation look-up tool, includes private and community foundation contact information and brief background data, such as type of foundation, assets, total giving, and EIN, Web address, as well as links to Forms 990-PF (IRS tax filings).

- *Philanthropy News Digest,* features current philanthropy-related articles abstracted from major media outlets, interviews, original content, and the PND Talk message board. PND is also available as a free weekly e-mail newsletter.

- *The Literature of the Nonprofit Sector Online,* a searchable bibliographical database, includes 23,000+ entries of works on the field of philanthropy, more than 15,000 of which are abstracted.

- Our Learning Lab features comprehensive answers to FAQs, an Online Librarian to field questions about grantseeking and the Foundation Center, Topical Resource Lists, and an Online Bookshelf with condensed versions of popular Foundation Center publications.

- Our popular Virtual Classroom allows visitors to link to online tutorials such as a Proposal Writing Short Course (in English and Spanish); Finding Foundation Support for Your Education; Establishing a Nonprofit Organization; Demystifying the 990-PF; and more.

- Information about Center-sponsored orientations, training programs, and seminars can be found on our library home pages and in the Marketplace.

- The locations of our 200+ Cooperating Collections nationwide, and the activities and resources at our five main libraries.

- A For Individual Grantseekers area introduces individuals to the grantseeking process and provides tools and resources to help individuals get started.

- A special section, For Grantmakers, offers funders the opportunity to help get the word out about their work, answers frequently asked questions, informs grantmakers on recent developments in the field, and describes how the Center assists grantees and grant applicants.

- Our Researching Philanthropy directory features PubHub, a searchable repository of reports and issue briefs created by or with foundation resources; a Funding Trends and Analysis section with the latest data available on U.S. foundation philanthropy; and FC Stats providing thousands of free statistical tables on foundations and their giving.

- The For the Media area provides journalists with current information on key developments in private philanthropy in the United States.

All this and more is available at our Web site. The Center's publications and electronic resources can be ordered at the site's Marketplace. Visit our Web site often for information on new products and services.

Appendix F

Foundation Center Cooperating Collections

Free Funding Information Centers

The Foundation Center is an independent national service organization established by foundations to provide an authoritative source of information on foundation and corporate giving. The New York, Washington, D.C., Atlanta, Cleveland, and San Francisco reference collections operated by the Foundation Center offer a wide variety of services and comprehensive collections of information on foundations and grants. Cooperating Collections are libraries, community foundations, and other nonprofit agencies that provide a core collection of Foundation Center publications and a variety of supplementary materials and services in areas useful to grantseekers. The core collection of print materials consists of:

The Board Member's Book

The Foundation 1000

The Foundation Center's Guide to Grantseeking on the Web

The Foundation Center's Guide to Proposal Writing

The Foundation Center's Guide to Winning Proposals

The Foundation Directory
The Foundation Directory, Part 2
The Foundation Directory Supplement
Foundation Fundamentals
Foundation Grants to Individuals
Foundations Today Series
*Guide to Funding for International and
    Foreign Programs*
*Guide to U.S. Foundations, Their Trustees,
    Officers, and Donors*

National Directory of Corporate Giving
*National Guide to Funding for Libraries and
    Information Services*
*National Guide to Funding for the
    Environment and Animal Welfare*
National Guide to Funding in AIDS
National Guide to Funding in Arts and Culture
National Guide to Funding in Health
National Guide to Funding in Religion
Securing Your Organization's Future

All five Foundation Center libraries have both *FC Search: The Foundation Center's Database on CD-ROM* and *Foundation Directory Online* available for public use. All Cooperating Collections have either *FC Search* or *Foundation Directory Online*, and all provide Internet access. Increasingly, those seeking information on fundraising and nonprofit management are referring to our Web site (http://www.fdncenter.org) for a wealth of data and advice on grantseeking, including links to foundation IRS information returns. Because the Cooperating Collections vary in their hours, it is recommended that you call a collection in advance of a visit. To check on new locations or current holdings, call toll-free 1-800-424-9836, or visit our site at http://www.fdncenter.org/collections/index.html.

Reference Collections Operated by the Foundation Center

HEADQUARTERS:

NEW YORK

79 Fifth Avenue/16th Street, 2nd Floor
New York, NY 10003-3076
Tel: (212) 620-4230
http://www.fdncenter.org
New York Library home page:
http://www.fdncenter.org/newyork

FIELD OFFICES:

ATLANTA

50 Hurt Plaza, Suite 150
Atlanta, GA 30303-2914
Tel: (404) 880-0094
http://www.fdncenter.org/atlanta

CLEVELAND

1422 Euclid Avenue, Suite 1600
Cleveland, OH 44115-2001
Tel: (216) 861-1934
http://www.fdncenter.org/cleveland

SAN FRANCISCO

312 Sutter Street, Suite 606
San Francisco, CA 94108-4314
Tel: (415) 397-0902
http://www.fdncenter.org/sanfrancisco

WASHINGTON, D.C.

1627 K Street, NW, 3rd Floor
Washington, D.C. 20006-1708
Tel: (202) 331-1400
http://www.fdncenter.org/washington

Cooperating Collections

ALABAMA

BIRMINGHAM PUBLIC LIBRARY
Government Documents Department
2100 Park Place
Birmingham, AL 35203
(205) 226-3620

HUNTSVILLE PUBLIC LIBRARY
Information & Periodical Department
915 Monroe St.
Huntsville, AL 35801
(256) 532-5940

MOBILE PUBLIC LIBRARY
West Regional Library
5555 Grelot Road
Mobile, AL 36609-3643
(251) 340-8555

AUBURN UNIVERSITY AT MONTGOMERY
LIBRARY
Information Services
74-40 East Drive
Montgomery, AL 36117-3596
(334) 244-3200

ALASKA

CONSORTIUM LIBRARY
3211 Providence Drive
Anchorage, AK 99508
(907) 786-1848

JUNEAU PUBLIC LIBRARY
Reference
292 Marine Way
Juneau, AK 99801
(907) 586-5267

ARIZONA

FLAGSTAFF CITY—COCONINO COUNTY
PUBLIC LIBRARY
300 W. Aspen Avenue
Flagstaff, AZ 86001
(928) 779-7670

PHOENIX PUBLIC LIBRARY
Information Services Department
1221 N. Central Avenue
Phoenix, AZ 85004
(602) 262-4636

TUCSON-PIMA PUBLIC LIBRARY
101 N. Stone Ave.
Tucson, AZ 85701
(520) 791-4393

ARKANSAS

UNIVERSITY OF ARKANSAS—FORT SMITH
BOREHAM LIBRARY
5210 Grand Avenue
Fort Smith, AR 72913
(479) 788-7204

CENTRAL ARKANSAS LIBRARY SYSTEM
100 Rock Street
Little Rock, AR 72201
(501) 918-3000

CALIFORNIA

KERN COUNTY LIBRARY
Beale Memorial Library
701 Truxtun Avenue
Bakersfield, CA 93301
(661) 868-0755

ROONEY RESOURCE CENTER
Humboldt Area Foundation
373 Indianola
Bayside, CA 95524
(707) 442-2993

VENTURA COUNTY COMMUNITY
    FOUNDATION
Resource Center for Nonprofit Organizations
1317 Del Norte Road, Suite 150
Camarillo, CA 93010
(805) 988-0196

FRESNO REGIONAL FOUNDATION
Nonprofit Advancement Center
3425 N. First Street, Suite 101
Fresno, CA 93726
(559) 226-0216

CENTER FOR NONPROFIT MANAGEMENT
    IN SOUTHERN CALIFORNIA
Nonprofit Resource Library
606 South Olive Street, #2450
Los Angeles, CA 90014
(213) 623-7080

LOS ANGELES PUBLIC LIBRARY
Mid-Valley Regional Branch Library
16244 Nordhoff Street
North Hills, CA 91343
(818) 895-3654

EAST BAY RESOURCE CENTER FOR
    NONPROFIT SUPPORT
359 Frank H. Ogawa Plaza
Oakland, CA 94612
(510) 834-1010

PHILANTHROPY RESOUCE CENTER
Flintridge Foundation
1040 Lincoln Avenue, Suite 100
Pasadena, CA 91103
(626) 449-0839

CENTER FOR NONPROFIT RESOURCES
Shasta Regional Community Foundation's
Center
2280 Benton Drive, Building C, Suite A
Redding, CA 96003
(530) 244-1219

RICHMOND PUBLIC LIBRARY
352 Civic Center Plaza
Richmond, CA 94804
(510) 620-6561

RIVERSIDE CITY PUBLIC LIBRARY
3581 Mission Inn Avenue
Riverside, CA 92501
(909) 826-5201

NONPROFIT RESOURCE CENTER
Sacramento Public Library
828 I Street, 2nd Floor
Sacramento, CA 95814
(916) 264-2772

SAN DIEGO FOUNDATION
Funding Information Center
1420 Kettner Boulevard, Suite 500
San Diego, CA 92101
(619) 235-2300

COMPASSPOINT NONPROFIT SERVICES
Nonprofit Development Library
1922 The Alameda, Suite 212
San Jose, CA 95126
(408) 248-9505

PENINSULA COMMUNITY FOUNDATION
Peninsula Nonprofit Center
1700 S. El Camino Real, R201
San Mateo, CA 94402-3049
(650) 358-9392

LOS ANGELES PUBLIC LIBRARY
San Pedro Regional Branch Library
931 S. Gaffey Street
San Pedro, CA 90731
(310) 548-7779

VOLUNTEER CENTER OF GREATER
    ORANGE COUNTY
Nonprofit Resource Center
1901 E. 4th Street, Suite 100
Santa Ana, CA 92705
(714) 953-5757

SANTA BARBARA PUBLIC LIBRARY
40 E. Anapamu Street
Santa Barbara, CA 93101-1019
(805) 962-7653

SANTA MONICA PUBLIC LIBRARY
1324 5th Street
Santa Monica, CA 90401
(310) 458-8600

SONOMA COUNTY LIBRARY
3rd and E. Streets
Santa Rosa, CA 95404
(707) 545-0831

SEASIDE BRANCH LIBRARY
550 Harcourt Avenue
Seaside, CA 93955
(831) 899-8131

SIERRA NONPROFIT SUPPORT CENTER
39 N. Washington Street, #F
Sonora, CA 95370-0905
(209) 533-1093

COLORADO

EL POMAR NONPROFIT RESOURCE CENTER
Penrose Library
20 N. Cascade Avenue
Colorado Springs, CO 80903
(719) 531-6333

DENVER PUBLIC LIBRARY
General Reference
10 W. 14th Avenue Parkway
Denver, CO 80204
(720) 865-1111

CONNECTICUT

DANBURY PUBLIC LIBRARY
170 Main Street
Danbury, CT 06810
(203) 797-4527

GREENWICH LIBRARY
101 W. Putnam Avenue
Greenwich, CT 06830
(203) 622-7900

HARTFORD PUBLIC LIBRARY
500 Main Street
Hartford, CT 06103
(860) 695-6300

NEW HAVEN FREE PUBLIC LIBRARY
Reference Department
133 Elm Street
New Haven, CT 06510-2057
(203) 946-7431

DELAWARE

UNIVERSITY OF DELAWARE
Hugh Morris Library
181 South College
Newark, DE 19717-5267
(302) 831-2432

FLORIDA

BARTOW PUBLIC LIBRARY
2151 S. Broadway Avenue
Bartow, FL 33830
(863) 534-0931

VOLUSIA COUNTY LIBRARY CENTER
City Island
105 E. Magnolia Avenue
Daytona Beach, FL 32114-4484
(386) 257-6036

NOVA SOUTHEASTERN UNIVERISTY
Research and Information Technology Library
3100 Ray Ferrero Jr. Boulevard
Fort Lauderdale, FL 33314
(954) 262-4613

INDIAN RIVER COMMUNITY COLLEGE
Learning Resources Center
3209 Virginia Avenue
Fort Pierce, FL 34981-5596
(561) 462-4757

JACKSONVILLE PUBLIC LIBRARIES
Grants Resource Center
122 N. Ocean Street
Jacksonville, FL 32202
(904) 630-2665

MIAMI-DADE PUBLIC LIBRARY
Humanities/Social Science Department
101 W. Flagler Street
Miami, FL 33130
(305) 375-5575

ORANGE COUNTY LIBRARY SYSTEM
Social Sciences Department
101 E. Central Boulevard
Orlando, FL 32801
(407) 425-4694

SELBY PUBLIC LIBRARY
Reference Department
1331 1st Street
Sarasota, FL 34236
(941) 861-1100

STATE LIBRARY OF FLORIDA
R.A. Gray Building
Tallahassee, FL 32399-0250
(850) 245-6600

HILLSBOROUGH COUNTY PUBLIC LIBRARY
COOPERATIVE
John F. Germany Public Library
900 N. Ashley Drive
Tampa, FL 33602
(813) 273-3652

COMMUNITY FOUNDATION OF PALM
BEACH & MARTIN COUNTIES
700 South Dixie Highway, Suite 200
West Palm Beach, FL 33401
(561) 659-6800

GEORGIA

HALL COUNTY LIBRARY SYSTEM
127 Main Street NW
Gainesville, GA 30501
(770) 532-3311

WASHINGTON MEMORIAL LIBRARY
1180 Washington Avenue
Macon, GA 31201
(478) 744-0828

THOMAS COUNTY PUBLIC LIBRARY
201 N. Madison Street
Thomasville, GA 31792
(229) 225-5252

HAWAII

UNIVERSITY OF HAWAII
Hamilton Library
General/Humanities/Social Science Reference
Department
2550 The Mall
Honolulu, HI 96822
(808) 956-7214

IDAHO

BOISE PUBLIC LIBRARY
Funding Information Center
715 S. Capitol Boulevard
Boise, ID 83702
(208) 384-4024

CALDWELL PUBLIC LIBRARY
1010 Dearborn Street
Caldwell, ID 83605
(208) 459-3242

ILLINOIS

DONORS FORUM OF CHICAGO LIBRARY
208 S. La Salle, Suite 735
Chicago, IL 60604
(312) 578-0175

EVANSTON PUBLIC LIBRARY
1703 Orrington Avenue
Evanston, IL 60201
(847) 866-0300

ROCK ISLAND PUBLIC LIBRARY
401 19th Street
Rock Island, IL 61201-8143
(309) 732-7323

UNIVERSITY OF ILLINOIS AT SPRINGFIELD
Nonprofit Resource Center, Brookens Library
One University Plaza, MS Lib 140
Springfield, IL 62703-5407
(217) 206-6633

INDIANA

EVANSVILLE-VANDERBURGH PUBLIC
LIBRARY
22 SE 5th Street
Evansville, IN 47708
(812) 428-8200

ALLEN COUNTY PUBLIC LIBRARY
200 East Berry Street
Fort Wayne, IN 46802
(260) 421-1238

INDIANAPOLIS-MARION COUNTY PUBLIC
LIBRARY
202 North Alabama Street
Indianapolis, IN 46206
(317) 269-1700

VIGO COUNTY PUBLIC LIBRARY
One Library Square
Terre Haute, IN 47807
(812) 232-1113

IOWA

CEDAR RAPIDS PUBLIC LIBRARY
500 1st Street SE
Cedar Rapids, IA 52401
(319) 398-5123

SOUTHWESTERN COMMUNITY COLLEGE
Learning Resource Center
1501 W. Townline Road
Creston, IA 50801
(641) 782-7081

DES MOINES PUBLIC LIBRARY
100 Locust Street
Des Moines, IA 50309-1791
(515) 283-4152 press 3

SIOUX CITY PUBLIC LIBRARY
Siouxland Funding Research Center
529 Pierce Street
Sioux City, IA 51101-1203
(712) 255-2933

KANSAS

PIONEER MEMORIAL LIBRARY
375 West 4th Street
Colby, KS 67701
(785) 462-4470

DODGE CITY PUBLIC LIBRARY
1001 2nd Avenue
Dodge City, KS 67801
(620) 225-0248

KEARNY COUNTY LIBRARY
101 East Prairie
Lakin, KS 67860
(620) 355-6674

SALINA PUBLIC LIBRARY
301 W. Elm
Salina, KS 67401
(785) 825-4624

TOPEKA AND SHAWNEE COUNTY PUBLIC
LIBRARY
1515 SW 10th Avenue
Topeka, KS 66604
(785) 580-4400

WICHITA PUBLIC LIBRARY
223 S. Main Street
Wichita, KS 67202
(316) 261-8500

KENTUCKY

WESTERN KENTUCKY UNIVERSITY
Helm-Cravens Library
110 Helm Library
Bowling Green, KY 42101-3576
(270) 745-6163

LEXINGTON PUBLIC LIBRARY
140 E. Main Street
Lexington, KY 40507-1376
(859) 231-5520

LOUISVILLE FREE PUBLIC LIBRARY
301 York Street
Louisville, KY 40203
(502) 574-1617

LOUISIANA

EAST BATON ROUGE PARISH LIBRARY
Centroplex Branch Grants Collection
120 St. Louis Street
Baton Rouge, LA 70802
(225) 389-4967

BEAUREGARD PARISH LIBRARY
205 S. Washington Avenue
DeRidder, LA 70634
(337) 463-6217

OUACHITA PARISH PUBLIC LIBRARY
1800 Stubbs Avenue
Monroe, LA 71201
(318) 327-1490

NEW ORLEANS PUBLIC LIBRARY
Business & Science Division
219 Loyola Avenue
New Orleans, LA 70112
(504) 596-2580

SHREVE MEMORIAL LIBRARY
424 Texas Street
Shreveport, LA 71120-1523
(318) 226-5894

MAINE

UNIVERSITY OF SOUTHERN MAINE LIBRARY
Maine Philanthropy Center
314 Forrest Avenue
Portland, ME 04104-9301
(207) 780-5029

MARYLAND

ENOCH PRATT FREE LIBRARY
Social Science & History Department
400 Cathedral Street
Baltimore, MD 21201
(410) 396-5320

MASSACHUSETTS

ASSOCIATED GRANT MAKERS OF
    MASSACHUSETTS
55 Court Street, Suite 520
Boston, MA 02108
(617) 426-2606

BOSTON PUBLIC LIBRARY
Social Sciences Reference Department
700 Boylston Street
Boston, MA 02116
(617) 536-5400

WESTERN MASSACHUSETTS FUNDING
    RESOURCE CENTER
65 Elliot Street
Springfield, MA 01101-1730
(413) 452-0697

WORCESTER PUBLIC LIBRARY
Grants Resource Center
3 Salem Square
Worcester, MA 01608
(508) 799-1655

MICHIGAN

ALPENA COUNTY LIBRARY
211 N. 1st Street
Alpena, MI 49707
(989) 356-6188

UNIVERSTIY OF MICHIGAN—ANN ARBOR
Graduate Library
Reference & Research Services Department
Ann Arbor, MI 48109-1205
(734) 763-1539

WILLARD PUBLIC LIBRARY
Nonprofit & Funding Resource Collections
7 W. Van Buren Street
Battle Creek, MI 49017
(269) 969-2100

HENRY FORD CENTENNIAL LIBRARY
Adult Services
16301 Michigan Avenue
Dearborn, MI 48126
(313) 943-2330

WAYNE STATE UNIVERSITY
134 Purdy/Kresge Library
Detroit, MI 48202
(313) 577-6424

MICHIGAN STATE UNIVERSITY LIBRARIES
Main Library Funding Center
100 Library
East Lansing, MI 48824-1048
(517) 432-6123

FARMINGTON COMMUNITY LIBRARY
32737 W. 12 Mile Road
Farmington Hills, MI 48334
(248) 553-0300

UNIVERSITY OF MICHIGAN—FLINT
Frances Willson Thompson Library
Flint, MI 48502-1950
(810) 762-3413

GRAND RAPIDS PUBLIC LIBRARY
Reference Department
111 Library Street NE
Grand Rapids, MI 49503-3268
(616) 988-5400

MICHIGAN TECHNOLOGICAL UNIVERSITY
Harold Meese Center, Corporate Services
1400 Townsend Drive
Houghton, MI 49931-1295
(906) 487-2228

WEST SHORE COMMUNITY COLLEGE
    LIBRARY
3000 North Stiles Road
Scottville, MI 49454-0277
(231) 845-6211

TRAVERSE AREA DISTRICT LIBRARY
610 Woodmere Avenue
Traverse City, MI 49686
(231) 932-8500

MINNESOTA

BRAINERD PUBLIC LIBRARY
416 S. 5th Street
Brainerd, MN 56401
(218) 829-5574

DULUTH PUBLIC LIBRARY
520 W. Superior Street
Duluth, MN 55802
(218) 723-3802

SOUTHWEST STATE UNIVERSITY
University Library
N. Highway 23
Marshall, MN 56253
(507) 537-6108

MINNEAPOLIS PUBLIC LIBRARY
Sociology Department
250 Marquette Avenue
Minneapolis, MN 55401
(612) 630-6000

ROCHESTER PUBLIC LIBRARY
101 2nd Street, SE
Rochester, MN 55904-3777
(507) 285-8002

ST. PAUL PUBLIC LIBRARY
90 W. 4th Street
St. Paul, MN 55102
(651) 266-7000

MISSISSIPPI

LIBRARY OF HATTIESBURG, PETAL AND
    FORREST COUNTY
329 Hardy Street
Hattiesburg, MS 39401-3824
(601) 582-4461

JACKSON/HINDS LIBRARY SYSTEM
300 N. State Street
Jackson, MS 39201
(601) 968-5803

MISSOURI

COUNCIL ON PHILANTHROPY
University of Missouri—Kansas City
4747 Troost, #207
Kansas City, MO 64171-0813
(816) 235-1176

KANSAS CITY PUBLIC LIBRARY
14 W. 10th Street
Kansas City, MO 64105-1702
(816) 701-3541

ST. LOUIS PUBLIC LIBRARY
1301 Olive Street
St. Louis, MO 63103
(314) 241-2288

SPRINGFIELD-GREENE COUNTY LIBRARY
The Library Center
4653 S. Campbell
Springfield, MO 65810
(417) 874-8110

MONTANA

MONTANA STATE UNIVERSITY—BILLINGS
Library-Special Collections
1500 N. 30th Street
Billings, MT 59101-0245
(406) 657-1687

BOZEMAN PUBLIC LIBRARY
220 E. Lamme
Bozeman, MT 59715
(406) 582-2402

MONTANA STATE LIBRARY
Library Information and Services Department
1515 E. 6th Avenue
Helena, MT 59620-1800
(406) 444-3115

LINCOLN COUNTY PUBLIC LIBRARIES
Libby Public Library
220 West 6th Street
Libby, MT 59923
(406) 293-2778

UNIVERSITY OF MONTANA
Maureen and Mike Mansfield Library
32 Campus Drive, #9936
Missoula, MT 59812-9936
(406) 243-6800

NEBRASKA

UNIVERSITY OF NEBRASKA—LINCOLN
14th & R Streets
Lincoln, NE 68588-2848
(402) 472-2848

OMAHA PUBLIC LIBRARY
W. Dale Clark Library
Social Science Department
215 S. 15th Street
Omaha, NE 68102
(402) 444-4826

NEVADA

GREAT BASIN COLLEGE LIBRARY
1500 College Parkway
Elko, NV 89801
(775) 753-2222

CLARK COUNTY LIBRARY
1401 E. Flamingo
Las Vegas, NV 89119
(702) 507-3400

WASHOE COUNTY LIBRARY
301 S. Center Street
Reno, NV 89501
(775) 327-8300

NEW HAMPSHIRE

CONCORD PUBLIC LIBRARY
45 Green Street
Concord, NH 03301
(603) 225-8670

PLYMOUTH STATE UNIVERSITY
Herbert H. Lamson Library
Plymouth, NH 03264
(603) 535-2258

NEW JERSEY

CUMBERLAND COUNTY LIBRARY
800 E. Commerce Street
Bridgeton, NJ 08302
(856) 453-2210

FREE PUBLIC LIBRARY OF ELIZABETH
11 S. Broad Street
Elizabeth, NJ 07202
(908) 354-6060

NEWARK ENTERPRISE COMMUNITY
    RESOURCE DEVELOPMENT CENTER
303-309 Washington Street, 5th Floor
Newark, NJ 07102
(973) 624-8300

COUNTY COLLEGE OF MORRIS
Learning Resource Center
214 Center Grove Road
Randolph, NJ 07869
(973) 328-5296

NEW JERSEY STATE LIBRARY
185 W. State Street
Trenton, NJ 08625-0520
(609) 292-6220

NEW MEXICO

ALBURQUERQUE/BERNALILLO COUNTY
    LIBRARY SYSTEM
501 Copper Avenue NW
Albuquerque, NM 87102
(505) 768-5141

NEW MEXICO STATE LIBRARY
Information Services
1209 Camino Carlos Rey
Santa Fe, NM 87507
(505) 476-9702

NEW YORK

NEW YORK STATE LIBRARY
Cultural Education Center, 6th Floor
Empire State Plaza
Albany, NY 12230
(518) 474-5355

BROOKLYN PUBLIC LIBRARY
Society, Science, and Technology Division
Grand Army Plaza
Brooklyn, NY 11238
(718) 230-2122

BUFFALO & ERIE COUNTY PUBLIC LIBRARY
Business, Science & Technology Department
1 Lafayette Square
Buffalo, NY 14203-1887
(716) 858-7097

SOUTHEAST STEUBEN COUNTY LIBRARY
300 Nasser Civic Center Plaza
Corning, NY 14830
(607) 936-3713

HUNTINGTON PUBLIC LIBRARY
338 Main Street
Huntington, NY 11743
(631) 427-5165

QUEENS BOROUGH PUBLIC LIBRARY
Social Sciences Division
89-11 Merrick Boulevard
Jamaica, NY 11432
(718) 990-0700

LEVITTOWN PUBLIC LIBRARY
1 Bluegrass Lane
Levittown, NY 11756
(516) 731-5728

ADRIANCE MEMORIAL LIBRARY
Special Services Department
93 Market Street
Poughkeepsie, NY 12601
(914) 485-3445

THE RIVERHEAD FREE LIBRARY
330 Court Street
Riverhead, NY 11901
(631) 727-3228

ROCHESTER PUBLIC LIBRARY
Social Sciences
115 S. Avenue
Rochester, NY 14604
(585) 428-8120

ONONDAGA COUNTY PUBLIC LIBRARY
447 S. Salina Street
Syracuse, NY 13202-2494
(315) 435-1900

UTICA PUBLIC LIBRARY
303 Genesee Street
Utica, NY 13501
(315) 735-2279

WHITE PLAINS PUBLIC LIBRARY
100 Martine Avenue
White Plains, NY 10601
(914) 422-1480

YONKERS PUBLIC LIBRARY
Riverfront Library
One Larkin Center
Yonkers, NY 10701
(914) 337-1500

NORTH CAROLINA

PACK MEMORIAL LIBRARY
Community Foundation of Western North Carolina
67 Haywood Street
Asheville, NC 28802
(828) 254-4960

THE DUKE ENDOWMENT LIBRARY
100 N. Tyron Street, Suite 3500
Charlotte, NC 28202-4012
(704) 376-0291

DURHAM COUNTY PUBLIC LIBRARY
300 N. Roxboro Street
Durham, NC 27702
(919) 560-0100

FORSYTH COUNTY PUBLIC LIBRARY
660 W. 5th Street
Winston-Salem, NC 27101
(336) 727-2264

NORTH DAKOTA

BISMARCK PUBLIC LIBRARY
515 N. 5th Street
Bismarck, ND 58501-4081
(701) 222-6410

FARGO PUBLIC LIBRARY
102 N. 3rd Street
Fargo, ND 58102
(701) 241-1491

MINOT PUBLIC LIBRARY
516 2nd Avenue SW
Minot, ND 58701-3792
(701) 852-1045

OHIO

STARK COUNTY DISTRICT LIBRARY
715 Market Avenue N.
Canton, OH 44702
(330) 452-0665

PUBLIC LIBRARY OF CINCINNATI &
  HAMILTON COUNTY
Grants Resource Center
800 Vine Street—Library Square
Cincinnati, OH 45202-2071
(513) 369-6000

COLUMBUS METROPOLITAN LIBRARY
Business and Technology Department
96 S. Grant Avenue
Columbus, OH 43215
(614) 645-2590

DAYTON METRO LIBRARY
Grants Information Center
215 E. 3rd Street
Dayton, OH 45402
(937) 227-9500

MANSFIELD/RICHLAND COUNTY PUBLIC
  LIBRARY
43 W. 3rd Street
Mansfield, OH 44902
(419) 521-3110

PORTSMOUTH PUBLIC LIBRARY
1220 Gallia Street
Portsmouth, OH 45662
(740) 354-5688

TOLEDO-LUCAS COUNTY PUBLIC LIBRARY
Business Science Society Department
325 N. Michigan
Toledo, OH 43612
(419) 259-5207

PUBLIC LIBRARY OF YOUNGSTOWN &
  MAHONING COUNTY
305 Wick Avenue
Youngstown, OH 44503
(330) 744-8636

OKLAHOMA

OKLAHOMA CITY UNIVERSITY
Dulaney Browne Library
2501 N. Blackwelder
Oklahoma City, OK 73106
(405) 521-5822

TULSA CITY-COUNTY LIBRARY
400 Civic Center
Tulsa, OK 74103
(918) 596-7977

OREGON

OREGON INSTITUTE OF TECHNOLOGY
  LIBRARY
3201 Campus Drive
Klamath Falls, OR 97601-8801
(541) 885-1770

PACIFIC NON-PROFIT NETWORK
Southern Oregon University
1600 N. Riverside, Suite 1001
Medford, OR 97501
(541) 779-6044

MULTNOMAH COUNTY LIBRARY
Science & Business Department
801 SW 10th Avenue
Portland, OR 97205
(503) 988-5123

OREGON STATE LIBRARY
State Library Building
250 Winter Street NE
Salem, OR 97301-3950
(503) 378-4277

PENNSYLVANIA

NORTHHAMPTON COMMUNITY COLLEGE
The Paul and Harriett Mack Library
3835 Green Pond Road
Bethlehem, PA 18017
(610) 861-5360

ERIE COUNTY LIBRARY SYSTEM
160 E. Front Street
Erie, PA 16507
(814) 451-6927

DAUPHIN COUNTY LIBRARY SYSTEM
East Shore Area Library
4501 Ethel Street
Harrisburg, PA 17109
(717) 652-9380

HAZLETON AREA PUBLIC LIBRARY
55 N. Church Street
Hazleton, PA 18201
(570) 454-2961

LANCASTER COUNTY LIBRARY
125 N. Duke Street
Lancaster, PA 17602
(717) 394-2651

FREE LIBRARY OF PHILADELPHIA
Regional Foundation Center
1901 Vine Street, 2nd Floor
Philadelphia, PA 19103-1189
(215) 686-5423

CARNEGIE LIBRARY OF PITTSBURGH
Foundation Center
Library Center
414 Wood Street
Pittsburgh, PA 15222-1818
(412) 281-7143

POCONO NORTHEAST DEVELOPMENT
FUND
James Pettinger Memorial Library
1151 Oak Street
Pittston, PA 18640
(570) 655-5581

READING PUBLIC LIBRARY
100 S. 5th Street
Reading, PA 19602
(610) 655-6355

JAMES V. BROWN LIBRARY
19 E. 4th Street
Williamsport, PA 17701
(570) 326-0536

MARTIN LIBRARY
159 E. Market Street
York, PA 17401
(717) 846-5300

PUERTO RICO

UNIVERSIDAD DEL SAGRADO CORAZON
M.M.T. Guevara Library
Santurce, PR 00914
(787) 728-1515

RHODE ISLAND

PROVIDENCE PUBLIC LIBRARY
225 Washington Street
Providence, RI 02906
(401) 455-8088

SOUTH CAROLINA

ANDERSON COUNTY LIBRARY
300 N. McDuffie Street
Anderson, SC 29622
(864) 260-4500

CHARLESTON COUNTY LIBRARY
68 Calhoun Street
Charleston, SC 29401
(843) 805-6930

SOUTH CAROLINA STATE LIBRARY
1500 Senate Street
Columbia, SC 29211
(803) 734-8666

GREENVILLE COUNTY LIBRARY SYSTEM
25 Heritage Green Place
Greenville, SC 29601-2034
(864) 242-5000

SOUTH DAKOTA

DAKOTA STATE UNIVERSITY
Nonprofit Management Institute
Nonprofit Grants Assistance
820 N. Washington
Madison, SD 57042
(605) 367-5382

SOUTH DAKOTA STATE LIBRARY
800 Governors Drive
Pierre, SD 57501-2294
(605) 773-3131

BLACK HILLS STATE UNIVERSITY
E.Y. Berry Library-Learning Center
1200 University Street, Unit 9676
Spearfish, SD 57799-9676
(605) 642-6834

TENNESSEE

UNITED WAY OF GREATER CHATTANOOGA
Center For Nonprofits
630 Market Street
Chattanooga, TN 37402
(423) 265-0514

KNOX COUNTY PUBLIC LIBRARY
500 W. Church Avenue
Knoxville, TN 37902
(865) 215-8751

MEMPHIS & SHELBY COUNTY PUBLIC
  LIBRARY
3030 Poplar Avenue
Memphis, TN 38111
(901) 415-2734

NASHVILLE PUBLIC LIBRARY
615 Church Street
Nashville, TN 37219
615 862-5800

TEXAS

AMARILLO AREA FOUNDATION
Grants Center
801 S. Filmore, Suite 700
Amarillo, TX 79101
(806) 376-4521

HOGG FOUNDATION FOR MENTAL HEALTH
Regional Foundation Library
3001 Lake Austin Boulevard, Suite 400
Austin, TX 78703
(512) 471-5041

BEAUMONT PUBLIC LIBRARY
801 Pearl Street
Beaumont, TX 77704-3827
(409) 838-6606

CORPUS CHRISTI PUBLIC LIBRARY
Funding Information Center
805 Comanche Street
Corpus Christi, TX 78401
(361) 880-7000

DALLAS PUBLIC LIBRARY
Urban Information
1515 Young Street
Dallas, TX 75201
(214) 670-1487

SOUTHWEST BORDER NONPROFIT
  RESOURCE CENTER
1201 W. University Drive
Edinburgh, TX 78539-2999
(956) 384-5920

UNIVERSITY OF TEXAS AT EL PASO
Institute for Community-Based Teaching And
Learning Community Non-profit Grant Library
500 W. University
El Paso, TX 79968-0547
(915) 747-7969

FUNDING INFORMATION CENTER OF
  FORTH WORTH
329 S. Henderson Street
Fort Worth, TX 76104
(817) 334-0228

HOUSTON PUBLIC LIBRARY
Bibliographic Information Center
500 McKinney Avenue
Houston, TX 77002
(832) 393-1313

LAREDO PUBLIC LIBRARY
Nonprofit Management and Volunteer
1120 E. Calton Road
Laredo, TX 78041
(956) 795-2400

LONGVIEW PUBLIC LIBRARY
222 W. Cotton Street
Longview, TX 75601
(903) 237-1350

LUBBOCK AREA FOUNDATION, INC.
1655 Main Street, Suite 209
Lubbock, TX 79401
(806) 762-8061

NONPROFIT RESOURCE CENTER OF TEXAS
7404 Highway 90 W.
San Antonio, TX 78212-8270
(210) 227-4333

WACO-MCLENNAN COUNTY LIBRARY
1717 Austin Avenue
Waco, TX 76701
(254) 750-5941

NONPROFIT MANAGEMENT CENTER OF
  WICHITA FALLS
2301 Kell Boulevard, Suite 218
Wichita Falls, TX 76308
(940) 322-4962

UTAH

GRAND COUNTY PUBLIC LIBRARY
25 South 100 East
Moab, UT 84532
(435) 259-5421

SALT LAKE CITY PUBLIC LIBRARY
210 E. 400 S.
Salt Lake City, UT 84111
(801) 524-8200

VERMONT

ILSLEY PUBLIC LIBRARY
75 Main Street
Middlebury, VT 05753
(802) 388-4095

VERMONT DEPARTMENT OF LIBRARIES
Reference & Law Information Services
109 State Street
Montpelier, VT 05609
(802) 828-3261

VIRGINIA

WASHINGTON COUNTY PUBLIC LIBRARY
205 Oak Hill Street
Abingdon, VA 24210
(276) 676-6222

HAMPTON PUBLIC LIBRARY
4207 Victoria Boulevard
Hampton, VA 23669
(757) 727-1314

RICHMOND PUBLIC LIBRARY
Business, Science & Technology Department
101 E. Franklin Street
Richmond, VA 23219
(804) 646-7223

ROANOKE CITY PUBLIC LIBRARY SYSTEM
Main Library
706 S. Jefferson Street
Roanoke, VA 24016
(540) 853-2471

WASHINGTON

MID-COLUMBIA LIBRARY
1620 S. Union Street
Kennewick, WA 99338
(509) 783-7878

KING COUNTY LIBRARY SYSTEM
Redmond Regional Library
Nonprofit & Philanthropy Resource Center
15990 NE 85th
Redmond, WA 98052
(425) 885-1861

SEATTLE PUBLIC LIBRARY
The Fundraising Resource Center
1000 4th Avenue
Seattle, WA 98104
(206) 386-4645

SPOKANE PUBLIC LIBRARY
Funding Information Center
906 West Main Avenue
Spokane, WA 99201
(509) 444-5300

UNIVERSITY OF WASHINGTON—
  TACOMA LIBRARY
1900 Commerce Street
Tacoma, WA 98402
(253)-692-4440

WENATCHEE VALLEY COLLEGE
John A. Brown Library
1300 5th Street
Wenatchee, WA 98807
(509) 664-2520

WEST VIRGINIA

KANAWHA COUNTY PUBLIC LIBRARY
123 Capitol Street
Charleston, WV 25301
(304) 343-4646

SHEPHERD COLLEGE
Ruth A. Scarborough Library
King Street
Shepherdstown, WV 25443-3210
(304) 876-5420

WISCONSIN

UNIVERSITY OF WISCONSIN—MADISON
Memorial Library, Grants Information Center
728 State Street
Madison, WI 53706
(608) 262-3242

MARQUETTE UNIVERSITY
Raynor Memorial Libraries
Funding Information Center
1355 W. Wisconsin Avenue
Milwaukee, WI 53201-3141
(414) 288-1515

UNIVERSITY OF WISCONSIN—
    STEVEN'S POINT
University Library-Foundation Center
900 Reserve Street
Stevens Point, WI 54481-3897
(715) 346-2540

WYOMING

CASPER COLLEGE
Goodstein Foundation Library
125 College Drive
Casper, WY 82601
(307) 268-2269

LARAMIE COUNTY COMMUNITY COLLEGE
Instructional Resources Center
1400 E. College Drive
Cheyenne, WY 82007-3299
(307) 778-1206

CAMPBELL COUNTY PUBLIC LIBRARY
2101 4-J Road
Gillette, WY 82718
(307) 687-0115

TETON COUNTY LIBRARY
125 Virginian Lane
Jackson, WY 83001
(307) 733-2164

SHERIDAN COUNTY FULMER PUBLIC
    LIBRARY
335 West Alger Street
Sheridan, WY 82801
(307) 674-8585